Jean-Paul Sartre

NLB

Between Existentialism
and Marxism, [by]

Translated from the French by John Matthews

The essays and interviews in this volume are taken from
Situations VIII and *IX*, published by Gallimard, Paris 1972
© Editions Gallimard 1972. English-language copyright
of the interview 'The Itinerary of a Thought', © *New Left Review*

This translation first published 1974
© NLB, 1974

NLB, 7 Carlisle Street, London W1

Typeset in Monotype Ehrhardt
and printed by Western Printing Services Ltd, Bristol
Designed by Gerald Cinamon

1. Self-Descriptions

The Purpose of Writing was originally an interview given by Sartre to Madeleine Chapsal in 1959, and published in her volume entitled *Les Ecrivains en Personne* (Paris 1960).

The Itinerary of a Thought was an interview given by Sartre a decade later, in 1969, to *New Left Review*, and published in *New Left Review* No 58. English-language copyright *NLR*.

The Purposes of Writing

I would like to ask you some questions about literature.

Good – hardly anyone ever discusses literature with me now. Philosophy is another story. . . .

It's known that you are currently working on several projects – a book on Mallarmé, a book on Tintoretto, a book on Flaubert, and an autobiography. You're working on all of them at once, without being able or – you might say – without wanting to bring any of them to a conclusion. Can you explain this?

Yes, I can – but it means leaving literature to one side and coming back to philosophy. For the last fifteen years I have been looking for something – I was trying, if you like, to lay the political foundations of anthropology. This project got bigger and bigger – it grew like a generalized cancer. Ideas came to me, and I wasn't sure what to do with them, so I put them anywhere – in whatever book I happened to be working on at the time.

Now I've finished with that. The ideas are all in place. I'm working on something that will relieve me of all of them – the *Critique of Dialectical Reason*. The first volume will be published within a month, and the second within a year. I no longer feel the need to make long digressions in my books, as if I were forever chasing after my own philosophy. It will now be deposited in little coffins, and I will feel completely emptied and at peace – as I felt after *Being and Nothingness*. A feeling of emptiness: a writer is fortunate if he can attain such a state. For when one has nothing to say, one can say *everything*.

When the book on anthropology is finally behind me, I will be able to write – on anything I like. As for philosophy, I will do no more than make brief mental notes about it, for my own purposes.

In your work, are philosophical ideas primary?

What is primary is what I haven't yet written – what I intend to write (not tomorrow, but the day after tomorrow) and what perhaps I will never write. . . .

Of course, since it takes a lot of time and effort to make a little headway in ideological questions, this does amount in a way to saying that philosophy is primary for me. But not always. When I wrote *Huis Clos*, for example – a one-act play that doesn't contain a word of philosophy – *Being and Nothingness* had already come out, or was at any rate in the process of being published. This story of mine about souls in torment was not symbolic – I had no wish to 'repeat' *Being and Nothingness* in different words. What would have been the point? I simply made up some stories with an imagination, sensibility and thought that the conception and writing of *Being and Nothingness* had united, integrated and organized in a certain way. If you like, my tome on philosophy was being narrated in the form of small non-philosophical stories. The audience believed *there was something in them they had to understand*. There was nothing of the sort.

But when one is writing works which are non-philosophical, while still ruminating on philosophy – as I have been doing for most of my time over the last ten years – every page, every line, suffers from hernia. Recently when I felt I was writing a hernia, I found it better to stop. That's why I have all these books waiting to be completed. Of course, I would very much like to finish them. Equally I would like to write something completely different. For example, to say the Truth. This is the dream of every aging writer. He thinks he has never told it – and yet he has never spoken of anything else; he is naked. Let us suppose that he insists, in any case, on doing a striptease himself. I have always produced a literature of occasional writings; I have always produced to order. Of course the employer can no longer be the State – nowadays it's everyone or someone: a political milieu in which I am involved, a particular event that calls for comment. The positive aspect of these orders is that they never allow the writer to 'indulge himself'. And by the same token, his public is automatically defined.

My present book on the Dialectic had its beginnings in an order. A

Polish review asked me to write an article on existentialism. I did so. Then I rewrote it for the readers of *Temps Modernes*. And then, on re-reading it, I saw that it lacked a foundation – the compass and validity of the Dialectic needed to be established. So then I got down and wrote the weighty tome that will be coming out soon. The ideas were there, but I lacked courage. . . . In earlier days I published books in complete innocence; but I have lost that now. Anyway the Polish order was the kick that despatches an apprentice parachutist into space.

Did you have to write about the Dialectic in order to be able to discuss Flaubert?

Yes. The fact that I couldn't stop myself discussing him in the Polish article proves it; and the fact that I transposed long passages from my book on him into the *Critique* confirms it. At the present moment the book on Flaubert is long and still not finished. But at least it now won't need a truss – it won't have any hernias.

Is this way of proceeding a personal characteristic of yours?

I think it depends on the situation, on the current preoccupation of the philosopher in question. Everything has changed: in Hegel's day history burst into philosophy in the form of tragedy; in Kierkegaard's, it was biography in the form or buffoonery, or drama.

Descartes saw his principal task as the search for the correct rules to guide the mind. What resulted from this was a Rationalism of Knowledge and of Ethics. Of course Cartesianism expressed and fashioned classical reason. But whatever may have been its relations with tragedy, it is clear that tragedy did not *directly* express the content of this universalism.

While today?

Today I think that philosophy is dramatic in nature. The time for contemplating the immobility of substances which are what they are, or for laying bare the laws underlying a succession of phenomena, is past. Philosophy is concerned with man – who is at once an *agent* and an *actor*, who produces and plays his drama while he lives the contradictions of his situation, until either his individuality is shatteied or his conflicts are resolved. A play (be it epic, such as Brecht's, or dramatic) is the most appropriate vehicle today for showing man *in action* – i.e. man full stop. It is with this man that philosophy, from its own point of view, should be concerned. That is why the theatre is philosophical and philosophy dramatic.

If this is what philosophy is to become, then why the rest of your literary output? Why don't you limit yourself to books on philosophy?

I wanted to write novels and plays a long time before I knew what philosophy was. I still want to; I've wanted to all my life.

Since school?

Even before that. I found philosophy at school so boring that I was convinced it was just a waste of time. My attitude owed something perhaps to the way the subject was taught in those days.

But in any case these perspectives on the reality of man are not interchangeable. Philosophy is dramatic but it does not study the individual as such. There is a certain amount of osmosis between my book on Flaubert and the *Critique*, but what will never be transferred from the first book to the second is the effort to understand Flaubert as an individual (it matters little in this respect, of course, if I fail or am partly successful). Again it's a question of an ordered interpretation. It would be impossible to philosophize on *Madame Bovary* because this is a unique book. More unique than its author – like all books. But it can be studied with *method*.

In What is Literature? *you said that, in your opinion, prose was no more than an instrument, an extension of one's arm or hand. Yet the writers who interest you are Flaubert, Genet, Mallarmé – all of whom seemed to regard writing as an end in itself. How do you reconcile this contradiction?*

There are differences between the three. As far as Flaubert is concerned, I use him to show that literature, understood as a pure art deriving all its rules from its own essence, conceals its author's commitment and his fiery opinions on every sort of subject – including social and political questions. Flaubert is a classic case. I'm sure that I will be attacked for taking advantage of him unduly. Whose fault is this? Flaubert is a very great writer. And after all, why shouldn't I try to explain the mixture of profound admiration and repulsion that *Madame Bovary* has inspired in me ever since my adolescence?

On the other hand, I am in complete sympathy with Mallarmé and Genet – they are both conscious of their commitment.

Mallarmé?

Yes, in my opinion. It is certain that Mallarmé bore little resemblance to the Mallarmé of literary history. He is our greatest poet. A wild, impassioned man. Yet so self-controlled that he could kill himself with a simple movement of his glottis! . . . His was an all-embracing commitment – social as much as poetic.

A commitment that was a rejection then?

Not just that. He rejected his epoch, but he preserved it in the form of a transition, a tunnel. He hoped that one day what he used to call 'the crowd' – by which he meant a mass public assembled in a godless cathedral rather than in a theatre – would see Tragedy played before them. The one and only Tragedy – at once the drama of man, the movement of the world, the tragic return of the seasons – a tragedy whose author (as anonymous as Homer) would be dead, or else be just one of the audience, present at the unfolding of a masterpiece that did not belong to him, one which *all* would stage for him as for all. Mallarmé linked his Orphic and tragic conceptions of Poetry to the communion of a people rather than to individual hermeticism. The latter was no more than a rejection of bourgeois stupidity. To be sure, Mallarmé did not think one could write 'openly' for a mass public. But he felt that for a united people, the obscure would become clear.

So what you're saying is that even writers who are considered to be detached are in reality committed? Did you study Flaubert and Mallarmé in order to demonstrate this?

This and other things. In the case of Mallarmé I have only just begun and won't be able to take him up again for a long time. I mention him only to indicate that 'pure' literature is a dream.

So you believe that literature is always committed?

If literature is not everything, it is worth nothing. This is what I mean by 'commitment'. It wilts if it is reduced to innocence, or to songs. If a written sentence does not reverberate at every level of man and society, then it makes no sense. What is the literature of an epoch but the epoch appropriated by its literature?

You have been accused of not taking literature seriously enough, of wanting to make it the vassal of politics. What do you say to that?

I think it would be more logical for people to accuse me of exaggerating its importance. The beauty of literature lies in its desire to be everything – and not in a sterile quest for beauty. Only a *whole* can be beautiful: those who can't understand this – whatever they may have said – have not attacked me in the name of art, but in the name of their particular commitment.

In your case, do you think that literature has fulfilled all its promises?

I don't believe it can fulfil them – not in my case, nor in that of anyone in particular. What I have in mind are the exigencies of pride. An insane pride is necessary to write – you can only afford to be modest after you've sunk your pride in your work. Having said this, it must be confessed that the author can miss his mark; he can also be interrupted in the middle of his work. So what? You have to aspire to *everything* to have hopes of doing *something*.

But isn't this what every writer dreams of – to write something that is everything?

I think so; I would hope so. But I'm afraid of the humility of certain writers. All those academies and legions of honour – a writer must be so humble to accept them! On the other hand, if others try to elicit everything out of nothing, they should say so.

Why?

If they maintain silence they perpetuate a contradiction which disturbs other writers. A writer has nothing in his hands, nothing in his pockets. If he's holding a pack of cards, he has to start by laying them on the table. I loathe all charlatans who try to make people believe that there is something magic about writing. They lead those who come after them astray – they mould them into sorcerers like themselves. Let writers begin by renouncing illusionism. What vanity and humility to want to be taken for conjurers! Let them say openly what they aspire to and what they're doing.

The critics encourage them never to admit to a soul – above all to themselves – the nature of their desires and the means at their disposal. They want to cling to the old romantic idea – the best of us must write as the bird sings. But a writer is not a bird.

Are there any writers today who are working in accordance with your ideas – towards greater freedom, within a full commitment? Which contemporary writers interest you?

If you put the question to me in that form, then I must confess there aren't too many. There are some very talented writers: Butor, Beckett. I'm very interested in the works of Robbe-Grillet and of Nathalie Sarraute. Still, if we examine their works from the point of view of totality, I would say that there is only one writer in France who has clearly formulated the problem and found an answer to the demands of the whole – and that is Butor.

I don't think the others are interested in the problem – they're looking for something else. And why not recognize their right to do so?

You feel that writers are wrong to restrict the field of their inquiries?

No, of course not. But they would be wrong to declare – as they do perhaps, but then what writer hasn't at some point in his life? – that there is only one thing worth doing: what they are doing at the moment. But inquiry and experience are valuable. There are so many of us in this country, creating together and alone the *real* totality of French literature today, as objective spirit! Individuals can linger over details – they won't contribute any less to the whole, thanks to the efforts of all the others.

Would you say that your research is more total in scope than that of others?

In its intention, yes; but its success is something else altogether! Many people have a sharp sight for details, but lose focus when they try to locate these details in the ensemble. I can say without any qualification whatever that I have always found what Nathalie Sarraute writes to be remarkable. But she believes that the protoplasmic exchanges which she describes enable her to grasp the elementary relations between individuals, whereas all she succeeds in revealing are the abstract and infinitesimal effects of a well defined social milieu: one that is leisured, bourgeois, somewhat worldly, in which work and idleness are never really distinguished. The paranoic structure which becomes more and more marked in her books, reveals a type of relationship characteristic of these milieus. But in her works the individual is not restored to his position within the milieu which conditions him; nor is the milieu restored within the individual. We are left on the undifferentiated and illusory plane of the immediate. In reality, all these inter-individual movements are defined by their relation to a totality – a whole that is mutely signified by their very pulverulence. But in Nathalie Sarraute's books, the totality is distinguished by its absence. The title of her latest work, *Planetarium*, proves that it has been excluded intentionally. For that matter the swarming quality of her *Planetarium* evokes a copy of Proust's *Temps Retrouvé* slowly decomposing under the action of lost Time (*Temps perdu*). In this, too, it is very much the work of a woman; for this pulverization is exactly the obverse of the refusal to assume responsibility for an atomized world – it is the rejection of action.

You just referred to 'the work of a woman'. Do you think women are incapable of writing anything but women's books?

Not at all. What I understand by a woman's book is one which refuses to take into account the activities of men. A lot of men have written nothing but feminine books. And by 'woman' I mean 'woman in society' – the woman who has been dispossessed of the right to say: 'I have no less an impact on the world than my male neighbour.' When I speak of a 'woman's novel', this is what I have in mind: the novelist has made her mark with her talent, but she has shown no desire to wrench herself out of her *disinherited* condition – both because of resentment and connivance with the enemy.

I referred a moment ago to paranoic structure. It must be stressed again that this imposes itself on an author involuntarily, perhaps unconsciously. Contemporary music has set itself the task of isolating these structures in sound-space, but our 'young novelists' are either unaware of the existence of such structures, or expel them from the universe of the novel. They have discovered that characters, qualities, substances never had any existence. It is positive that each generation should rediscover this. But does it mean that there is no synchronic or diachronic structure in the societies which produced them? Don't these novelists realize that what they are eliminating from their works forms the very foundation of anthropology and anthropological research?

It is said, for example, that Robbe-Grillet's aim is to decondition our literary vision by sweeping away all its pre-established significations. Fashionable critics on the left who support Robbe-Grillet have even gone so far as to say that this deconditioning will liberate us from any *bourgeois* vision of the world. Unfortunately, this deconditioning may be possible in a musical work – as in the case of Webern – but only in the sense that it liberates the listener from his expectations. But the total object that figures in a novel is a *human* object, and it is nothing without its human significations. Robbe-Grillet's deconditioned objects float between two levels of signification, between two extremes. On the one hand, he may deal with topographies, mechanical measurements, strictly objective descriptions – yet nothing is more human than the use of landmarks, calculations and surveys. Take away man, and things are no longer near or far off – they are no longer things at all. The affirmation that we can describe things, classify them, find an order in them is the primary moment of mathematical Reason. Alternatively – and this is Robbe-Grillet's other extreme – these highly rigorous descriptions suddenly assume the guise of symbols of an obsessional and rigorously subjective universe. This universe has to deploy a particular symbol-object because the obsessive subject's thinking cannot – as Lacan would say – achieve articulation. A case in point is the famous rape in Robbe-Grillet's *Voyeur*. This story shows children walking along a beach; the author's attention seems to be concentrated solely on the intersection of two movements – the movement of the waves, and perpendicular to this, that of the children's footprints in the wet sand. Suddenly everything capsizes into a symbol; the mere chiming of a bell is enough to make us see the children's walk as undefined, aimless, and yet ordered by certain appeals which may be real or may be dreams – we will never know; a walk which seems to be unique and at the same time begins over and over again. What we have here is quite simply a rather flat symbol of our condition; in other words, René Char's *man, an imitated illusion*.

I find a strange attraction in objects like this – ones which betray their makers. It remains true that they are the product of a laboratory-type schematization. No one has the right to choose between all the diverse significations whose dense sweeps constitute human reality. They have to be there – all of them. It is not necessary to name them. But literature finds its *initial* impulse in silence.

You don't feel that all things are always present in this silence, even when the writer selects only one or two of them? If you were writing a review of one of Robbe-Grillet's or Nathalie Sarraute's books, would you demonstrate that the universe is there, in its totality, around their every phrase?

Yes. Perhaps. But it would be a waste of time. On the other hand, we should recognize that someone is alive today in France who has the ambition and every possibility of becoming a great writer – our first great writer since 1945: Butor. He's the man we should be trying to help – although I suspect he needs no assistance – by attempting to interpret his intentions and communicating them to the public. He is proud – he writes to live. He aims to capture in his writing men who seem at times to come straight out of a populist novel, *through the totality* in which they are lost. And, because of this, none of these men turns out to be what we took him to be at first: each one, lost at first in the whole, ends up by interiorizing and expressing it; each one ends up by writing.

I'm in the middle of reading *Degrés* at the moment. Never before have I come across such an able and profound attempt to seize an individual in the light of the family and work relations which produce and condition him, and which he transforms. A new life comes into existence: in this novel, a man cannot be reduced to a series of *social* attributes, nor is he properly an individual reality. Nor yet a mere mixture of social and individual characteristics. In fact, the principle of individuality is abandoned. Within professional and traditional groups we find recurrent groups and indeterminate groups appearing – *and they are all the same*. This book is certainly out of the ordinary. If I were a critic, I would very much like to discuss it.

I am struck all the more in that I saw great promise in his earlier work, *La Modification*. Butor has given the objects which in Robbe-

Grillet's hands are no more than an index of obsession, their *true meaning* (through a technique which is hardly new, but which reveals an extreme rigour): they become instruments which transform whoever uses them. An intention to catch a train acts as a centre of indetermination. But *for the moment* it is the train which *acts*: its trajectory, its stops, its traditions, the station and its irreversibility (both departure and destination are equally irreversible – while topographically the two stations are equivalent), the distances to the other people – all these factors *modify* the characters.

I get the feeling from Butor's first three books that we are confronted here with a premeditated attempt – the perfectly hopeless attempt that only a true writer is capable of – to master everything. He has already covered a lot of ground, and he will go further.

But what about you? What has your own experience of literary activity been? Have you used literature in the way you hoped to? Are you content, optimistic? Or do you feel disappointed?

No, I've never felt disappointed. My work has always gone well. There have been books I had to abandon half-way through because I didn't know how to go on. Others that I had hopes for were published but got a bad reception – and I realized that I was wrong and the critics were right. But that's all part of the job. One way or another, you get the same frustrations in any profession.

What I mean is that writing in itself *cannot* entail disappointment. In what follows I'm going to appear a bit confused, but the subject would take up too much time otherwise. So to be brief: in the domain of expression, success is necessarily failure. I'm not referring to those misunderstandings to which the aristocratic authors of the last century attributed their large circulations. I'm speaking of technical success. It is *impossible* to succeed, since at the outset you set yourself the goal of failure (to capture movement in immobile objects, for instance); after all the lies, you always come back to this in the end – so many little faults accumulate that the moment comes when you just can't take the work any further; all is lost. At this point, my friend Giacometti explains, you can throw your piece of sculpture in the rubbish bin or exhibit it in a gallery. So there it is. You never quite grasp what you set out to achieve.

And then suddenly it's a statue or a book. The opposite of what you wanted. If its faults are inscribed methodically in the negative which you present to the public, they at least point to what it might have been. And the spectator becomes the real sculptor, fashioning his model in thin air, or reading the book between the lines.

Since you mention the public, how would you describe your relation to it? How has this relation evolved? Haven't you said that the public plays an important role in the life of a written work?

One has so many links – not only to one's time but, in this epoch of nationalism, to national society as well – that a writer's personal history is inevitably that of his public. One day, when we were young, Simone de Beauvoir and myself decided to go skiing – a serious and deliberate decision, which we thought quite original. The day we left, we discovered that all the older school-children in Paris together with all their teachers had been just as original as ourselves. What this means is that I would never say what *I* felt unless I were sure that *everyone* felt the same. I don't want to express my public in spite of myself, after the fashion of those *fin de siècle* aristocrats of sensibility who aspired to an exquisite sense of Toledo or of Goya – and who, in the end, merely expressed a bourgeois preciosity that was soon throttled by the First World War. My aim is to express, to the best of my ability, *what I feel as an ordinary person.*

Who makes up your public?

Students, teachers, people who love reading, who have a weakness for it – they make up a very small circle. My print-run is of no significance; it can be large or small, but this particular readership is still the same. Not *my* readership but *ours*: that of everyone who is afflicted with the vice of writing.

Journalists have an odd approach: they compile a list of circulations, calculate averages and make statistical comparisons (of dubious accuracy since they are generally based on incorrect data), and then draw conclusions. What they've done is confuse the meaning of the print-run of a book with that of their own newspaper. In a country like the USSR where there are State publishing ventures, the circulation of a book has a real meaning: if the public demands a new translation of Zola, this means that people really want to read or re-read Zola. Whereas here, under conditions of liberal capitalism and free enterprise, circulation figures have no meaning. What relationship is there between a book like Schwarz-Bart's recent novel – a thoughtful, relentless, profound work, an attempt devoid of any illusions to recover all the dead we have killed – and the smartly dressed young woman with a hard, stupid face I saw the other day reading *The Last of the Just* in the dining car as she ate a pastry? She was reading his book, but she wasn't part of *his* public.

You haven't quite answered my question. Do you personally feel you have succeeded or failed? Would you say that anything has changed because of what you have written?

Not a thing. On the contrary, ever since my youth I have experienced utter impotence. But that's neither here nor there. You could say, if you like, that to begin with I wrote a few books which weren't directly concerned with social problems; then came the Occupation – people began to think it was necessary to act. After the war, we felt once more that books, articles, etc. could be of use. In fact they were of no use whatever. Then we came to feel – or at least I did – that books conceived and written without any specific relation to the immediate situation could be of long-term use. And these turned out to be just as useless, for the purpose of acting on people – all you found was a distortion of your own thoughts and feelings. You find your own words turned against you and changed out of all recognition by a young man taking a casual swipe at you. Fair enough – I did the same myself. That's literary endeavour for you – you can see that it doesn't produce the results you wanted it to.

All the same, those you have influenced haven't all turned round and attacked you. Don't you ever come across writers in whom you recognize yourself with pleasure?

Of course. But you must understand – if I am to approve of them they must be making something new out of what I've made myself; and since I am still alive, this can only be in opposition to what I am doing myself. People worthy of esteem could never be the passive recipients of someone else's influence. If I really recognized *myself* in someone, it would vex me – why begin what I have done all over again? On the contrary, if a writer (or a young reader who is not a writer) pleases me, it's usually because he disconcerts me somewhat initially. So much the better if I subsequently discover behind the novelty of his thoughts an image of my former self – though altered and half-obscured with age.

In a word, what is honourable about reading is this: the reader freely allows himself to be influenced. This fact alone is enough to quash the fable of his passivity. The reader invents us: he uses our words to set his own traps for himself. He is active, he transcends us – that is why we write. And that precisely is why I have never been disappointed by my craft. Of course, I had to endure the apprenticeship of impotence – but this was because in 1940 or thereabouts I still innocently believed in Father Christmas.

Perhaps this will surprise you, but I have sometimes had the feeling that you yourself were somewhat imprisoned within this epoch, this society, and within your work as well. When I saw Les Sequestrés d'Altona *I said to myself that the real victim of sequestration was yourself.*

Myself? I should welcome it. Hitherto, I've never been sequestered enough for my liking. If I were Frantz, I wouldn't be consumed with remorse. Fundamentally, he represents the negative of one of my fondest dreams – to be in a cell, and to be able to write in peace. I shall nourish this sweet regret until the day I die . . . !

No, what I actually wanted to do was pass on something that I felt – in common, I believe, with everyone. The men of my generation and those a little younger than ourselves (I'm 54) were gripped by a feeling of consternation when we looked upon this epoch we all helped to build, and we said: 'So, that's what it was.' I'm not talking about what a young Russian might have felt, but of what a Frenchman felt when he looked back.

You must understand; in our youth we were gentle – the problem of violence tormented us. The upshot was that the whole of the younger generation espoused a violent creed and so disposed of the problem. That's what I was trying to say to you – how difficult it is to recognize oneself in others! Because one is *other*.

Precisely. One has the feeling that you whom the problem of violence 'tor-

mented' are still worse at ease in this gloomy society of ours than others, that you feel restricted in it, that it stifles you – and that you 'secrete' your work as a kind of refuge from it. This is why I asked you whether you felt 'sequestered'.

No. The sense of gloom in *Les Sequestrés* was essentially inspired by the current state of French society. It's a frightful wreckage – and like anyone else, I'm inescapably part of it. If I'm a prisoner – together with all who have said no and who go on saying no – it is of the present regime.

What do you call violence?

The people of my generation had lived through two periods of sacred violence by the time they reached their adolescence. In 1914 there was the war: we were told that it was just and that God was on our side. And in 1917 there was the Russian Revolution. In the interim, in fact, we had become a little less mystified, and by 1919 our hopes rested on the Revolution. Don't get the idea that I am confusing the violence of a capitalist war with that of the insurrection of Petrograd. Today I firmly believe that the month of October 1917 irreversibly transformed the world. But I'm discussing how we felt as children. We were steeped in the violence of our fathers. From 1914 to 1918 I lived at La Rochelle: at that time children were in power – they thought they were at the front. One of my school-friends chased after his mother with a knife – she had given him potatoes, and he didn't like them. In other respects, they were very sensible boys. But these events had in some way turned their heads – they were asked to *interiorize* this sacred violence. They did so and, in their ensuing disgust, many of them – including myself – experienced little difficulty in substituting a holy revolution for this holy war. When I became a student at the Ecole Normale, no one – not even a *thala** – would have dared to openly reject violence. We were concerned above all to channel it, to restrict it. We sought a well-behaved and profitable violence. Most of us were very mild and yet we became violent beings. For one of our problems was this: could a particular act be described as one of revolutionary violence or did it rather go beyond the violence necessary for the revolution? This problem has stayed with us all our lives – we will never surmount it.

*Translator's note: A militant Catholic student – from 'ceux qui vont à la messe'.

Do you see what I mean? After that, many of us had children. Not myself, but then I taught other people's children – I was a teacher. All of us shared the responsibility for bringing them up. And then these children had children of their own. Now, it seems to me that these children have grown up under our influence and that many of them have radicalized the whole phenomenon of violence. The young people in London who recently started to lynch West Indians, young German anti-semites or young French fascists all share a common indulgence in an absolutely pure and unconditioned violence. Such a brand of violence never calls itself into question. It makes no effort to criticize itself. It is *in love* with itself. It is as much an explosion of hate provoked by poverty as a sport. There are *blousons noirs* – juvenile delinquents – who are bored out of their minds in the housing estates of the Paris suburbs. They form gangs; and then everything is so cosy, so sinisterly cosy in these high-rise apartment blocks – carefully built by the neo-paternalism of our capitalists – that there's nothing for them to do but smash everything.

This is what staggers us. One used to think – or at least we thought – of violence as born of exploitation and oppression, and as directed against them. In a certain sense, there was a *political* motivation behind the construction of these apartment blocks, directed – like all paternalist policies – against the interests of the workers. Now we, older ones, would understand it if young people broke doors and windows in them as protest against this paternalism. I'm not saying they would be right, but that we would understand them. But no, they pick fights with each other, or beat up passers-by. It is certainly their situation which provokes this violence. But it only appears legitimate to them because it is anarchic. If it acquired the slightest political direction, they would begin to suspect it. In our eyes, violence could be justified if it were being used to safe-guard the interests of the masses, a revolution, etc. But for these de-linquents, violence can never be put to use: it is good only when it's *senseless*.

I don't want to go on and discuss this: I'm merely giving you an example of influence at work. And of course these young people weren't con-ditioned by *our* conceptions, but by the Cold War. But then we were the ones who waged the Cold War.

Do you believe that one fashions one's epoch?

When you reach the age of 54, you can be excused for speaking in the past tense. But it doesn't matter how old you are, it always remains true that History makes man and man makes History.

Would you say that we are responsible for it?

Yes, both responsible and complicit. The whole of French society is responsible for the Algerian War, and for the way it is being conducted (torture, internment camps, etc.) – the whole of the society, including the men and women who have never stopped protesting against it. We are inextricably involved: the slightest discussion between the left-wing groups who were gradually assassinating each other had the effect of encouraging torture, or a putsch. All these soft and well-meaning gentlemen we have become – we have all had to interiorize the war. The result is that we are solidary with it, plunged ever more deeply in violence. This, among other things, is what I was trying to convey in *Les Sequestrés*. The dying Frantz, the executioner – he is us, he is myself.

None of this stops a man from writing.

What do you see as the function of literature, if you have this feeling of impotence, in a century that has seen more violence than any before it?

Man lives in the midst of images. Literature offers him a critical image of himself.

Then it's a mirror?

A critical mirror. If literature is to be engaged, it must reveal, demonstrate, represent. After that, people can look at each other face to face, and act as they want. In the eighteenth century, writers were carried along by history, but not today; now they have become suspect. We should try to keep this role for ourselves – what would become of a society if it had no suspects?

You think writers are 'suspect'! Aren't you over-estimating the importance accorded to them?

They are suspected of having a mirror in their pocket, of wanting to take it out and hold it up to their neighbour – who might have a stroke if he saw himself as he really is. . . .

Writers are suspect because Poetry and Prose have become critical Arts: it was Mallarmé who called his own body of work, 'critical poetry'. Writing, today as in the past, has always meant calling the whole of writing into question. The same is true of Painting, Sculpture, Music: Art in its totality is engaged in the activity of a single man, as he tests and pushes back its limits. But writing cannot be critical without calling everything into question: this is its content. The adventure of writing undertaken by each writer challenges the whole of mankind. Both those who read and those who do not. Any string of words *whatsoever* (assuming the writer has talent) – even a sentence describing the virgin forest – calls everything we have done into question, and poses the issue of *legitimacy* (which particular one is of little importance – all are shapes of human power). Compare these suspects to ethnologists: ethnologists describe, but writers can *no longer* describe. They must take sides.

Isn't the writer's occupation a strange one? Of course, writing demands a lot of energy, but at the same time it seems to derive from the writer's weakness.

In my case, I chose writing in place of death, and because I lacked faith. That was certainly a sort of weakness.

When I was seven or eight years old, I lived with my widowed mother together with a Catholic grandmother and a Protestant grandfather. At the dinner table, each poked fun at the other's religion. No malice was involved – it was simply a family tradition. But a child reasons in a straightforward fashion: I concluded from these exchanges that the two faiths were equally valueless. Even though my family saw it as their duty to bring me up as a Catholic, religion never had any weight with me.

Now about the same age I was terrified of death. Why? Perhaps, understandably, because I had no beneficent myth of eternal life to fall back on (beneficent for children, that is). I was already writing, in my childish way. I was already pouring my longing for immortality – literary immortality, of course – into writing. I have since abandoned the idea of literary survival, but it was certainly the initial focus of my cathexis.

The Christian, in principle, has no fear of death because he knows he has to die in order to begin true life. Life on earth is merely a period of trial to earn glory in heaven. Various precise obligations go with this. There are rites to be observed, and vows can be taken, such as those of obedience, chastity, poverty. I inherited all this and transposed it bodily into literary terms – I would be unknown all my life, but I would merit immortality through my dedication to writing and my professional integrity. My glory as a writer would date from the time of my death. I had some stirring debates with my conscience: was it necessary for me to experience everything before I could write about everything? Or should I live a monk's life in order to devote all my time to polishing my phrases? In either case what was at stake was everything. In my imagination, literary life was modelled on religious life. I dreamt only of ensuring my salvation. . . .

I wasn't aware of any of this until I was forty – simply because I had never inquired into my motives for writing. I contested everything save my own profession. Then one day I was writing down some thoughts on morality when it struck me that I was propounding a writer's ethics for the benefit of writers – though I was supposed to be addressing people who never did any writing! That forced me to go back to the origins of this bizarre attitude, to unearth its presuppositions – or, if you like, my childhood cathexes. Today I'm sure I came to the right conclusion – that I had transposed religious needs into literary longings. The more so since writers a little older than myself followed the same trajectory – it was the epoch that fashioned its future writers.

So you're right in effect; writing is an escape, a sign of weakness. 'What does it matter to me, if I can write *Paludes* . . . ?'

But didn't you just say that you no longer have any interest in literary glory?

It's not that I no longer have any interest in it, but that from a certain point in my life onwards, it no longer made any sense. The more death became a *reality*, the more this glory became pure mystification. Someone said recently that he knew of nothing more ignominious than posthumous rehabilitation: one of our number is trapped, he dies from rage or grief and then, a quarter of a century later, a monument is erected in his honour. And the jackals who make the speeches over his effigy are the *very ones* who killed him in the first place – they honour death in order to poison the living.

As a matter of fact, no one – nothing – can be rehabilitated, especially not an assassin. As for the dead man: he suffers until the very end, he perishes in despair, and that's the end of it for him. In their own time, Nietzsche and Baudelaire were made wretched and senile – and now people turn round and tell us that one was the prophet of the twentieth century, and the other was France's greatest poet! . . . What do these titles change? Death cannot be recuperated.

But what did you mean when you spoke of weakness? I don't think I've touched upon what you had in mind.

I feel a writer always has a recourse to fall back on. He writes his work, good or bad (you said a moment ago that literary labour in itself cannot disappoint); when he finds reality disagreeable he can retreat and seek refuge with his pen and paper. While a man who involves himself in action is liable to lose everything.

You speak as if a choice were possible. The fact is that – save in the case of a restricted circle of leisured members of the ruling class – you cannot choose between writing and politics. It's the situation that decides. Take the men who form the Algerian FLN, for example: for them the political problem was posed as something violent and immediate. A whole generation knew nothing but war from their earliest childhood. Recourse to violence, in such a case, is not an option, but a course of action imposed by the situation. When the war is over, some of them will doubtless become writers. But politics and war will have been their lot *initially*.

In France, it's the middle classes that supply both the literary and political personnel of the nation. The nation is rather shop-worn – and has been for many years. Therefore hesitation is permitted. You know the result – the wretchedness of French politicians. At this level there is no distinction between the two activities: bad literature is redeemed by its political content, and politics is turned into bad literature. This lack of differentiation is such that writers are attacked – as I have been – for having lost wars (a right-wing attack) or for not urging the masses to the assault of our Bastilles (a left-wing attack). A few years ago a journalist came to see me, at a time when the affairs of State or Universe weren't going too well. 'What I need is a cry from the heart,' he told me, 'would you be so good as to make it?' Can you believe it – sometimes I did! But with varied results – which depended on other people: on the number of those who had decided – *before* my intervention, of course – to join the demonstration. But this is the very grandeur and weakness of a literature of pathos – in politics, it depends for its effect entirely on others. It is other people – who perhaps have not even read the writer – who swell his words with their passion. The real work of the committed writer is, as I said before, to reveal, demonstrate, demystify, and dissolve myths and fetishes in a critical acid bath. With a bit of luck, other people will utilize him to create new myths; or else – as happened in the case of Pushkin and of the Elizabethans – the purest or most flamboyant style can become the equivalent of political action because the writer enables the nation to discover its own language, as the ultimate moment of its unification. We were not given such opportunities. I feel that fewer and fewer young people are driven to write these days. In my time, you could hope to die in your bed. I felt assured of a long life when I looked at my ancient but active grandfather: I had the right to adopt a literary religion, as I had sixty years of faith and needs in front of me. But since the Cold War, young people have been brought up to believe that death could come any day. God has regained the upper hand over literature – he can save a soul at a moment's notice, whereas my God, a crueller deity, demanded a lifetime's work. . . . And so the mystification begins all over again – history is full of such cycles and eddies. I've said all this to show you that explanations of literature based on psychological concepts of weakness or strength – or any other subjective notion – are at once superficially correct and far too simple. Don't forget that a man carries a whole epoch within him, just as a wave carries the whole of the sea. . . .

You think people are becoming less inclined to write?

There's no lack of inclination, certainly. But do writers today want to do *nothing else* but write? Maybe one day the faculty of writing will belong to everyone – someone will make use of it somewhere, then it will disappear and reappear in their neighbour. Full-time writers will be a thing of the past – there will simply be people who do several things, including writing. This will be a much more satisfactory situation – one which will go far closer to fulfilling the basic *need to write* that is present in everyone – even today. Just who are we, the professionals? We claim to have received a mandate; people let us do the writing – instead of doing it themselves. We put ourselves forward as elected representatives. But this is a lie. And with today's huge print-runs, the publishing houses accentuate the fraud – every book bought becomes a vote in favour of its author. In reality, people read because they want to write. Anyway, reading is a sort of rewriting.

From this point of view, yes, people discover that they have a need to express their lives. During my time as a prisoner of war in a German Stalag, I came across a little poacher. He'd really been through the mill – abandoned child, brought up by the State, every sort of misfortune. One day, after he had joined up in the Army, he got a letter telling him his wife was deceiving him. He left at once with his gun, found her in bed in the arms of her lover, and shot the two of them on the spot. Then he came back and gave himself up. This was in May 1940. He was thrown into a military prison. Then the Germans came, and packed him off to a prison camp in Germany. His story of passion and crime, no longer subject to sanction, remained unresolved. We, his comrades, knew all about it – an official from the Military Tribunal was able to confirm it. But this wasn't enough – the man felt cheated. All the more so since mourning was doing its work inside him, and there would soon be nothing left of the experience but an abstract memory. He then *invented* the idea of writing it down in order to express it – in other words, to possess it in all its clarity and distinction, and at the same time to let the story take possession of him and so survive – with its author, frozen and objectified within it. Of course, he wrote it *very badly* – this is where the difficulties start. Read Blanchot's *Le Paradoxe d'Ayrté* – he explains marvellously how this initial desire to *say everything* results in *everything* being *hidden*. But that's another question. What I'm trying to say is that people – people everywhere – wish their own life, with all its dark places that they sense, to be an experience not only lived, but *presented*. They would like to see it disengaged from all the elements that crush it; and rendered essential by an *expression* that reduces what crushes them to inessential conditions of their person. Everyone wants to write because everyone has a need to be *meaningful* – to signify what they *experience*. Otherwise it all slips away –

you go about with your nose to the ground, like the pig made to dig for truffles – and you find nothing.

I've shed a lot of literary illusions – that literature has an absolute value, for instance, that it can save a man or simply change men (except in special circumstances). Today all this seems long out of date to me. But the writer goes on writing, having lost these illusions, because – as the psychoanalysts say – he has invested everything in his occupation. He goes on writing for the same reason that others go on living with people of whom they are no longer fond, or are fond in a different way – because they are their family. But I still possess one conviction, one only, and I shall never be shaken from it: writing is a need felt by everyone. It's the highest form of the basic need to communicate.

In that case, shouldn't those who have chosen writing as a career be the most satisfied of people, since they spend their whole time doing what others only dream of?

No, because it's their *job*. Every person is always faced in his own lifetime with the task of wresting his life from the various forms of night.

Is a reader necessary?

Of course. The *cri écrit* – written cry – to use Cocteau's phrase, only becomes an absolute when it is preserved in other people's memories, when it is integrated into the *objective spirit*. It goes without saying that the public you aim to reach (it may be imaginary) will never coincide exactly with the public you actually reach. But perhaps this real public takes the place of the one you aimed at.

Deep down, then, everyone would like to be a writer?

Yes and no. A writer alienates himself to his writing – which is unfortunate. When I was eight, I thought that Nature herself was not insensible to the appearance of a good book. When an author finished his manuscript with the words 'the end', I fancied a falling star would appear in the sky! Today I feel that writing, as a job, is an activity that is more or less the same as any other. But I must repeat, this is not the point: what is important is that every single person feels, perhaps only unconsciously, the need to be a witness of his time, of his life – before the eyes of all, to be a witness to himself. And you should never forget that our feelings and acts are always ambiguous and confused – something inside us obstructs their development, or interferes with them like crackle on a radio. Tragedy is not lived tragically, nor pleasure pleasurably. The need to write is fundamentally a quest for purification.

The Itinerary of a Thought

How do you envisage the relationship between your early philosophical writings, above all L'Etre et Le Néant, *and your present theoretical work, from the* Critique de la Raison Dialectique *onwards? In the* Critique, *the typical concepts of* L'Etre et Le Néant *have disappeared, and a completely new vocabulary has taken their place. Yet when reading the passages of your forthcoming study of Flaubert published in* Les Temps Modernes *one is struck by the sudden re-emergence of the characteristic idiom of the early work – thetic consciousness, ego, nihilation, being, nothingness. These notions are now juxtaposed in the text with the distinct set of concepts which derive from the* Critique *– serialization, totalization, practico-inert, collectives. What is the precise relationship between the two in your current thought?*

The basic question here, of course, is my relationship to Marxism. I will try to explain autobiographically certain aspects of my early work, which may help to clarify the reasons why my outlook changed so fundamentally after the Second World War. A simple formula would be to say that life taught me *la force des choses* – the power of circumstances. In a way, *L'Etre et Le Néant* itself should have been the beginning of a discovery of this power of circumstances, since I had already been made a soldier, when I had not wanted to be one. Thus I had already encountered something that was my freedom and which steered me from without. Then I was taken prisoner, a fate which I had sought to escape. Hence I started to learn what I have called human reality among things: Being-in-the-world.

Then, little by little, I found that the world was more complicated than this, for during the Resistance there appeared to be a possibility of free decision. For my state of mind during those years, I think that the first plays I wrote are very symptomatic: I called them a 'theatre of freedom'. The other day, I re-read a prefatory note of mine to a collection of these plays – *Les Mouches*, *Huis Clos* and others – and was truly scandalized. I had written: 'Whatever the circumstances, and wherever the site, a man is always free to choose to be a traitor or not. . . .' When I read this, I said to myself: it's incredible, I actually believed that!

To understand how I could have done so, you must remember that there was a very simple problem during the Resistance – ultimately, only a question of courage. One had to accept the risks involved in what one was doing, that is, of being imprisoned or deported. But beyond this? A Frenchman was either for the Germans or against them, there was no other option. The real political problems, of being 'for, but' or 'against, but', were not posed by this experience. The result was that I concluded that in any circumstances, there is always a possible choice. Which is false. Indeed, it is so false that I later wanted precisely to refute myself by creating a character in *Le Diable et Le Bon Dieu*, Heinrich, who cannot choose. He wants to choose, of course, but he cannot choose either the Church, which has abandoned the poor, or the poor, who have abandoned the Church. He is thus a living contradiction, who will never choose. He is totally conditioned by his situation.

However, I understood all this only much later. What the drama of the war gave me, as it did everyone who participated in it, was the experience of heroism. Not my own, of course – all I did was a few errands. But the militant in the Resistance who was caught and tortured became a myth for us. Such militants existed, of course, but they represented a sort of personal myth as well. Would we be able to hold out against torture too? The problem then was solely that of physical endurance – it was not the ruses of history or the paths of alienation. A man is tortured: what will he do? He either speaks or refuses to speak. This is what I mean by the experience of heroism, which is a false experience.

After the war came the true experience, that of *society*. But I think it was necessary for me to pass via the myth of heroism first. That is to say, the pre-war personage who was more or less Stendhal's egotistical individualist had to be plunged into circumstances against his will, yet where he still had the power to say yes or no, in order to encounter the inextricable entanglements of the post-war years as a man totally conditioned by his social existence and yet sufficiently capable of decision to reassume all this conditioning and to become responsible for it. For the idea which I have never ceased to develop is that in the end one is always responsible for what is made of one. Even if one can do nothing else besides assume this responsibility. For I believe that a man can always make something out of what is made of him. This is the limit I would today accord to freedom: the small movement which makes of a totally conditioned social being someone who does not render back completely what his conditioning has given him. Which makes of Genet a poet when he had been rigorously conditioned to be a thief.

Perhaps the book where I have best explained what I mean by freedom is, in fact, *Saint Genet*. For Genet was made a thief, he said 'I am a thief', and this tiny change was the start of a process whereby he became a poet and then eventually a being no longer even on the margin of society, someone who no longer knows where he is, who falls silent. It cannot be a happy freedom, in a case like this. Freedom is not a triumph. For Genet, it simply marked out certain routes which were not initially given.

L'Etre et Le Néant traced an interior experience, without any co-ordination with the exterior experience of a petty-bourgeois intellectual, which had become historically catastrophic at a certain moment. For I wrote *L'Etre et Le Néant* after the defeat of France, after all. But catastrophes have no lessons, unless they are the culmination of a praxis. Then one can say, my action has failed. But the disaster which overwhelmed the country had taught us nothing. Thus, in *L'Etre et Le Néant*, what you could call 'subjectivity' is not what it would be for me now, the small margin in an operation whereby an interiorization re-exteriorizes itself in an act. But 'subjectivity' and 'objectivity' seem to me entirely useless notions today, anyway. I might still use the term 'objectivity', I suppose, but only to emphasize that everything is objective. The individual interiorizes his social determinations: he interiorizes the relations of production, the family of his childhood, the historical past, the contemporary institutions, and he then re-exteriorizes these in acts and options which necessarily refer us back to them. None of this existed in *L'Etre et Le Néant*.

In L'Etre et Le Néant, *you radically rejected the concept of the unconscious, saying that it was a philosophical contradiction. The model of consciousness in your early work effectively excludes any idea of it whatever. Consciousness is always transparent to itself, even if the subject creates a false screen of 'bad faith'. Since then, you have among other things written a film-script on Freud –*

– I broke with Huston precisely because Huston did not understand what the unconscious was. That was the whole problem. He wanted to suppress it, to replace it with the pre-conscious. He did not want the unconscious at any price –

The question one would like to ask is how you conceive the precise theoretical statute of the work of Freud today? Given your class position, it is not perhaps so surprising that you did not discover Marx before the war. But how did you miss Freud? Surely the opaque evidence of the unconscious, its resistances, should have been accessible to you even then? They are not exactly comparable to the class struggle.

The two questions are linked, however. The thought of both Marx and Freud is a theory of conditioning in exteriority. When Marx says: 'It matters little what the bourgeoisie thinks it does, the important thing is what it does', one could replace the 'bourgeoisie' by 'a hysteric', and the formula would be one of Freud. Having said this, I must try to recount my relationship to Freud's work biographically. I will begin by saying that I undoubtedly had a deep repugnance for psychoanalysis in my youth, which needs to be explained as much as my innocence of the class struggle. The fact that I was a petty-bourgeois was responsible for the latter; one might say that the fact that I was French was responsible for the former. There would certainly be a lot of truth in this. You must never forget the weight of Cartesian rationalism in France. When you have just taken the *bachot* at the age of 17, with the 'I think, therefore I am' of Descartes as your set text, and you open *The Psychopathology of Everyday Life*, and you read the famous episode of Signorelli with its substitutions, combinations and displacements, implying that Freud was simultaneously thinking of a patient who had committed suicide and of certain Turkish mores, and so on – when you read all that, your breath is simply taken away.

Such investigations were completely outside my preoccupations at the time, which were at bottom to provide a philosophical foundation for realism. Which in my opinion is possible today, and which I have tried to do all my life. In other words, how to give man both his autonomy and his reality among real objects, avoiding idealism without lapsing into a mechanistic materialism. I posed the problem in this way because I was ignorant of dialectical materialism, although I should add that this later allowed me to assign certain limits to it – to validate the historical dialectic while rejecting a dialectic of nature, in the sense of a natural process which produces and resolves man into an ensemble of physical laws.

To return to Freud, however, I have to say that I was incapable of understanding him because I was a Frenchman with a good Cartesian tradition behind me, imbued with a certain rationalism, and I was therefore deeply shocked by the idea of the unconscious. However, I will not say *only* this because I must add that I remain shocked by what was inevitable in Freud – the biological and physiological language with which he underpinned thoughts which were not translatable into without mediation. Right up to the time of Fliess, as you know, he wrote physiological studies designed to provide an equivalent of the cathexes and equilibria he had found in psychoanalysis. The result is that the manner in which he describes the psychoanalytic object suffers from a kind of mechanistic cramp. This is not always true, for there are moments when he transcends this. But in general this language produces a *mythology* of the unconscious which I cannot accept. I am completely in agreement with the *facts* of disguise and repression, as facts. But the *words* 'repression', 'censorship', or 'drive' – words which express one moment a sort of finalism and the next moment a sort of mechanism, these I reject. Let us take the example of 'condensation', for instance, which is an ambivalent term in Freud. One can interpret it simply as a phenomenon of association in the same way as your English philosophers and psychologists of the 18th and 19th centuries. Two images are drawn together externally, they condense and form a third: this is classical psychological atomism. But one can also interpret the term on the contrary as expressive of a finality. Condensation occurs because two images combined answer a desire, a need. This sort of ambiguity occurs again and again in Freud. The result is a strange representation of the unconscious as a set of rigorous mechanistic determinations, in any event a causality, and at the same time as a mysterious finality, such that there are 'ruses' of the unconscious, as there are 'ruses' of history; yet it is impossible to reunite the two in the work of many analysts – at least early analysts. I think that there is always a fundamental ambiguity in them; the unconscious is one moment *another consciousness*, and the next moment *other than consciousness*. What is other than consciousness then becomes simply a mechanism.

Thus I would reproach psychoanalytic theory with being a syncretic and not a dialectical thought. The word 'complex', indeed, indicates this very evidently: interpenetration without contradiction. I agree, of course, that there may exist an enormous number of 'larval' contradictions within individuals, which are often translated in certain situations by interpenetrations and not by confrontations. But this does not mean these contradictions do not exist. The results of syncretism, on the contrary, can be seen in the idea of the Oedipus complex, for instance: the fact is that analysts manage to find everything in it, equally well the fixation on the mother, love of the mother, or hatred of the mother, as Melanie Klein argues. In other words, anything can be derived from it, since it is not *structured*. The consequence is that an analyst can say one thing and then the contrary immediately afterwards, without in any way worrying about lack of logic, since after all 'opposites interpenetrate'. A phenomenon can mean this, while its contrary can also mean the same thing. Psychoanalytic theory is thus a 'soft' thought. It has no dialectical logic to it. Psychoanalysts will tell me that this is because there is no such logic in reality. But this is precisely what I am not sure of: I am convinced that complexes exist, but I am not so certain that they are not structured.

In particular, I believe that if complexes are true structures, 'analytic scepticism' would have to be abandoned. What I call the 'affective scepticism' of psychoanalysts is the belief of so many of them that the relationship which unites two people is only a 'reference' to an original relationship which is an absolute: an allusion to a primal scene, incomparable and unforgettable – yet forgotten – between father and mother. Ultimately, any sentiment experienced by an adult becomes for the analyst a sort of occasion for the rebirth of another. Now, there is a real truth in this: the fixation of a girl on an older man may well come from her father, or the fixation of a young man on a girl may derive from a profusion of original relationships. But what is missing in conventional psychoanalytic accounts is the idea of dialectical irreducibility. In a truly dialectical theory, such as historical materialism, phenomena derive from each other dialectically: there are different configurations of dialectical reality, and each of these configurations is rigorously conditioned by the previous one, while preserving and superseding it at the same time. This supersession is, however, precisely irreducible. While one configuration may preserve another, it can never simply be reduced to its predecessor. It is the idea of this *autonomy* that is lacking in psychoanalytic theory. A sentiment or a passion between two persons is certainly highly conditioned by their relationship to the 'primal object', and one can locate this object within it and explain the new relationship by it; but the relationship itself remains irreducible.

Thus there is an essential difference in my relationship to Marx and my relationship to Freud. When I discovered the class struggle, this was a *true* discovery, in which I now believe totally, in the very form of the descriptions which Marx gave of it. Only the epoch has changed; otherwise it is the same struggle with the same classes and the same road to victory. Whereas I do not believe in the unconscious in the form in which psychoanalysis presents it to us. In my present book on Flaubert, I have replaced my earlier notion of consciousness (although I still use the word a lot), with what I call *le vécu* – lived experience. I will try to describe in a moment what I mean by this term, which is neither the precautions of the preconscious, nor the unconscious, nor consciousness, but the terrain in which the individual is perpetually overflowed by himself and his riches and consciousness plays the trick of determining itself by forgetfulness.

In L'Etre et Le Néant, *there is not much room for the phenomenon of dreams. For Freud dreams were a privileged 'space' of the unconscious, the zone where psychoanalysis was discovered. Do you try to situate the space of dreams in your current works? This would be a concrete test of your present relationship to Freud.*

My work on Flaubert deals with dreams. Unfortunately Flaubert himself reports very few of his dreams. But there are two extremely striking ones – both nightmares, which he recounts in *Mémoires d'un Fou*, an autobiography he wrote at the age of 17, and which are thus perhaps partly invented. One concerns his father, the other his mother: both reveal his relationship to his parents with an extraordinary evidence. The interesting thing, however, is that otherwise Flaubert virtually never mentions his parents in his writings. In fact, he had very bad relationships with both his father and his mother, for a whole number of reasons which I try to analyse. He says nothing about them. They do not exist in his early works. The only time that he speaks of them, he speaks of them precisely where a psychoanalyst would like him to do so, in the narrative of a dream. Yet it is Flaubert himself who spontaneously does so. Thereafter, at the very end of his life, five years before he died, he published a novella called *La Légende de Saint Julien l'Hospitalier*, which he said he had wanted to write for thirty years: it is in effect the story of a man who kills his father and his mother and who becomes a writer by doing so.

Thus Flaubert has two quite different conceptions of himself. One is at the level of banal description, for example when he writes to his mistress Louise: 'What am I? Am I intelligent or am I stupid? Am I sensitive or am I stolid? Am I mean or am I generous? Am I selfish or am I selfless? I have no idea, I suppose I am like everyone else, I waver between all these. . . .' In other words, at this level he is completely lost. Why? Because none of these notions has any meaning in themselves. They only acquire a meaning from inter-subjectivity, in other words what I have called in the *Critique* the 'objective spirit' within which each member of a group or society refers to himself and appears to others, establishing relations of interiority between persons which derive from the same information or the same context.

Yet one cannot say that Flaubert did not have, at the very height of his activity, a comprehension of the most obscure origins of his own history. He once wrote a remarkable sentence: 'You are doubtless like myself, you all have the same terrifying and tedious depths' – *les mêmes profondeurs terribles et ennuyeuses*. What could be a better formula for the whole world of psychoanalysis, in which one makes terrifying discoveries, yet which always tediously come to the same thing? His awareness of these depths was not an intellectual one. He later wrote that he often had fulgurating intuitions, akin to a dazzling bolt of lightning in which one simultaneously sees nothing and sees everything. Each time they went out, he tried to retrace the paths revealed to him by this blinding light, stumbling and falling in the subsequent darkness.

For me, these formulations define the relationship which Flaubert had with what is ordinarily called the unconscious, and what I would call a total absence of knowledge, but a real comprehension. I distinguish here between comprehension and intellection: there can be intellection of a practical conduct, but only comprehension of a passion. What I call *le vécu* – lived experience – is precisely the ensemble of the dialectical process of psychic life, in so far as this process is obscure to itself because it is a constant totalization, thus necessarily a totalization which cannot be conscious of what it is. One can be conscious of an external totalization, but one cannot be conscious of a totalization which also totalizes consciousness. 'Lived experience', in this sense, is perpetually susceptible of comprehension, but never of knowledge. Taking it as a point of departure, one can know certain psychic phenomena by concepts, but not this experience itself. The highest form of comprehension of lived experience can forge its own language – which will always be inadequate, and yet which will often have the metaphorical structure of the dream itself. Comprehension of a dream occurs when a man can express it in a language which is itself dreamt. Lacan says that the unconscious is structured like a language. I would say that the language which expresses it has the structure of a dream. In other words, comprehension of the unconscious in most cases never achieves explicit expression. Flaubert constantly speaks of *l'indisable*, which means the 'unsayable', only the word does not exist in French, it should be *l'indicible* (perhaps it was a regional usage in Flaubert's time, but in any case it is not the normal word). The 'unsayable', however, was something very definite for him. When he gave his autobiography to his mistress at the age of 25, he wrote to her: 'You will suspect all the unsayable.' Which did not mean family secrets or anything like that. Of course, he hated his elder brother, but this is not what he was talking about. He meant precisely this kind of comprehension of oneself which cannot be named and which perpetually escapes one.

The conception of 'lived experience' marks my change since *L'Etre et Le Néant*. My early work was a rationalist philosophy of consciousness. It was all very well for me to dabble in apparently non-rational processes in the individual, the fact remains that *L'Etre et Le Néant* is a monument of rationality. But in the end it becomes an irrationalism, because it cannot account rationally for those processes which are 'below' consciousness and which are also rational, but lived as irrational. Today, the notion of 'lived experience' represents an effort to preserve that presence to itself which seems to me indispensable for the existence of any psychic fact, while at the same time this presence is so opaque and blind before itself that it is also an absence from itself. Lived experience is always simultaneously present to itself and absent from itself. In developing this notion, I have tried to surpass the traditional psychoanalytic ambiguity of psychic facts which are both teleological and mechanical, by showing that every psychic fact involves an intentionality which aims at something, while among them a certain number can only exist if they are comprehended, but neither named nor known. The latter include what I call the 'stress' of a neurosis. A neurosis is in the first instance a specific wound, a defective structure which is a certain way of living a childhood. But this is only the initial wound: it is then patched up and bandaged by a system which covers and soothes the wound, and which then, like anti-bodies in certain cases, suddenly does something abominable to the organism. The unity of this system is the neurosis. The work of its 'stress' is intentional, but it cannot be seized as such without disappearing. It is precisely for this reason that if it is transferred into the domain of knowledge, by analytic treatment, it can no longer be reproduced in the same manner.

There is an obvious question raised by your work on Flaubert. You have already written a study of Baudelaire –

– A very inadequate, an extremely bad one –

Then a long book on Genet, after that an essay on Tintoretto and then an autobiography, Les Mots. *After this succession of writings, what will be the methodological novelty of the book on Flaubert? Why exactly did you decide to return once again to the project of explaining a life?*

In the *Question de Méthode*, I discussed the different mediations and procedures which could permit an advance in our knowledge of men if they were taken together. In fact, everyone knows and everyone admits, for instance, that psychoanalysis and Marxism should be able to find the mediations necessary to allow a combination of the two. Everyone adds, of course, that psychoanalysis is not primary, but that correctly coupled and rationalized with Marxism, it can be useful. Likewise, everyone says that there are American sociological notions which have a certain validity, and that sociology in general should be used – not, of course, the Russian variety which is no more than an enumeration or nomenclature. Everyone agrees on all this. Everyone in fact *says* it – but who has tried to *do* it?

I myself was in general only repeating these irreproachable maxims in *Question de Méthode*. The idea of the book on Flaubert was to abandon these theoretical disquisitions, because they were ultimately getting us nowhere, and to try to give a concrete example of how it might be done. The result can look after itself. Even if it is a failure, it can thereby give others the idea of redoing it, better. For the question the book seeks to answer is: how shall I study a man with all these methods, and how in this study will these methods condition each other and find their respective place?

You feel you did not have these keys when you wrote Saint Genet, *for example?*

No, I did not have them all. It is obvious that the study of the conditioning of Genet at the level of institutions and of history is inadequate – very, very inadequate. The main lines of the interpretation, that Genet was an orphan of Public Assistance, who was sent to a peasant home and who owned nothing, remain true, doubtless. But all the same, this happened in 1925 or so and there was a whole context to this life which is quite absent. The Public Assistance, a foundling, represent specific social phenomena, and anyway Genet is a product of the twentieth century; yet none of this is registered in the book.

Whereas today I would like the reader to feel the presence of Flaubert the whole time; my ideal would be that the reader simultaneously feels, comprehends and knows the personality of Flaubert, totally as an individual and yet totally as an expression of his time. In other words, Flaubert can only be understood by his difference from his neighbours.

Do you see what I mean by this? For example, there were a consider-able number of writers who elaborated analogous theories at the time and produced more or less valid works inspired by them, Leconte de Lisle or the Goncourts, for example: it is necessary to try to study how they were all determined to produce this particular vision, and how Flaubert was determined similarly yet otherwise, and saw it in another fashion. My aim is to try to demonstrate the encounter between the development of the person, as psychoanalysis has shown it to us, and the development of history. For at a certain moment, an individual in his very deepest and most intimate conditioning, by the family, can fulfil a historical role. Robespierre could be taken as an example, for instance. But it would be impossible to pursue such a study of him, because there are no materials for doing so. What would be necessary to know is what was the encounter of the revolution which created the Committee of Public Safety, and the son of Monsieur and Madame Robespierre of Arras.

This is the theoretical aim of your present work. But why exactly the choice of Flaubert?

Because he is the imaginary. With him, I am at the border, the barrier of dreams.

There have been writers or politicians who have left a certain work and who could equally well provide the material for such a study –

In theory, yes. There were a number of reasons, however, which led me to select Flaubert. Firstly, to give the strictly circumstantial cause of this selection: Flaubert is one of the very rare historical or literary personages who have left behind so much information about themselves. There are no less than 13 volumes of correspondence, each of 600 pages or so. He often wrote letters to several persons the same day, with slight variations between them which are often very amusing. Apart from this, there are numerous reports and witnesses of him; the Goncourt brothers kept a diary and saw Flaubert very frequently, so that we see him from the outside through the Goncourts and we also have a record of what he said to others about himself, recorded by the Goncourts – not an altogether trustworthy source, of course, since they were rancorous imbeciles in many ways. Nevertheless, there are many facts in their *Journal*. Besides this, of course, there is a complete correspondence with George Sand, letters of George Sand on Flaubert, memoirs of him, and so on. All this is completely circumstantial, but it is of great importance.

Secondly, however, Flaubert represents for me the exact opposite of my own conception of literature: a total disengagement and a certain idea of form, which is not that which I admire. For example, Stendhal is a writer whom I greatly prefer to Flaubert, while Flaubert is probably much more important for the development of the novel than Stendhal. I mean that Stendhal is much finer and stronger. One can give oneself completely to him – his style is acceptable, his heroes are sympathetic, his vision of the world is true and the historical conception behind it is very acute. There is nothing like this in Flaubert. Only, Flaubert is much more significant than Stendhal for the history of the novel. If Stendhal had not existed, it would still have been possible to go straight from Laclos to Balzac. Whereas, let us say, Zola or the Nouveau Roman are inconceivable without Flaubert. Stendhal is greatly loved by the French, but his influence on the novel is minimal. Flaubert's influence by contrast is immense, and for this reason alone it is important to study him. Given that, he began to fascinate me precisely because I saw him in every way as the contrary of myself. I found myself wondering: 'How was he possible?' For then I rediscovered another dimension of Flaubert, which is besides the very source of his talent. I was used to reading Stendhal and company, where one is in complete accord with the hero, whether he is Julien Sorel or Fabrice.

Reading Flaubert one is plunged into persons with whom one is in complete disaccord, who are irksome. Sometimes one feels with them, and then somehow they suddenly reject one's sympathy and one finds oneself once again antagonistic to them. Obviously it was this that fascinated me, because it made me curious. This is precisely Flaubert's art. It is clear that he detested himself, and when he speaks of his principal characters, he has a terrible attitude of sadism and masochism towards them: he tortures them because they are himself, and also to show that other people and the world torture him. He also tortures them because they are not him and he is anyway vicious and sadistic and wants to torture others. His unfortunate characters have very little luck, submitted to all this.

At the same time, Flaubert writes from within his characters and is always speaking of himself in a certain fashion. He thus succeeds in speaking of himself in a way that is unique. This type of discomfited, refused confession, with its self-hatred, its constant reversion to things he comprehends without knowing, wanting to be completely lucid and yet always grating – Flaubert's testimony about himself is something exceptional, which had never been seen before and has not been seen since. This is another motive for studying him.

The third reason for choosing Flaubert is that he represents a sequel to *L'Imaginaire*. You may remember that in my very early book *L'Imaginaire* I tried to show that an image is not a sensation reawakened, or re-worked by the intellect, or even a former perception altered and attenuated by knowledge, but is something entirely different – an absent reality, focused in its absence through what I called an *analogon*: that is to say, an object which serves as an analogy and is traversed by an intention. For example, when you are going to sleep, the little dots in your eyes – phosphenes – may serve as an analogy for every kind of oneiric or hypnagogic image. Between waking and sleeping, some people see vague shapes pass, which are phosphenes through which they focus on an imagined person or a thing. In *L'Imaginaire*, I tried to prove that imaginary objects – images – are an absence. In my book on Flaubert, I am studying imaginary persons – people who like Flaubert act out roles. A man is like a leak of gas, escaping into the imaginary. Flaubert did so perpetually; yet he also had to see reality because he hated it, so there is the whole question of the relationship between the real and the imaginary which I try to study in his life and work.

Finally, via all this, it is possible to ask the question: what was the *imaginary social world* of the dreamy bourgeoisie of 1848? This is an intriguing subject in itself. Between 1830 and 1840 Flaubert was in a Lycée in Rouen, and all his texts speak of his fellow-pupils there as contemptible, mediocre bourgeois. It so happens, however, that there were five years of violent, historic fights in the lycées of that time! After the revolution of 1830, there were boys who launched political struggles in the schools, who fought and were defeated. The reading of the romantics, of which Flaubert speaks so often as a challenge to their parents, is only explicable in this perspective: when these youths finally become *blasés*, they have been recuperated as 'ironic' bourgeois, and they have failed. The extraordinary thing is that Flaubert does not say a word about any of this. He simply describes the boys who surround him as if they were future adults – in other words, abject. He writes: 'I saw defects which would become vices, needs which would become manias, follies which would become crimes – in short, children would become men.' The only history of the school for him was the passage from childhood to maturity. The reality is, however, that this history was that of a bourgeoisie seized with shame at itself in its sons, of the defeat of these sons and thereby the suppression of its shame. The end result of this history will be the massacre of 1848.

Before 1830, the bourgeoisie was hiding under its blankets. When it finally emerged, its sons cried 'Bravo! We are going to declare the Republic,' but their fathers found they needed an eiderdown after all. Louis-Philippe became king. The sons persuaded themselves their fathers had been duped, and continued the struggle. The result was an uproar in the schools: in vain, they were expelled. In 1831, when Louis-Philippe dismisses Lafayette and the road to reaction is open, there were boys of 13 or 14 in Flaubert's school, who calmly refused to go to confession, having decided that this was an excellent pretext for a confrontation with the authorities, since after all the bourgeoisie was still officially Voltairean. Confession was a survival from Louis XVIII and Charles X, and raised awkward questions about compulsory religious instruction, which might eventually get as far as the Chamber of Deputies. I take off my hat to these boys of 14 who planned this strategy, knowing very well that they would be expelled from the school. The chaplain descended on them – 'Confess!' 'No!' – then another functionary – 'No, No, No!' – they were taken to the principal and thrown out of the school. Whereupon there was a gigantic uproar in the whole college, which was what they had hoped for. The fourth year class threw rotten eggs at the vice-principal, and two more boys were expelled. Then the day-boys of the class met at dawn and took an oath to avenge their comrades. The next day at six in the morning, the boarders opened the doors to them. Together, they seized and occupied the building.

Already, in 1831! From their fortress there, they bombarded the Academic Council which was deliberating in another building within reach of their windows.

The principal was meanwhile throwing himself at the feet of the older pupils, imploring them not to solidarize with the occupation – successfully. Eventually, the fourth year class did not achieve the reinstatement of their comrades, but the authorities had to promise that there would be no sanctions against them for the occupation. Three days later, they found they had been tricked: the college was closed for two months. Exactly like today!

The next year, when they came back, they were naturally raging and there was constant turbulence in the Lycée. This was the time in which Flaubert lived, and yet he did not experience it like that. He wrote a great deal about his childhood and youth – but there is not a single text which refers to this history. In fact, what happened, of course, was that he lived the same evolution of this generation in his own way. He was unaffected by this violent episode and yet he arrived at the same result by a different route somewhat later. The philosophy teacher in the school fell ill, and a substitute took over for him. The pupils decided the substitute was an incompetent and made life impossible for him. The principal tried to victimize two or three, and the whole class solidarized with them: Flaubert now wrote their collective letter to the principal, denouncing the quality of the course and the threats of punishment. The upshot was that he and two or three others were expelled from the school. The meaning of the protest this time is very clear: Flaubert and his class-mates were young bourgeois demanding a proper bourgeois education – 'Our fathers are paying enough, after all.' The evolution of a generation and of a class are manifest in this second episode. These different experiences produce a bitter literature on the bourgeoisie and then this generation resigns itself to becoming merely ironic – another way of being bourgeois.

Why have you opted for biography and the theatre in recent years, and abandoned the novel? Is it that you think Marxism and psychoanalysis have rendered the novel as a form impossible, by the weight of their concepts?

I have often asked myself that question. It is, in fact, true that there is no technique that can account for a character in a novel as one can account for a real person, who has existed, by means of a Marxist or psychoanalytic interpretation. But if an author has recourse to these two systems within a novel, without an adequate formal device for doing so, the novel disappears. These devices are lacking, and I do not know if they are possible.

You think that the existence of Marxism and of psychoanalysis prevents any novelist from writing, so to speak, naïvely today?

By no means. But if he does so, the novel will all the same be classified as 'naïve'. In other words, a natural universe of the novel will not exist, only a certain specific type of novel – the 'spontaneous', 'naïve' novel. There are excellent examples of the latter, but the author who writes them has to make a conscious decision to ignore these interpretative techniques. Thereby he necessarily becomes less naïve. There is another type of novel today in which the work is conceived as a sort of infernal machine – fake novels like those of Gombrowicz, for example. Gombrowicz is aware of psychoanalysis, and of Marxism and many other things, but he remains sceptical about them, and hence constructs objects which destroy themselves in their very act of construction – creating a model for what might be a novel with an analytic and materialist foundation.

Why have you personally stopped writing novels?

Because I have felt no urge to do so. Writers have always more or less chosen the imaginary. They have a need for a certain ration of fiction. Writing on Flaubert is enough for me by way of fiction – it might indeed be called a novel. Only I would like people to say that it was a true novel. I try to achieve a certain level of comprehension of Flaubert by means of hypotheses. Thus I use fiction – guided and controlled, but nonetheless fiction – to explore why, let us say, Flaubert wrote one thing on the 15th March and the exact opposite on the 21st March, to the same correspondent, without worrying about the contradiction. My hypotheses are in this sense a sort of invention of the personage.

You have reproached a book like The Children of Sanchez *for not being a literary work because the people in it spoke a language like that of all of us when we are not writers. You think such works lack invention?*

The Children of Sanchez is not a literary work, but it renders a mass of literary works redundant. Why write a novel on its characters or their milieu? They tell us much more by themselves, with a much greater self-understanding and eloquence. The book is not literature because there is no quest for a form that is also a meaning in it: for me the two – form and meaning – are always linked. There is no production of an object, a constructed object.

You continue to write plays?

Yes, because plays are something else again. For me the theatre is essentially a myth. Take the example of a petty-bourgeois and his wife who quarrel with each other the whole time. If you tape their disputes, you will record not only the two of them, but the petty-bourgeoisie and its world, what society has made of it, and so on. Two or three such studies and any possible novel on the life of a petty-bourgeois couple would be outclassed. By contrast, the relationship between man and woman as we see it in Strindberg's *Dance of Death* will never be outclassed. The subject is the same, but taken to the level of myth. The playwright presents to men the *eidos* of their daily existence: their own life in such a way that they see it as if externally. This was the genius of Brecht, indeed. Brecht would have protested violently if anyone said to him that his plays were myths. Yet what else is *Mother Courage* – an anti-myth that despite itself becomes a myth?

You discussed the theatre with Brecht?

I saw Brecht three or four times in a political context, but we never had a chance to discuss the theatre. I admire Brecht's plays very much, but I think that what Brecht said about them is not always true. His theory of *Entfremdung* – distanciation – is one thing: the actual relationship between the public and his characters is another. The blind and deaf girl in *Mother Courage* calls to the people when she falls from the roof, dying. This is a scene of pathos, and yet it is precisely a passage of the play

where Brecht most wants to establish a contestation and recoil from
the drama. Mother Courage herself is an anti-heroine who – unavoidably,
by her very mystification – becomes a heroine. The *Caucasian Chalk
Circle* presents the same paradox – scenes such as the flight of the servant
or the adjudication of the child, which despite all Brecht's efforts are
extremely moving in the most classical tradition of the theatre. Brecht
was tremendously astute in his use of theatre, but he could not always
control the final result of his writing.

The Critique de la Raison Dialectique *appears to be constructed on the idea
that there is a fundamental homogeneity between the individual and history:
the central theme of the book is the reversible relationships – interversions –
between the individual, worked matter, the group, the series, the practico-inert,
collectives. To adopt its vocabulary, your formal aim is to show how the
totalizing acts of every individual are totalized in exteriority by others and
become other to their agents, just as groups become other to themselves through
serialization. The* Critique *deals in a very systematic way with that aspect of
history which presents itself as alienation and degradation of intentional
projects, whether by individuals or groups, in their encounter with materiality
and alterity, in the world of scarcity. There is, however, another aspect of
history which is not accounted for by the* Critique. *Social facts are not simply
a totalization in exteriority of the totalizing acts of a multiplicity of individuals
and groups, which may during certain privileged moments achieve an apocalyp-
tic sovereignty, but which normally fall into the practico-inert. They have an
intrinsic order of their own, which is not deducible from the criss-crossing of
innumerable individual totalizations. The most obvious example of this is
language – which can in no way be described as a simple totalization of all the
speech-acts of linguistic agents. The subject who speaks never totalizes linguistic
laws by his words. Language has its own intelligibility as a system which
appears* heterogeneous *to the subject. Can the themes of 'totalization' and
the 'practico-inert' ever account for the emergence of ordered social structures
not merely random alienation of subjective projects?*

But there is totalization in language. You cannot say a single sentence
which does not refer, by its elements, to opposites. Thereby the whole
of language, as a system of differential meanings, is present in its very
absence, as linguists themselves admit. Every sentence is a levy on the

entire resources of speech, for words only exist by their opposition to each other. There is thus certainly totalization in language.

The question is whether there is only totalization? There are two central ex-
amples in the Critique *of a multiplicity of totalizations which fall into the*
practico-inert and become an alien power denaturing the intentions of their
agents. One is that of different Chinese peasants cutting down trees to enlarge
their cultivation of land, thus creating erosion, which thereby causes floods
which then ruin their lands. The other is of the impact of gold in 16th-century
Spain – whereby the individual decisions of each single producer to raise
prices caused an uncontrollable general inflation which eventually resulted in
the collective impoverishment of all of them. These two examples do not have
the same type of intelligibility –

I agree. The deforestation of the Chinese peasants is a product of in-dividuals, each acting on their own, directly on nature, in ignorance of the others. They are not united by any collective object, and it is only gradually that the end-result of their acts imposes itself on them. The counter-finality of these peasants is cultural, but it concerns above all the relationship of a multiplicity of individuals with nature. Whereas the impact of gold in Spain presupposes money, which is a social in-stitution. Money has nothing natural about it, it is a conventional system in some ways very similar to language. Thus gold is a pre-eminently social fact. I therefore am perfectly in agreement that there is a specific reality of social facts. This reality implies precisely that every totalization of the individual in relation to this reality either fails, is deviated by it or is a negative totalization. When I speak, I never say completely what I want to say and I often do not know what I say, given that my words are robbed from me and revealed to me as other than what I intended. But the important thing is that these social facts are, in spite of everything, the product of the social activity of collective ensembles. I will be dis-cussing this in the second volume of the *Critique*. Language exists only as a convention.

But where does the order of this convention come from? To ask the same
question in a different way: by the end of the Critique *the reader has been*
taken through all the different reversible relationships of individuals, groups,

series and the practico-inei t, which constitute for you 'the formal elements of
any history'. Yet from this perspective there seems to be no reason why history
should not then be an arbitrary chaos of inter-blocking projects, a sort of
colossal traffic-jam?

There are a number of reasons. The first is that accumulation exists.
There are crucial domains where accumulation occurs: science, capital,
goods – which thereby produce a history: change. This is something
different from a mere transition. There are periods which are transitions,
until something is invented that changes. For example, the whole feudal
period of the 11th, 12th and 13th centuries is a perpetual turmoil:
there were events everywhere, yet there was no emergence from the
Middle Ages because the elements for doing so did not exist. Then, one
day, a certain number of processes coincided, social and economic facts
like the indebtedness of the lords, the ruin of the Church, the change
in the nature of Catholicism, the peasant revolts, scientific discoveries,
and a spiral development of history resulted. Science, of course, in a
sense advanced in a straight line through all its conversions, hesitations
and errors. These mistakes and confusions might be classified as 'subjective' – they have little importance in the development of science. On
the other hand, they whirl about every level of science and deform its
discoveries and practices, changing them into other than themselves: a
discovery made because of war in time of war will serve in peace, while
a discovery in time of peace will serve for war. Simultaneously, there are
whole plateaux where the class struggle changes because there is a new
mode of production. I have not discussed any of this in the first volume
of the *Critique*, both because I believe in the general schema provided by
Marx and because I intend to study it at the level of history proper. For
it is at the level of history that one should determine to what extent there
is or is not progress, to what extent progress exists only where there is
accumulation, and whether it produces in its train total modifications
which are not necessarily progressive.

What is going to be the architecture of the second volume of the Critique *?*

I will simply try to show the dialectical intelligibility of a movement of
historical temporalization.

A *movement?*

The movement. The difference between the first and second volume is this: the first is an abstract work where I show the possibilities of exchange, degradation, the practico-inert, series, collectives, recurrence and so on. It is concerned only with the theoretical possibilities of their combinations. The object of the second volume is history itself. But I know no other history than our own, so the question 'What is history?' becomes 'What is our history?' – the history in which Mahomet was born and not one in which he never lived. It is irrelevant to wonder whether there are other histories in other galaxies. Perhaps there are, but we know nothing of them, and they consequently have no importance for us. Thus all the notions which will emerge from the second volume will be rigorously applied to our own history; my aim will be to prove that there is a dialectical intelligibility of the singular. For ours is a singular history. It is determined by the forces of production and the relations of production, their correspondences and their conflicts. It is possible that in completely primitive societies there exist the 'global facts' of which Mauss speaks – a kind of undifferentiated social conditioning. But even if this were so, it is not the history that I will be studying. What I will seek to show is the dialectical intelligibility of that which is not universalizable.

It is still very difficult to see how a multiplicity of individual acts can never give birth to social structures which have their own laws, discontinuous from the acts which for you formally constitute a historical dialect? A tribe can speak a language for centuries and then be discovered by an anthropologist who can decipher its phonological laws, which have been forever unknown to the totality of the subjects speaking the language. How can these objective laws be deduced merely from words spoken?

I believe that all the same language is a totalized and detotalized result of the ensemble of human activities during a certain time. Language is imposed on each of us as a practico-inert.

The connotation of 'practico-inert' is precisely that of a brute, random mass alien to human agents. The problem is, how does this mass happen to have a rigorous structure – the laws of grammar, or more fundamentally, the relations of production? These structures are never intentional objects – they are heterogeneous to the historical acts of individuals?

There is a historical problem of the passage from non-language to language in early human communities: it is impossible to reconstruct this passage, but probably it was accomplished within certain early institutions. For language sustains institutions, institutions are a language, and language is itself an institution. From the moment that a limited system of signs exists, which has an institutional character, both invented by the group and already dividing the group, language can change men into collectives. I have tried to explain this in the *Critique*. An institution or collective object is always a product of the activity of the group in *matter*, whether verbal matter or physico-chemical matter, and is thereby sealed and surpassed by an inertia which separates the group and imposes itself on it as the instituted and sacred. The subjective here capsizes into the objective and the objective into the subjective: the result is an instituted object. Thus I am in complete agreement that social facts have their own structures and laws that dominate individuals, but I only see in this the reply of worked matter to the agents who work it.

Why is this 'reply' a coherent discourse?

For me the fact of being worked does not endow matter with a system, but the fact of becoming inert converts work into a system.

Not everything that is inert is a system.

Structures are created by activity which has no structure, but suffers its results as a structure.

How can individual acts result in ordered structures, and not a tangled labyrinth – unless you believe in a sort of pre-established harmony between them?

You are forgetting the level of power and therefore of generality. If a decision is taken at a certain level of political or religious power, an objective unity is given by the project at that level. What then happens is that others deviate and deform the project, but they simultaneously create something else by their work: other structures with their own internal relations which constitute a queer kind of object, but a potent and significant one. In the last chapter of the *Critique*, entitled 'Towards History', I started to discuss this problem. I tried to argue that an object created by a plurality of different or antagonistic groups is nevertheless, in the very moment of their shock against each other, intelligible. In the second volume, I was going to take the elementary example of a battle, which remains intelligible after the confusion of the two armies engaged in combat in it. From there I planned to develop a study of the objects constituted by entire collectivities with their own interests. In particular, I want to analyse the example of Stalin to see how the objects which constituted Stalinist institutions were created through the ensemble of relationships between groups and within groups in Soviet society, and through the relationship of all these to Stalin and of Stalin to them. Finally, I was going to end by studying the unity of objects in a society completely rent asunder by class struggle, and considering several classes and their actions to show how these objects were completely deviated and always represented a detotalization while at the same time preserving a determinate intelligibility. Once one has reached this, one has reached history. Hence I had the embryo of an answer to the question you have been asking me. There is an institutional order which is necessarily – unless we are to believe in God the father or an organicist mythology – the product of masses of men constituting a social unity and which at the same time is radically distinct from all of them, becoming an implacable demand and an ambiguous means of communication and noncommunication between them. Aesop said that language is both. The same is true of institutions. Indeed, I would like to write a study of work and technology to show exactly what happens to material in industry, how it becomes an inhuman image of man, by its demands. For I believe that the existence of different ethics in different epochs is due to matter: it is because of inert, inanimate objects that there are demands in us. A demand is fixed and inert: a duty has no life in it, it is always immobile and imbecile, because whenever anyone tries to do his so-called duty, he always finds himself in opposition to others. This contradiction ultimately derives from the demands of materiality in us. To sum up what I have been saying in a sentence: my aim in the second volume of the *Critique* was precisely a study of the paradoxical object which is an institutional ensemble that is perpetually detotalized.

There is another dimension of the Critique *which must be striking for any new reader of it today. The book in some respects appears an anticipation of two of the major historical events of recent years, the May Revolt in France and the Cultural Revolution in China. There are long analyses of the dialectical relationship between class, cadres, trade-unions and political party during factory occupations, taking 1936 as a model, which often seem to prefigure the trajectory of the French proletariat in May 1968. At the same time, there is a passage where you evoke the official parades in Tien An Minh Square in the Peking of the early sixties as a sort of pyramidal 'mineralization of man', whereby a bureaucratic order manipulates dispersed series beneath it to confer on them a false semblance of groups. Do you then today interpret the Cultural Revolution as an attempt to reverse the deterioration of the Chinese Revolution into a set of bureaucratically institutionalized groups manipulating passive masses, by a sort of gigantic 'apocalypse' throughout China which recreates 'fused groups' such as once made the Long March and the People's War – to use the language of the* Critique?

I should say that I regard myself as very inadequately informed about the Cultural Revolution. The specific level of the phenomenon is that of ideology, culture and politics – in other words, superstructures which are the higher instances of any dialectical scale. But what happened at the level of infrastructures in China which led to the initiation of this movement in the superstructures? There must have been determinate contradictions at the base of the Chinese socialist economy which produced the movement for a return to something like a perpetual fused group. It is possible that the origins of the Cultural Revolution are to be found in the conflicts over the Great Leap Forward, and the investment policies undertaken at that time: Japanese Marxists have often maintained this. But I nevertheless must confess that I have not succeeded in understanding the causes of the phenomenon in its totality. The idea of a perpetual apocalypse is naturally very attractive – but I am convinced that it is not exactly this, and that the infrastructural reasons for the Cultural Revolution must be sought.

You do not think that Sino-Soviet conflict was a crucial determinant? Part of the Chinese leadership appears to have consciously been determined to avoid any reproduction of the present state of the USSR in China. Is it

*necessary to assume insurmountable contradictions within the Chinese economy
to explain the Cultural Revolution?*

I certainly do not think that the Cultural Revolution is in any way a
mechanical reflection of infrastructural contradictions: but I think that
to understand its total meaning one should be able to reconstruct the
precise moment of the historical process and of the economy at which it
exploded. It is perfectly clear, for instance, that Mao was virtually
marginalized for a certain time and that he has now reassumed power.
This change is undoubtedly linked to internal Chinese conflicts, which
go back at least to the Great Leap Forward.

Equally striking are the contradictions within the Cultural Revolution.
There is a central discordance between the unleashing of mass initiatives
and the cult of the leader. On the one side, there is the perpetual maintenance of the fused group with unlimited personal initiatives within it,
with the possibility of writing anything in big-character posters, even
'Chou En-lai to the gallows' – which did, in fact happen in Peking; on
the other side, there is the fetichization of the little red book, read aloud
in waiting rooms, in airplanes, in railway stations, read before others
who repeat it in chorus, read by taxi-drivers who stop their cab to read
it to passengers – a hallucinating collective catechism which resounds
from one end of China to the other.

*Your own analysis of the fundamental reason for the degradation of groups
into series in the* Critique *is that scarcity ultimately renders inevitable the
fall of any collective project into the practico-inert. China remains a very
poor country, with a low level of development of productive forces. Your own
account of the reign of scarcity leads to the conclusion that it is impossible to
abolish bureaucracy in such a country; any attempt to overcome bureaucratic
degradation of the revolution will inevitably be profoundly marked by the
objective limits imposed by scarcity. This line of argument would explain the
bureaucratic safety-rails, whether institutional like the army or ideological
like the cult of personality, which trammel mass initiative in China?*

It is evident that completely untrammelled initiatives can lead to a sort
of madness. Because the free and anarchic development of the individual
– not the social individual of the future, but the free practical organism

of today – may not endanger his own reason, but can endanger a society. But to insist on his total freedom within a fused group and at the same time to put pebbles in his head, called the Thoughts of Mao, is not to create a whole man. The two halves of the process are in complete contradiction.

Perhaps the paradox of a cultural revolution is that it is ultimately impossible in China, where it was invented, but is somewhat more possible in the advanced countries of the West?

I think that is correct. With one qualification: is a cultural revolution possible without making *the* revolution? French youth during May wanted a cultural revolution – what was missing for them to achieve one? The ability to make a real revolution. In other words, a revolution which is no way initially cultural, but is the seizure of power by violent class struggle. Which is not to say that the idea of cultural revolution in France was merely a mirage: on the contrary, it expressed a radical contestation of every established value of the university and society, a way of looking at them as if they had already perished. It is very important that this contestation be maintained.

What were the main lessons of the May Revolt for you?

I have always been convinced that the origins of May lie in the Vietnamese Revolution. For the French students who unleashed the process of May, the Vietnamese war was not merely a question of taking the side of the National Liberation Front or the people of Vietnam against US imperialism. The fundamental impact of the war on European or US militants was its enlargement of the field of the possible. It had previously seemed impossible that the Vietnamese could resist successfully such an enormous military machine and win. Yet that is what they did and by doing so they completely changed the horizon of French students, among others: they now knew that there were possibilities that remained unknown. Not that everything was possible, but that one can only know something is impossible once one has tried it and failed. This was a profound discovery, rich in its eventual consequences and revolutionary in the West.

Today, over a year later, it is clear that to a certain extent we have discovered the impossible. In particular, as long as the French Communist Party is the largest conservative party in France, and as long as it has the confidence of the workers, it will be impossible to make the free revolution that was missed in May. Which only means that it is necessary to pursue the struggle, however protracted it may be, with the same persistence as the Vietnamese, who after all are continuing to fight and continuing to win.

May was not a revolution: it did not destroy the bourgeois state. To make the revolution next time, organization will be necessary to co-ordinate and lead the struggle. What sort of political organization do you judge to be the appropriate instrument today?

It is obvious that anarchism leads nowhere, today as yesterday. The central question is whether in the end the only possible type of political organization is that which we know in the shape of the present CPs: hierarchical division between leadership and rank-and-file, communications and instructions proceeding from above downwards only, isolation of each cell from every other, vertical powers of dissolution and discipline, separation of workers and intellectuals? This pattern developed from a form of organization which was born in clandestinity in the time of the Tsars. What are the objective justifications of its existence in the West today? Its purpose here appears merely to ensure an authoritarian centralism which excludes any democratic practice. Of course, in a civil war situation, a militarized discipline is necessary. But does a proletarian party have to resemble the present-day Communist Parties? Is it not possible to conceive of a type of political organization where men are not barred and stifled? Such an organization would contain different currents, and would be capable of closing itself in moments of danger, to reopen thereafter.

It is always true, of course, that to fight something one must change oneself into it; in other words one must become its true opposite and not merely other than it. A revolutionary party must necessarily reproduce – up to a certain limit – the centralization and coercion of the bourgeois state which it is its mission to overthrow. However, the whole problem – the history of our century is there to prove it – is that once a party dialectically undergoes this ordeal, it may become arrested there. The result is then that it has enormous difficulty in ever escaping from the bureaucratic rut which it initially accepted to make the revolution against a bureaucratic-military machine. From that moment on, only a cultural revolution against the new order can prevent a degradation of it. It is not a benevolent reform that is occurring in China today, it is the violent destruction of a whole system of privilege. Yet we know nothing of what the future will be in China. The danger of a bureaucratic deterioration will be powerfully present in any Western country, if we succeed in making the revolution: that is absolutely inevitable, since both external imperialist encirclement and the internal class struggle will continue to exist. The idea of an instant and total liberation is a utopia. We can already foresee some of the limits and constraints of a future revolution. But he who takes these as an excuse not to make the revolution and who fails to struggle for it now, is simply a counter-revolutionary.

Abroad, you are often seen as a classical product of French university culture. The university system in which you were educated and made your early career was the exact target of the first explosion which set off the upheaval of May. What is your judgment of it now?

It is certainly true that I am a product of this system, and I am very aware of it: although I hope I am not only that. When I was a student, only a very small élite got to university, and if one had the additional 'luck' to get into the Ecole Normale, one had every material advantage. In a sense the French university *system* formed me more than its professors, because in my time the latter, with only one or two exceptions, were very mediocre. But the system, above all the Ecole Normale, I accepted as absolutely natural: son and grandson of petty-bourgeois intellectuals, it never occurred to me to question it. The lectures of the *cours magistral* seemed idiotic to us, but only because the teachers who gave it had nothing to tell us. Later, others saw that the lecture course itself was irredeemable. We merely abstained from ever going to the Sorbonne: only once, when law students threatened to invade it, did we go to the lectures there – otherwise never. Most of the Ecole Normale students of my time were very proud if they became *agregés*, for instance (although there were a few who thought the hierarchy of *agregés* and *licenciés* was monstrous). Nizan was an exception, of course. He detested the Ecole Normale, for very good reasons – its class function in creating a privileged élite. Although he was academically 'successful', he never, never fitted into the system. By the third year he was in such a state of malaise that he escaped to Aden. Of course, this was related to neurotic problems in his personal history, but the fundamental fact was that he could not breathe within these institutions designed to perpetuate a monopoly of knowledge.

What is your view of a correct Marxist practice within the institutions of bourgeois culture – the educational system – after May?

Is a positive revolutionary culture conceivable today? For me, this is the most difficult problem posed by your question. My frank opinion is that everything within bourgeois culture that will be surpassed by a revolutionary culture will nevertheless ultimately also be preserved by it. I do not believe that a revolutionary culture will forget Rimbaud, Baudelaire or Flaubert, merely because they were very bourgeois and not exactly friends of the people. They will have their place in any future socialist culture, but it will be a *new* place determined by new needs and relations. They will not be great principal values, but they will be part of a tradition reassessed by a different praxis and a different culture.

But how can they be reassessed today, when a revolutionary culture does not exist? They have only one place within existing society – the site assigned to them by bourgeois culture. What is the 'correct use' of Rimbaud for a young socialist militant in Vincennes or Nanterre? The question is unanswerable. It is true that a certain number of university intellectuals of an older generation became revolutionaries within a society that dispensed this culture to them. But the situation has changed radically since then. To take only the material conditions of a university education: in my time an orthodox lecture course was trundled out to perhaps 15 or 20 people. It was less shocking, because it could formally be contested: a student could interrupt and say he disagreed, and the lecturer would tolerate this because it hid the completely authoritarian character of the whole course. Today, there are 100 or 200 students where there were once 15. There is no longer any chance of this. Where it was once possible to turn bourgeois culture against itself, showing that Liberty, Equality and Fraternity had become their opposites, today the only possibility is to be against bourgeois culture. For the traditional system is collapsing. The Baccalauréat in France is something incredible, in its antiquation. In Rouen-Le Havre recently, the subject of the philosophy paper was: 'Epictetus said to a disciple: "Live Hidden"'. Comment.' Can you imagine – giving a question like that to school-children of sixteen in this day and age! Not only the reference is outrageous, of course. Ten per cent to 20 per cent of the candidates thought that *Vis Caché* (Live Hidden) was *Vices Cachés* (Hidden Vices), imagining perhaps that this was ancient orthography, and interpreted the quotation to mean: 'Hide your Vices.' They then developed at length the idea of Epictetus along the lines 'If you have vices, satisfy them, but secretly.' The funniest, and saddest thing of all is that they approved the formula of Epictetus! 'For it is like that in society, one can have a vice, but one should practise it in solitude.' Innocent answers, showing what bourgeois morality is in fact like; pitiful answers because these pupils obviously thought, 'Epictetus must be famous, if I criticize him I might get 4 out of 20 and fail, the only thing to do is to agree with him.' There is no relationship, no contact whatever between these young people and their teachers. Bourgeois culture in France is destroying itself. Thus for the moment, regardless of the eventual future, I believe that a radical negation of the existing culture is the only possible option for young militants – a negation which will often take the form of violent contestation.

Are you going to write sequel to Les Mots? *What are your future plans?*

No, I do not think that a sequel to *Les Mots* would be of much interest. The reason why I produced *Les Mots* is the reason why I have studied Genet or Flaubert: how does a man become someone who writes, who wants to speak of the imaginary? This is what I sought to answer in my own case, as I sought it in that of others. What could there be to say of my existence since 1939? How I became the writer who produced the particular works I have signed. But the reason why I wrote *La Nausée* rather than some other book is of little importance. It is the birth of the decision to write that is of interest. Thereafter, what is equally interesting are the reasons why I was to write exactly the contrary to what I wanted to write. But this is another subject altogether

– the relationship of a man to the history of his time. Thus what I will write one day is a political testament. The title is perhaps a bad one, since a testament implies the idea of giving advice; here it will simply be the end of a life. What I would like to show is how a man comes to politics, how he is caught by them, and how he is remade other by them; because you must remember that I was not made for politics, and yet I was remade by politics so that I eventually had to enter them. It is this which is curious. I will recount what I did politically, what mistakes I committed, and what resulted from it. In doing so, I will try to define what constitutes politics today, in our own phase of history.

2. Politics

Vietnam: Imperialism and Genocide was written by Sartre in December 1967, in his capacity as President of the International War Crimes Tribunal created by Bertrand Russell. Sartre was charged by the Tribunal with setting out the grounds for its verdict that the United States government had committed genocide in Vietnam. The text was first published in English in *New Left Review* 48.

Czechoslovakia: The Socialism that Came in from the Cold was written in 1970, as an introduction to a volume of interviews with Czechoslovak intellectuals edited by Antonin Liehm, entitled *Trois Generations* (Paris 1970).

France: Masses, Spontaneity, Party was an interview-discussion with the Italian journal *Il Manifesto*, given in August 1969. It was first published in English in *The Socialist Register 1970*; the translation below is used by permission of Merlin Press.

Vietnam: Imperialism and Genocide

The *word* 'genocide' has not been in existence for very long: it was coined by the jurist Lemkin between the two world wars. The *thing* is as old as mankind and so far no society has existed whose structure has prevented it from committing this crime. In any case, genocide is a product of history and it bears the mark of the society from which it comes. The example which we are to consider is the work of the greatest capitalist power in the present-day world: it is as such that we must try and examine it – in other words, in so far as it expresses both the economic infrastructure of this power, its political aims and the contradictions of the present set of circumstances.

In particular we must try to understand the *intentions*, in respect to *genocide*, of the American government in its war against Vietnam. Because Article 2 of the 1948 Convention defines genocide on the basis of intent. The Convention made tacit reference to events that were fresh in everyone's memories: Hitler had openly proclaimed his deliberate intention of exterminating the Jews. He used genocide as a *political means* and did not disguise the fact. The Jew had to be put to death wherever he came from not because he had been caught preparing to fight, or because he was taking part in resistance movements, but simply *because he was Jewish*. Now the American government has naturally been careful not to say anything so explicit. It even claimed that it was rushing to the support of its allies, the South Vietnamese, attacked by the Communists of the North. After studying the facts, can we objectively discover such an unspoken aim? Can we say, after this investigation, that the American armed forces are killing the Vietnamese for the simple reason that they are Vietnamese? This can be established only after a short historical discussion: the structures of war change with the infrastructures of society. Between 1860 and the present day, military thinking and objectives have undergone profound changes, and the outcome of this

metamorphosis is, in fact, the 'cautionary' war the United States is fighting in Vietnam. 1856 – convention to protect the goods of neutral countries;
1864 – attempt at Geneva to protect the wounded; 1899, 1907 – two
conferences at The Hague to try to regulate fighting generally. It was no
coincidence that jurists and governments should have been increasing
the attempts to 'humanize war' on the eve of the most frightful massacres
mankind has ever known. In his work *On Military Conventions*, V. Dedijer
has shown clearly that capitalist societies were also simultaneously
engaged in the process of giving birth to the monster of total war – which
expresses their true nature. This is because:

(1) Rivalry between industrialized nations, who fight over the new
markets, engenders the permanent hostility which is expressed in the
theory and practice of what is known as 'bourgeois nationalism'.

(2) The development of industry, which is at the root of these antagonisms, supplies the means of resolving them to the benefit of one of the
competitors, by producing devices that kill on an ever more *massive* scale.

The result of this development is that it becomes more and more difficult to distinguish between the front and the rest of the country, between
combatants and civilian population.

(3) All the more so since new military objectives are now appearing
near the towns – i.e. the *factories* which, even when they are not actually
working for the army, are nonetheless to some degree the storehouses
of the country's economic potential. The destruction of this potential
is precisely the aim of conflict and the means of winning it.

(4) For this reason, everyone is mobilized: the peasant fights on the
front, the worker supports him behind the lines, the peasant women
take their men's places in the fields. In the *total* struggle mounted by one
nation against another, the worker tends to become a combatant because,
in the final analysis, it is the power that is strongest economically that
has the most chance of winning.

(5) Lastly the democratic development of the bourgeois countries tends
to involve the masses in political life. They do not control the decisions
of those in power, and yet little by little they become self-aware. When
a war breaks out, they no longer feel remote from it. Reformulated,
often distorted by propaganda, it becomes a focus of moral effort for
the whole community: in each belligerent nation everyone, or almost

everyone, after a certain amount of manipulation, becomes the enemy of all the members of the other – which is the last step in the evolution of total war.

(6) These same societies in full technological growth continue to broaden the field of competition by multiplying means of communication. The famous 'One World' of the Americans already existed by the end of the 19th century, when American wheat finally brought about the ruin of the English farmer. Total war is no longer the war waged by all members of one national community against all those of another. It is total *for another reason*: because it may well involve the whole world.

So that war between (bourgeois) *nations* – of which the 1914 war was the first example but which had been threatening Europe since 1900 – was not the *invention* of a single man or a single government, but the simple need for total effort which became obligatory, from the beginning of the century onward, for those who wished to continue politics by other means. In other words, the choice was clear: no war or that war. It was *that war* that our fathers fought. And the governments – who saw it coming without having the intelligence or the courage to avoid it – tried in vain to humanize it.

Yet during the first world conflict, the intention of genocide appeared only sporadically. It was primarily a question – as in previous centuries – of shattering the military power of a country, even if the underlying aim was to ruin its economy. But, if it was true to say that one could no longer distinguish clearly between civilians and soldiers, it was rarely – for this very reason – that the population was overtly aimed at, with the exception of a few terror raids. In any case the belligerents – at any rate those who were actively conducting the war – were industrial powers, which implied a certain balance at the outset: each possessed a force for the dissuasion of possible exterminations – i.e. the power to apply the law of retaliation; this explains why, even in the midst of the massacre, a sort of prudence still reigned.

*

However, after 1830 and during the whole of the last century, there were many examples of genocide outside Europe. Some of these were the expression of authoritarian political structures and the others – those relevant for the understanding of the sources of United States imperialism and the nature of the war in Vietnam – had their origin in the internal structures of the capitalist democracies. To export goods and capital, the great powers – England and France in particular – built themselves colonial empires. The name given by the French to their 'conquests' – *possessions d'outre mer* (overseas possessions) – indicates clearly that they had managed to obtain them only by wars *of aggression*. The aggressor seeks out the adversary on his own ground, in Africa, in Asia, in the under-developed countries; and, far from waging a 'total war', which would presuppose a certain reciprocity at the outset, he takes advantage of his *absolute* superiority in arms to commit only an expeditionary corps to the conflict. This gains an easy victory over the regular armies – if there are any – but as this uncalled-for aggression arouses the hatred of the civilian population, and since the latter is always a mine of rebels or soldiers, the colonial troops hold sway by terror, that is to say, by constantly renewed massacres. These massacres are genocidal in character: they involve destroying 'a part of the group' (ethnic, national, religious) to terrorize the rest and to *destructure* the native society. When in the last century the French, after wreaking havoc in Algeria, imposed on its tribal society – where each community owned the land jointly – the practice of the *Code Civile,* which introduced the legal norms of bourgeois ownership and enforced the dividing up of inheritances, they systematically destroyed the economic infrastructure of the country and the land soon passed from the peasant clans into the hands of traders from the parent country. In point of fact colonization is not a matter of mere conquest – like the annexation in 1870 by Germany of Alsace-Lorraine; it is, of necessity, cultural genocide. Colonization cannot take place without the systematic elimination of the distinctive features of the native society, combined with the refusal to allow its members integration with the parent country, or to benefit from its advantages. Colonialism is, in fact, a system: the colony sells raw materials and foodstuffs at preferential rates to the colonizing power which, in return, sells the colony industrial goods at the price current on the world market. This curious system of exchange can be established only if work is imposed on a colonial sub-proletariat for starvation wages.

The inevitable consequence is that the colonized peoples lose their national individuality, their culture and their customs, sometimes even their language, and live, in abject poverty, like shadows, ceaselessly reminded of their 'sub-humanity'.

However, their value as almost free manpower protects them to some degree against genocide. Just before the Nuremberg trials the French, to set an example, massacred seventy thousand Algerians at Sétif. This was such a matter of course at the time that no one took it into their heads to judge the French government as they were to judge the Nazis. But this 'deliberate destruction of a part of the national group' could not be extended without damaging the colonialists' own interests. By exterminating their sub-proletariat, they would have ruined themselves. It was because they could not liquidate the Algerian population and, equally, because they could not integrate it, that the French lost the Algerian war.

*

These observations help us to understand that the structure of colonial wars changed after the Second World War. It was about this time, in fact, that the colonial peoples, enlightened by that conflict and its effects upon the 'Empires', and subsequently by the victory of Mao Tse Tung, determined to reconquer their national independence. The characteristics of the struggle were laid down in advance: the colonialists had superiority in arms, the natives in numbers. Even in Algeria – a colony which the French had not merely exploited but also settled – the ratio in terms of numbers was 1 to 9. During the two world wars, many native Algerians had been trained as soldiers and had become seasoned fighters. However, the scarcity and poor quality of arms – at least at first – meant that fighting units were necessarily few in number. Their action too was dictated by those objective conditions: terrorism, ambushes, harassment of the enemy, hence extreme mobility of the combat groups, who had to strike suddenly and then vanish immediately. This was possible only with the participation of the entire population – hence the famous symbiosis of the liberation forces and the people in general. Everywhere the army of liberation organized agrarian reform, political power, education; the people supported them, fed them, hid their soldiers and gave them their young men to make good their losses. It is no coincidence that the people's war made its appearance, with its principles, its strategy, its tactics and its theoreticians, just when the industrial powers were taking total war to its limits with the industrial production of atomic power. Nor is it a coincidence that this should have resulted in the collapse of colonialism. The contradiction which gave victory to the Algerian FLN can be seen to have been present in many other places at the time: as a matter of fact, the People's War tolled the knell of classical warfare (just as the hydrogen bomb did at the same time). Colonial armies were powerless against partisans backed by the entire population. They had only one means of escaping the harassment that was demoralizing them and threatening to end in new Dien-Bien-Phu's, and that was to 'get rid of the water as well as the fish' – meaning the civilian population. Indeed, the soldiers of the parent country soon learned to regard these silent, obstinate peasants who, half a mile away from an ambush, knew nothing, had seen nothing, as their most formidable enemies. And since it was a whole and united people which was holding the classical army at bay, the only *anti-guerrilla* strategy that could pay off would be the destruction of this people, i.e. of civilians, of women and children. Torture and genocide: this was the response of the colonial powers to the revolt of their subject peoples. And this response, we know, is useless if it is not radical and total: that determined population, unified by its army of partisans, politicized, savage, will no longer be intimidated, as in the heyday of colonialism, by a 'cautionary' massacre. Quite the reverse, its hatred will simply be redoubled: therefore it is no longer a question of terrorizing but of physically *liquidating* a whole people. But this is not possible without at the same time liquidating the colonial economy, and therefore, as a direct and logical result, the whole colonial system. So the settlers panic, the parent countries weary of sinking men and money into an endless war, the masses within them ultimately oppose the continuation of a barbarous conflict, and the colonies become sovereign states.

*

However, there do exist cases where genocide as a response to a people's war is not restrained by infrastructural contradictions. Total genocide then emerges as the absolute basis of anti-guerrilla strategy. And, in certain circumstances, it may even appear as the ultimate objective – to be attained immediately or gradually. This is exactly what is happening in the war in Vietnam. This is a new moment in the imperialist process which is usually called neo-colonialism – because it can be defined as aggression against a former colony, which has already obtained its independence, to subject it once again to colonial rule. From the outset it is ensured – by the financing of a putsch, or by some other machination – that the new rulers of the State will not represent the interests of the masses but those of a thin layer of privileged people and, consequently, those of foreign capital. In the case of Vietnam, what happened was the appearance of Diem – imposed, supported and armed by the US – and the announcement of his decision to reject the Geneva agreements and to set up the Vietnamese territory situated below the Seventeenth Parallel as an independent State. What followed was the necessary consequence of these premises: a police force and an army were needed to hunt down former combatants who, balked of their victory, became *ipso facto* and *before* any effective resistance the enemies of the new regime; in short there was a reign of terror, which provoked a new uprising in the South and rekindled the people's war. Did the United States ever believe that Diem would crush the revolt in the bud? Be that as it may, they did not hesitate to send in first experts and then troops; and promptly found themselves involved in the struggle up to the neck. And we find once again more or less the pattern of the war that Ho-Chi-Minh fought against the French, although the American government declared, at the beginning, that it was sending troops only out of generosity and to fulfil its duties towards an ally.

That is how things appear on the surface. But looked at more closely, these two successive struggles appear basically different: the United States, unlike the French, have no economic interests in Vietnam, apart from a few private firms who have invested a certain amount there. And these interests are not so considerable that, if the need arose, they could not be sacrificed – without harm to the American nation as a whole and without really damaging the monopolies. So that, since the government of the United States is not engaged in the struggle for *directly* economic reasons, it has no reason to hesitate to end it by an absolute strategy, i.e. by genocide. Obviously this is not enough to prove that it is envisaging such a strategy – merely that there is nothing to prevent it from doing so.

In fact, according to the Americans themselves, this conflict has two objectives. Quite recently, Rusk stated: 'It is ourselves we are defending.' It is no longer Diem, the ally in danger, nor Ky whom they are so generously assisting: it is the United States which is in danger in Vietnam. This means clearly that their first aim is military: to encircle communist China, the main obstacle to their expansionism. For this reason they will not allow south-east Asia to slip through their fingers. They have put their men in power in Thailand, they control two thirds of Laos and threaten to invade Cambodia. But these conquests will have been to no avail if they find themselves faced with a free, united Vietnam with a population of thirty-one million. This is why military chiefs are apt to talk of a 'key-position'; this is why Dean Rusk says, with unwitting irony, that the American armed forces are fighting in Vietnam 'to avoid a third world war'; either this phrase has absolutely no meaning, or one must interpret: 'to *win* it'. In short, the first objective is dictated by the need to establish a *Pacific defence line*. A need, be it added, that only arises within the framework of the general policy of imperialism.

. The second objective is economic. General Westmoreland defined it in these terms at the end of last October: 'We are waging war in Vietnam to show that guerrilla warfare does not pay.' To show this *to whom?* To the Vietnamese themselves? This would be odd, to say the least: is it necessary to consume so many lives and so much money to prove this to a nation of poor peasants fighting thousands of miles away from San Francisco? And, above all, seeing that the interests of the big companies there are more or less negligible, what need was there to *attack* that nation, to provoke it to conflict just to be able to crush it and prove the futility of its struggle? Westmoreland's phrase – like Rusk's quoted above – needs completing. It is *the others* who must be shown that guerrilla warfare does not pay. All the exploited and oppressed nations who might be tempted to throw off the Yankee yoke by a people's war, waged first against their pseudo-government and the *compradores* supported by a national army, then against the 'special forces' of the United States, and lastly against the GIs. In other words, in the first place Latin America. And, more generally, the Third World as a whole. Replying to Guevara who said 'We need several Vietnams', the United States government says: 'They will all be crushed as I crush this one.' In other terms, *America's* war, above all, is *an example and a warning.* An example for three continents and perhaps for four – after all Greece too is a peasant nation, a dictatorship has just been set up there, one must anticipate: submission or radical liquidation. So this cautionary genocide is addressed to all mankind; it is by this warning that 6 per cent of mankind hope to succeed, without too much expense, in controlling the remaining 94 per cent. Of course, it would be preferable – for propaganda purposes – that the Vietnamese should give in before being annihilated. And yet even that is not so certain – if Vietnam were to be scrubbed off the face of the map, the situation would be clearer. Submission could conceivably be due to some *avoidable* failing; but if these peasants do not weaken for an instant, and if they pay for their heroism with an *inevitable* death, then guerrillas still unborn will be discouraged more surely. At this stage in the argument, three points have been established: what the United States government wants is a base and an example. To attain its first objective it *can*, with no difficulty other than the resistance of the Vietnamese themselves, liquidate a whole people and establish the *Pax Americana* over a deserted Vietnam; to achieve the second, it *must* effect this extermination – at least in part.

*

The statements of American statesmen lack the outspokenness of those made by Hitler in his time. But such frankness is not vital: it is enough that the facts should speak. The speeches that accompany them, *ad usum internum*, will be believed only by the American people; the rest of the world understands quite well. Those governments which are accomplices keep silent; the others denounce the genocide, but the United States government finds it only too easy simply to tell them that there has never been any question of such a thing, that they are simply revealing their biased attitudes by these unproven accusations. In truth, say the Americans, all we have ever done is to put this option to the Vietnamese – North and South: either you cease your agression or we break you. There is no longer any need to point out that this proposition is absurd, *since the agression* is American and since, consequently, only the

Americans can put an end to it. And this absurdity is not uncalculated: it is clever to formulate, with apparent innocence, a demand which the Vietnamese cannot satisfy. In this way the United States government retains the power of deciding whether or not to cease hostilities. But even if one translated this as meaning: 'Declare yourselves beaten or we'll bomb you back into the stone age', the second term of the alternative is still *genocide*.

It has been said: genocide, yes, but *conditional*. Is this objection legally valid? Is it even convincing? If the argument did make sense legally, the United States government would just escape the accusation of genocide. But the law, in distinguishing intention from pretext, leaves no place for this loophole. Genocide – particularly if it has been continuing for several years – may well be motivated by blackmail. One may well say that one will call a halt if the victim submits; these are pretexts and the act is still – absolutely and completely – genocide in intent. In particular since – as is the case – a part of the group has been annihilated to force the remainder into submission.

But let us look at the whole matter and consider the terms of the alternative. In the South, this is the choice: villages are burnt, the population is subjected to massive and deliberately murderous bombardments, their cattle are killed, vegetation is ruined by defoliants, crops are sprayed with poisons and destroyed, machine-gunning is indiscriminate, there is murder, rape, pillaging: this is genocide in the strictest sense of the word – mass extermination. What is the alternative? What must the people of Vietnam do to escape this atrocious death? They must rally to the armed forces of the United States or of Saigon, and allow themselves to be shut up in strategic hamlets or in those 'New Life' hamlets which differ from the first only in name – in fact in concentration camps. We have a good deal of evidence about these camps from many witnesses. They are surrounded by barbed wire. The most elementary needs are not catered for: there is undernourishment, complete absence of sanitation. The prisoners are thrown together in tents or cramped airless quarters. Social structures are destroyed: husbands are separated from their wives, mothers from their children, family life – so deeply respected by the Vietnamese – no longer exists. Since households were broken up, the birthrate has dropped. Every possibility of religious or cultural life has been suppressed. Even work – work to ensure *the continuation* of their own lives and those of their families – is denied them. These unfortunate people are not even slaves: slavery did not prevent a rich culture from existing among the Negroes in the United States. Here the group is reduced to the state of a formless mass, to the extremes of vegetative existence. If it wishes to emerge from this state, the bonds re-established among these pulverized, hate-ridden men can only be *political*: they form clandestine groups of resistance. The enemy guesses this. The result: even these camps themselves are combed through two or three times; *even there*, security is never attained and the pulverizing forces have to work relentlessly. If by chance a fatherless family is freed, children with an older sister or a young mother, they go to swell the sub-proletariat of the big towns. The oldest sister or the mother, without a breadwinner and with other mouths to feed, complete their degradation by prostituting themselves to the enemy. What I have just described – the lot of *a third* of the population in the South, according to the evidence of Donald Duncan – is in fact another sort of genocide, equally condemned by the 1948 Convention:

ARTICLE II

(b) Causing serious bodily or mental harm to members of the group;
(c) Deliberately inflicting on the group conditions of life calculated to bring about its physical destruction in whole or in part;
(d) Imposing measures intended to prevent births within the group;
(e) Forcibly transferring children. . . .

In other words it is not true to say that the choice turns on death or submission. Because submission itself, in these circumstances, is genocide. It would be more apt to say that they must choose between immediate death by violence and slow death at the end of a period of physical and mental degradation. Or rather, *there is no choice*, there is no condition to be fulfilled: the blind chance of an 'operation', or sometimes indiscriminate terror, may decide the type of genocide that an individual will undergo.

Is it different in the North?

On the one hand, there is *extermination*: not merely the daily risk of death but the systematic destruction of economic infrastructures, from dikes to factories, of which 'not a stone must be left standing'. Deliberate attacks on the civilian population, especially in rural districts. Destruction of hospitals, schools, places of worship, a sustained effort to annihilate the achievements of 20 years of socialism. Is it simply to terrorize the population? But this can be achieved only by the daily extermination of an ever-growing part of the group. And then this terrorism itself, in its psycho-social consequences, *is genocide*: there is no way of knowing if, among children in particular, it may not cause mental disturbances which will long, indeed possibly always, damage mental balance.

The alternative is surrender. This means that they accept that their country should be cut into two and that American dictatorship, directly or through intermediaries, should be imposed upon their compatriots, even upon members of their own families whom war has separated from them. Would this intolerable humiliation end the war? It is far from certain: the National Liberation Front and the Democratic Republic of Vietnam, although closely allied, have a different strategy and different tactics, because their situations within the war are different. If the National Liberation Front continued the struggle, the American bombers, despite the surrender of the Democratic Republic of Vietnam, would continue attacking the latter. But if the war were to end, we know – from official declarations – that the United States would be eager generously to pour mountains of dollars into the reconstruction of the Democratic Republic of Vietnam. This means quite simply that they would destroy, by private investment or conditional loans, the whole economic basis of socialism. And this too is genocide: you cut a sovereign state into two parts; you occupy one of the two halves, and rule there by terror; you ruin the enterprise achieved at such a price by the other half and, by means of calculated investments, you keep it nicely at heel. The national group known as 'Vietnam' is not *physically* eliminated, yet it no longer exists: it has been economically, politically and culturally suppressed.

In the North as in the South, there is a choice only between two types of destruction: collective death or disintegration. The most significant thing is that the American government has been able to test the resistance of the National Liberation Front and of the Democratic Republic of Vietnam. It knows that destruction – unless it is total – will always be ineffectual. The Front is more powerful than ever; North Vietnam is unshakeable. For this very reason, the calculated extermination of the Vietnamese people cannot be aimed at making them capitulate. They are being offered an 'honourable peace' with the knowledge that they will not accept it; and this apparent alternative is concealing the real intention of imperialism, which is gradually to push escalation to its utmost limits, i.e. to total genocide. It may be objected that the United States government could have gone about it more directly and 'cleaned up' Vietnam by a *Blitzkrieg* of all its inhabitants. But, apart from the fact that this extermination required the setting up of a complex logistic apparatus – for example, the creation and free use in Thailand of air bases, shortening the bombers' journey by several thousand miles – the essential aim of 'escalation' was and still is to prepare bourgeois opinion for the idea of genocide. From this point of view, the Americans have succeeded only too well. Repeated and systematic bombings of crowded districts of Haiphong and Hanoi which two years ago would have aroused violent protests, are carried out today amid a sort of general indifference that is more like paralysis than apathy. The trick has come off: what is, in fact, the preparation of public opinion for the final genocide is seen by that opinion as a gentle and continually increasing pressure. Is this genocide possible? No. But that depends on the Vietnamese and on them alone, on their courage, on the admirable effectiveness of their organization. As far as the United States government is concerned, no one can exculpate it from its crime with the pretext that the intelligence and heroism of its victim enable him to limit its effects. One may conclude: faced with a people's war – a product of our time, a reply to imperialist aggression and a demand for sovereignty made by a people which values its unity – two attitudes are possible. Either the aggressor withdraws and makes peace, recognizing that a whole nation is rising up against him; or else, aware of the uselessness of classical strategy, he has recourse, if he can do so without damaging his interests, to extermination pure and simple. There is no third choice; but this choice, at least, is always *possible*. Since the armed forces of the United States are sinking ever deeper into the mud of Vietnam, since they are intensifying bombardments and massacres, since they are trying to gain control of Laos and are planning to invade Cambodia, when they could withdraw, there is no doubt that the American government, despite its hypocritical denials, has opted for genocide.

*

The intention becomes apparent from a consideration of the facts. It is necessarily *premeditated*. It is possible that, in other ages, genocide may have been realized suddenly, in a moment of violent emotion, during tribal or feudal struggles. Anti-guerrilla genocide, a product of our time, presupposes organization, bases and therefore accomplices (it takes place only at a distance), a special budget. It must therefore be thought out, planned. Does this mean that its authors are clearly aware of what they want? It is hard to decide about this: one would have to probe deep into men's hearts, and Puritan bad faith can work wonders. Perhaps certain members of the State Department are so used to lying to themselves that they still manage to believe that they are working for the good of Vietnam. After the recent declarations of their spokesmen, one may imagine that these self-deluding innocents are rapidly decreasing in numbers; 'It is ourselves we are defending'; 'Even if the Saigon government asked us to, we would not leave Vietnam', etc. In any case, we do not need to concern ourselves with this game of psychological hide and seek. The truth is to be found *on the spot*, in the racism of the American forces. Of course, this racism – anti-Negro, anti-Asiatic, anti-Mexican – is a fundamental fact which goes very deep and which existed, potentially or in fact, long before the Vietnam war. The proof of this is that the United States government refused to ratify the Convention against genocide. This does not mean that, as early as 1948, it was thinking of exterminating a people, but – according to its own statements – that this pledge would have gone against the internal legislation of many of its States. In other words – and it all links up – the present rulers think they have a free hand in Vietnam because their predecessors refused to take a stand against the anti-Negro racism of the Southern whites. In any case, since 1965, the racism of the American soldiers, from Saigon to the Seventeenth Parallel, has been intensifying. The young Americans torture, they utilize the current from their field telephones unflinchingly, they fire on unarmed women for target-practice, they kick wounded Vietnamese in the testicles, they cut the ears off the dead as trophies. The officers are even worse: a general boasted – in front of a Frenchman who reported this in evidence before the Tribunal – that he pursued the 'vc' from his helicopter and shot them, in the ricefields. These, of course, were not fighters in the National Liberation Front, who know how to protect themselves, but peasants cultivating their rice. The 'Vietcong' and the Vietnamese are tending to merge in the minds of these confused men, who regularly declare that 'The only good Vietnamese is a dead Vietnamese' – or, the inverse of this but which comes to the same thing, 'Every dead Vietnamese is a Vietcong'. Peasants are preparing to harvest the rice to the south of the Seventeenth Parallel. American soldiers appear, set fire to their houses and want to transfer them to a strategic village. The peasants protest. What else can they do, bare-handed against these Martians? They say: 'The rice crop is so good. We want to stay to eat our rice.' Nothing else; but that is enough to exasperate the young Americans. 'The Vietcong put these ideas into your heads. They've been teaching you to resist.' These soldiers are so confused that they see 'subversive' violence in the feeble protests that their own violence has aroused. At the root of all this there is probably a certain disappointment. They have come to save Vietnam, to free it from Communist aggressors; they soon see that the Vietnamese do not like them; from the becoming role of liberators they are pushed into that of occupying forces. It is a sort of dawning of awareness: they don't want us, there's nothing we can do here. But the moment of hesitation takes them no further. Their anger boils up and they say to themselves quite simply that any Vietnamese is, by definition, suspect. And this is true, from the neo-colonialists' point of view: they understand vaguely that, in a people's war, the civilians are the only *visible* enemy. They begin to hate them; racism does the rest. They thought they were there to save these men; they discover with vicious glee that they are there to kill them. Every one of them is a potential Communist: the proof is that they hate the Americans. From that point on, the truth of the Vietnamese war is to be found in these confused and remotely-controlled minds: and it begins to resemble Hitler's utterances. Hitler killed the Jews because they were Jews. The armed forces of the United States torture and kill the men, women and children of Vietnam *because they are Vietnamese.* In this way, whatever the lies and verbal precautions taken by the government, the drive to genocide is lodged in the heads of the soldiers. And this is their way of living out the murderous situation the government has put them in. The witness Martinsen, a 23-year-old student who had 'interrogated' prisoners for six months and who found the memory of it intolerable, told us: 'I am the stereotype of an American college student, and I find myself a war criminal.' And he was right to add: 'Anyone would have become like me, in my place.' His only mistake was to attribute his degrading crimes to the influence of war in general. For they were not attributable to war in the abstract, unspecified, but to *this* war, fought by the world's greatest power against a people of poor peasants, and which forces those fighting it to *live it out* as the only form of relationship possible between a highly industrialized country and an under-developed one, i.e. as a relationship of genocide expressed through racism. The only relationship – short of calling a halt and leaving.

Total war presupposes a certain balance of forces, a certain reciprocity. Colonial wars were fought without this, but colonial interests restricted genocide. The present example of genocide, the latest result of the unequal development of societies, is *total* war fought to the bitter end *by one side only* and *without the slightest degree of reciprocity.*

The American government is not guilty of having invented modern genocide, nor even of having selected it, chosen it from among other possible and effective replies to guerrilla warfare. It is not guilty – for instance – of having preferred it for strategic or economic reasons. In fact, genocide appears as the *only possible reaction* to the rebellion of *a whole people* against its oppressors. The American government is guilty of having preferred, of still preferring a policy of aggression and of war, aiming at total genocide, to a policy of peace, the only real alternative – because the latter would necessarily imply a reconsideration of the main objectives imposed on it by the big imperialist companies through their pressure groups. It is guilty of continuing and intensifying the war, although each of its members understands more clearly each day, from the reports of the military chiefs, that the only means of winning is to 'liberate' Vietnam from all of the Vietnamese. It is guilty, by plotting, misrepresenting, lying and self-deceiving, of becoming more deeply committed every instant, despite the lessons of this unique and intolerable experience, to a course which is leading it to the point of no return. It is guilty, self-confessedly, of knowingly carrying on this *cautionary* war to make genocide a challenge and a threat to peoples everywhere. We have seen that one of the features of total war was a constant growth in the number and speed of means of transport: since 1914, war can no longer remain localized, it must spread throughout the world. Today the process is becoming intensified; the links of the *One World*, this universe upon which the United States wishes to impose its hegemony, are ever closer. For this reason, of which the American government is well aware, the present act of genocide – as a reply to a people's war – is conceived and perpetuated in Vietnam not only against the Vietnamese but against humanity. When a peasant falls in his ricefield, mown down by a machine gun, we are all struck. In this way the Vietnamese are fighting for all men, and the Americans against all men. Not in the figurative sense or the abstract. And not only because genocide in Vietnam would be a crime universally condemned by the law of nations. But because, gradually, the threat of genocide is extended to the whole human race, backed up by the threat of atomic warfare, i.e. the absolute point of total war, and because this crime, perpetrated every day before the eyes of all, makes all those who do not denounce it the accomplices of those who commit it and, the better to bring us under control, begins by degrading us. In this sense, imperialist genocide can only become more radical – because the group aimed at, to be terrorized, *through the Vietnamese nation*, is the human group in its entirety

Czechoslovakia:
The Socialism that Came in from the Cold

The voices we are about to hear were raised between 1966 and the first months of 1968; a timorous first light crept over the Carpathians of Slovakia, the plains of Moravia, the mountains of Bohemia. A little more time, and we might have seen in broad daylight men who had been hidden from us by clouds ever since we delivered them to the Nazis for twelve months of peace – in 1938.

Dawn, however, never came; no lark sang. Since then socialism has fallen back into the long night of its Middle Ages. I remember a Soviet friend saying to me towards 1960: 'Have patience; improvements will take time perhaps, but you will see that progress is irreversible.' Today I sometimes feel that nothing was irreversible except the steady, remorseless degeneration of Soviet socialism. These Slovak and Czech voices remain, bouquets of caught breath, still warm and alive, disavowed, unrefuted. We cannot hear them without unease. They speak of a sinister and grotesque past, they tell us that it is buried forever, and yet this resuscitated past has once again become the interminable present of Czechoslovakia. They cautiously announce a better future that, soon afterwards, a great wind blew out like a candle. It is tempting to compare them to the light that falls from dead stars, all the more so since they bore a message, before the country was once again plunged into silence, that was not addressed to us. However, it is now that we must understand them; I shall try to explain here why these voices concern us.

Thirteen interviews, fourteen accounts, or if you like, fourteen confessions. For a confession, in the sense which Rousseau gave to the word, is the exact opposite of a self-criticism. Those who speak here – novelists, playwrights, poets, essayists; there is even a philosopher – seem relaxed, measured, rarely harsh, often ironic; if they burn with revolutionary rage, they scarcely reveal it. They assert less than they question, and question themselves. Apart from this, they differ in every respect. Some of them are sons of workers, of peasants, of teachers. Mucha's father was a painter, and Kundera's a musician; Havel is a descendant of the upper bourgeoisie of the pre-war epoch. Some are Czechs, others Moravians, and others Slovaks. The eldest, Novomesky, was sixty-two when these interviews took place; the youngest, Havel, was thirty-two and could have been his son. Novomesky witnessed the birth and death of the first Czechoslovak Republic; he was one of the three main leaders of the Slovak Uprising in 1944; then as a Cabinet Minister after the war he helped make his country what it became, which did not prevent him a little later from ending, like so many others, in prison. Havel was two years old at the time of the surrender at Munich, fifteen when the trials began. Men of mature age range between these two. Three generations of which the first formed the destiny of the third, and the third willingly made itself the judge of the two others; the second, victim and accomplice, was attracted to both by undeniable affinities and yet separated from them by particular antagonisms. Such is the content of this work: intellectuals look about themselves and within themselves and ask 'What happened?'

I fear that these last words may put off more than one reader: 'Intellectuals? A mandarin caste that has no right to speak in the name of the people.' Precisely, they are very careful not to; citizens of Czechoslovakia, they speak to their fellow citizens. Not to you. Their real interlocutors seem to have been less supercilious than you, since for years culture had, as Liehm says, performed the function of politics. Thus in spite of their divergences or oppositions, and through their very nuances, hesitations, and diversity of characters, it is possible to reconstruct a common implicit discourse on twenty-five years of Czechoslovak history from them. It is this discourse – such as I understand it – that I would like to trace with you, before you read the individual accounts themselves.

Novomesky, the first to question himself, goes straight to the nub of the problem: the present misfortune of Czechoslovakia is due to its adoption of a ready-made socialism. He is in the best position to speak to us of the years that immediately followed the Second World War. In 1945, nobody wanted to restore the First Republic: it had collapsed *before* the occupation, at Munich. For the angry young men of the time, the capitulation of 1938 was not merely the fault of their allies, it was first and foremost the responsibility of their own bourgeoisie. The humanism of Beneš had proved a mere plaster mask. It was now pulverized; and behind it there was not a human face, not even a ruthless one – only mechanical cogs. Why else had a united people not risen up against the German Diktat in 1938? Would resistance have been useless? Would insurrection have been drowned in blood? Perhaps. But perhaps, too, an uprising would have forced the Allies to change their policies. In any event, resistance was preferable to passivity. But what was the cause of this passivity? Indubitably, the relations of production, that is to say, the bourgeois institutions of the First Republic. The high degree of industrialization of the country developed 'massifying' forces that sapped the unity of the workers and tended to make each of them a solitary molecule; the reign of profit, which is a thing, imposed on men the dispersal and inertia of things. When the insurgents came to power after the liberation, they swore that this society of impotence would never return.

Socialism for them was thus initially the overthrow of the golden calf, the integration of all into a *human* collectivity, full citizenship for each member of it, full rights to participate in the economic, social, and political administration of the country. They would create in the heat of the battle the national unity that they had been unable to obtain when circumstances demanded it, by putting the fate of all in the hands of all, which could be done on only one basis: the socialization of the means of production.

The reasons why a people chooses socialism matter comparatively little; what is essential is that they build it with their own hands. 'What is true', said Hegel, 'is only what has *become* so.' This is also, of course, the principle of psychoanalysis: it would be futile or harmful, even if *per impossibile* one knew the secrets of a patient, to reveal them to him – to *administer* his truth to him like a blow on the head with a cudgel; the patient must rather always search for it himself and change himself by his very search, in such a way that he will discover the truth when he is prepared to bear it. What holds for the individual also in this respect holds for great collective movements. The proletariat must emancipate itself by its own means, forge its own arms and class consciousness in daily battle, in order to take power when it is capable of exercising it. This was not entirely the case in the USSR; but it should be added that a people makes itself socialist by making socialism, as much as by its efforts to install necessary new structures and break old ones, outside itself and within itself, as by any functioning of established institutions. Lenin said of the Russian masses – confused, still imbued with ideologies of the old regime, most of them illiterate – that the new society could only be built *with them* and *by them*. It was just this that the revolutionaries of Bohemia, of Slovakia wanted to achieve: to change themselves by changing the world, to make themselves, by a patient and tenacious construction of *their* socialism, men *become* socialists. Today, as you will see below, several of them call Yalta 'another Munich'. At the time, they were full of gratitude towards the USSR, which had just freed them from German rule, and dazzled by a military victory which they saw as the triumph of a liberated society over a great capitalist power, or more simply, of Good over Evil. They asked no more than to remain within the zone of Soviet influence, and never dreamt of contesting the leadership of the state that was their 'elder brother'. They wanted to benefit from its experience and advice, but to do the work of the revolution themselves, on the basis of their own problems, their own particular situation, their own resources, their own history, and their own culture. Czechoslovakia, a small binational country, highly industrialized, a hundred times invaded and enslaved, had no model to copy. It was necessary for it to invent its own path, wending through errors surmounted, deviations corrected, distortions redressed – as Cuba was to do fifteen years later – in order to be able one day to recognize itself in its work.

It was spared the trouble. The two great powers each made a contribution: after Yalta, the Marshall Plan. We know what followed. In 1948 the Communists took power and the elder brother bestowed on the cadet the gift of a prefabricated socialism. In the USSR, this socialism had developed for better or for worse, in practice very badly rather than reasonably well. At least it was an answer – during the first years – to the difficulties of a huge and overwhelmingly agrarian country in the process of industrialization, without a bourgeoisie and, after the Civil War and its massacres, virtually without a proletariat, on which imperialist blockade imposed economic autarky, and with it official sacrifice of the peasantry to the creation of heavy industry. Since the working class, now absent, could not exercise its dictatorship, the Party believed itself constrained to exercise it in its place, or rather in place of a future working class. The extraordinary demographic upheaval that was both the means and effect of socialist accumulation is well known. To rebuild the secondary sector, resources were squeezed from the primary sector, as always happens, but the metamorphosis was so swift that the Party had to forge the new working class by radically recasting the peasants needed in industry. These mutants had none of the traditions of the old revolutionary proletariat: where could they have acquired them? An accelerated acculturation had to be imposed by various manipulations: to combat the stubborn survival of old ideologies and primordial customs that presented themselves as the spontaneous nature of the people, the Bolshevik Party sought to create a 'second nature' that would suppress the first by conditioning reflexes and loading memories with a ballast of mini-Marxist maxims to confer the necessary stability, weight, and inertia on the thought of the masses. Driven by the necessities of the time, the Party, far from *expressing* the consciousness of the workers, was obliged to *produce* it. The only real force in this immense invertebrate country, it found itself impelled to concentrate power. Instead of assisting the withering away of the State by a critical independence of it, the Party reinforced the State by identifying itself with it, but was thereby overcome with administrative sclerosis. Controlling a majority in all elected assemblies, this gigantic apparatus was semi-paralysed by its own omnipotence: in its ubiquity and solitude, it ceased any longer to be able to *see itself*. All this was at first only a stop-gap remedy, a provisional deviation of whose perils Lenin was well aware, and which he believed could be corrected. Soon, however, the Soviet bureaucracy that was the inevitable product of this accumulation of responsibilities, transformed it into a definitive system. Soviet society gradually consolidated its structure around this spinal cord and in a half-century became what it is today. We are all now familiar with this history; it is futile to wonder whether things could have turned out differently. What is certain is that new relations of production were instituted in the USSR under the pressure of a vital need: to produce at all costs. This end, at least, was *imposed* upon an almost entirely agricultural country which had just socialized the means of production. Electrification devoured the Soviets. But it was at least a partial success, to the extent that it was a necessity at that time, in that space.

Czechoslovakia, by contrast, had long since passed the phase of primitive accumulation and was merely encumbered by the type of socialism so kindly bestowed on it. The country had no urgent need to develop heavy industry since its resources were already mainly derived before the war from prosperous manufactures. As for autarky – the horse medicine that the USSR had initially administered to itself under duress[1] – this small nation that depended on foreign trade, exporting consumer goods and importing most of its heavy equipment, had neither reason nor (despite the wealth of its subsoil) resources to achieve it. Now integrated into the socialist zone, all it needed to do was to change customers.[2] In fact, the inordinate expansion of its output and especially the absurd reversal of its priorities rapidly forced it to *produce for the sake of production*, when it should on the contrary have reorganized its existing industries to satisfy the needs of its own people and to meet the *legitimate* demands of its new clients abroad, and above all should have sought to improve its productivity. The identification of Party and State might have been necessary – or appeared to be necessary – 'in fatal circumstances'[3] in Russia, to control the demographic transformation of an agricultural country in the throes of industrialization. But what sense did it make for a nation of fourteen million inhabitants, with a considerable and intact proletariat that had acquired, by its struggles, its defeats, its very impotence under the First Republic, an incontestable class consciousness and strong workers' traditions? Czechoslovakia could have been the first power to accomplish a successful transition from an advanced capitalist economy to a socialist economy, offering the proletariat of the West, if not a model, at least an embodiment of its own revolutionary future. It lacked nothing, neither the means nor the men; if genuine workers' control was possible anywhere, it was in Prague and Bratislava.

To its misfortune, the manipulators in Moscow, manipulated by their own manipulations, could not even understand the idea of such a socialism. They imposed their *system* instead. This imported, disadapted model, with no real foundations in the country, was sustained from the

1. The country also, of course, had the necessary resources to be self-sufficient.
2. Which in point of fact it did, substituting the USSR for Germany, but under conditions that are common knowledge.
3. Rosa Luxemburg.

outside by the solicitude of the 'elder brother'. It was installed as an idol – that is to say, a fixed set of unconditional demands, indisputable, undisputed, inexplicable, unexplained. The Czechoslovak workers had freed themselves from the reign of profit only to fall under that of fetichized production. One nail drives out another; the 'Thing in power' in the old republic was evicted and replaced by another 'Thing', one alienation substituted by another alienation. Once its heavy machinery was installed, it dislocated every structure – slowly, at first, then with increasing speed – and ravaged the country.

It could, of course, be said that this socialism conferred on Czechoslovakia was made by Czechs and Slovaks, or rather through them. The trouble is that it did not socialize them. Let there be no misunderstanding: the men of 1945 were convinced revolutionaries and most of them remained so, but the system forbade them the experience of building socialism themselves. In order to change them, the experience would have had to take them as they were; the system took them as they were not. Instead of presenting itself as an open set of problems calling for both a rational transformation of structures and a constant modification of ideas (in other words a reciprocal and dialectical interaction of practice and theory), it posed with incredible complacency as a gracious gift of providence, a socialism without tears – in other words, without revolution or any contestation whatever. The tasks were already defined; it only remained to execute them. All knowledge was already complete: it only remained to memorize it.

Under such conditions, it is not surprising that the men of the first generation, those who had been militants in the Communist Party (CSK) before the War and had fought in the Resistance during the Occupation, should have reverted after 1956, as Novomesky says, to their options of 1920. Prevented from building anything, they had altered nothing of them. Buried and hidden beneath the stonework of slogans above them, the memories of their past, the hopes of their youth, lay intact; all the more so, in that they became for many a soundless refuge from the official line. Alas, such memories, however fresh for their bearers, inevitably acquire mould: it is a folly to try to relive one's twenties when one is sixty. But in the same way, and for the same reason, the collective fund of old conservative customs in the country was not touched. Our fourteen witnesses are categorical about this: families, churches, local or national traditions, patterns of thought, ideologies – the whole heritage that would have been superseded or modified by a socialism in the process of becoming – either survived or actually strengthened under the established order. Skacel points out the growing influence of catholicism in Brno, while others report that relations between Bohemia and Slovakia, always somewhat tense, progressively declined rather than improved, as they should have done in a great common undertaking. Yet if old mores remained virulent beneath a cloak of semi-clandestinity, we must not conclude that human relations were in no way changed by the new regime. From 1948 to 1956 they grew worse every day; false relations of production were established under a rigged economy and a reified apparatus of power.

It is clear, first of all, that the system deprived its citizens of any real participation in the national enterprise in which it was at the same moment calling on them to work together. Naturally, there was no question of self-government by workers, or of control exercised by regularly elected assemblies; the system, as we have seen, is by definition allergic to such leftist aberrations. I am thinking rather of another inevitable corollary of imported socialism: the vertiginous and radical depoliticization of a country which the Occupation and Resistance had profoundly politicized. All our witnesses agree on this phenomenon. The 'Thing', of course, could not function without men: it recruited men who were things, blockheads that it changed into pinheads. These became creatures possessed by power, hierarchized bureaucrats, each of whom commanded in the name of another – his superior, this other in the name of yet another, and the highest of all in the name of the 'Thing' itself. The latter was, by essence, incapable of adaptation or progress: the smallest change risked undoing it. It therefore never needed to renew its cadres, or rather, it needed never to renew them. If a bureaucrat disappeared, he was replaced by another who resembled him like a brother and was scarcely any younger. The 'system' conserved and conserved itself; it had no other end than to persevere in its being. It thus naturally tended to produce a gerontocracy, for the old are generally conservative. Consequently, the 'first generation', which imported the system, carefully kept the second generation out of all key posts. 'We were eternal *dauphins*,' remarks a forty-year-old witness. Kundera writes: 'My generation was deeply divided. . . . Some emigrated, others fell silent; some adapted, still others (I was one) resorted to a kind of legal and constructive opposition. All these attitudes, however, lacked dignity. . . . External emigration ended in impasse; internal emigration withered in solitude and impotence; loyal opposition, where it continued to publish, was condemned to inconsequence and compromise; as for those who submitted . . . they became corpses. None of us can be satisfied with ourselves, and the bitterness of this experience is the common bond of a whole generation . . . which no longer even has the desire to defend itself, when attacked by the young.'

Impotent and compromised, virtually excluded from public affairs by their elders, attacked by their youngers for nevertheless having participated unduly in them – such is the 'middle' generation. Its members rarely judge their elders very severely, however; after registering the complete bankruptcy and fraud of the regime, they sometimes add, with a pity that is not without tenderness: 'They had so little chance to have any effect on anything.' As for the aggressive youth which occasionally insults them – much less than they suggest – they are afraid of it and afraid for it. The younger generation is sceptical and cynical, they explain, because it feels that it can do nothing about anything. They feared that this age-group, raised in ignorance, when knowledge was debased, would suffer a destiny worse than their own; it would regret the First Republic because it would never have known its corruption, and then would be progressively recuperated by the regime, which it would finally – because it is necessary to live somehow – in turn perpetuate without believing in it. That at least was what adults were predicting for adolescents before the winter of 1967–1968. They were right about one thing: this third generation rejected with horror and disgust the prefabricated socialism proffered to it. The rejection was ineffective because prior to 1967, this generation had no purchase on anything. But what its elders did not understand – except perhaps Skacel – was that one day the opening of a breach, the appearance of any possibility of undertaking a common action, would be enough for this impotent cynicism to change into revolutionary demands and for this 'absurdist' youth to become, in the eyes of everyone, the generation of Jan Palach.

For within this generation, in effect, the mineralization of man had scarcely begun.

Kosik and Kundera give us precious information about the nature of this process of mineralization, which is all the more instructive in that they consider it from different standpoints. Its essential feature was that the 'Thing' thought Man, through the intermediary of its servants, and it goes without saying, conceived him as a thing. Not as a subject of history, but, necessarily, as its object. Blind and deaf to all properly human dimensions, it reduced him to a mechanical system: not merely in theory, but in its everyday practice. 'The regime had no consciously defined concept of Man,' Kosik says, 'it merely presupposed an effigy of him and mass-produced it because it needed precisely that sort of citizen.' What distinguishes *homo bureaucraticus* is an ensemble of negative traits. He does not laugh. 'The ruling group considered laughter incompatible with its station.' In other words, it had unlearned how to laugh. If one of its members, contrary to his institutional character, permitted himself any display of gaiety, he risked both himself and his entourage. An example of the official attitude was the misadventure – recounted by Liehm – of the impudent youngsters who thought that they could make fun of Nezval with impunity. This grotesque episode, I imagine, was the origin of *The Joke*. It was forbidden *to want* to laugh. An illuminating imperative, which follows rigorously from its premises: laughter contests, so when the revolution is conservative, it is counter-revolutionary. 'Official man', in Kosik's phrase, does not die either, 'because ideology does not acknowledge death'. For good reason: a robot is not alive, and hence cannot die; when it goes wrong, it is repaired or scrapped. 'In a sense,' Kosik adds, 'he possesses no body either.' Naturally: the system has cog-wheels and transmission belts but no organs; those who 'think' for it have no eyes to see organisms, those antibureaucratic integers that might take themselves for ends if undue attention were paid to them. The Czech philosopher adds that *homo bureaucraticus* knows neither the grotesque, nor the tragic, nor the absurd, because these existential categories have no discernible relationship to production, and consequently no reality; they are mere misty mirages of the dreamy bourgeoisies of the West. He concludes: 'Official man has no conscience, and no need of one.' What on earth would he have done with one, indeed? His paths are laid out; his tasks are preordained; his reflexes are conditioned by tried and tested methods, including the cerebral reflex improperly known as thought. This superb object, external to itself and moved by external forces, is regulated solely by Pavlovian mechanics; it is eminently manipulable and infinitely *corvéable*. 'Yet men,' Kosik writes, 'are not born careerists, mean, blinkered, insensible, incapable of reflection, amenable to corruption. It was the system that needed such men and procured them, to assure its own operation.'

The men of the system, as products of fetichized production, are suspect by *definition*: doubly suspect, both because they are reified and because they are never completely so. Robots are designed to be manipulated and are therefore potentially treacherous instruments; since the holders of power know how to work their controls, why should not foreign agents find out how to do so too? Then who is to know who is actually pulling the strings? But at the same time to the very extent that mineralization is not complete – and it never is, for these mineral bipeds are men who must live their mineralization as human beings – their very existence is a danger to the regime. To laugh, to weep, to die, even to sneeze, is to reveal a malignant and possibly bourgeois spontaneity. To *live*, in short, is to contest; if not in fact, at least in principle. Hence the necessity for constant surveillance. The regime benefited doubly from its double suspicion. First of all, it had no other end than itself and hence, lacking any controls or mediations, became a victim of its own unlimited power – unable either to perceive itself, or to conceive that it might be criticized. It therefore made it an axiom that men should be doubted rather than institutions. Consequently, it suited the regime that in these animal-machines the animal should sometimes reappear beneath the machinery: animality is Evil, the irreducible residue of a succession of corrupted millennia. Criticism never revealed an imperfection of the system, but rather the profound vice of the critic, the serf-will which leads every man to sin sooner or later, at least in spirit, against the building of socialism. But, above all, the principle of the permanent corruptibility of *homo bureaucraticus* had two manifest advantages: it justified recourse to the Machiavellian practices of buying or terrorizing men, and it allowed the 'Thing' to liquidate its own ministers when the need arose. When the machine rattled or stalled, it eliminated a few leaders rather than sought repair – which would anyway have been futile. Such leaders were traitors in the pay of the enemy; the motor itself was working well, its inexplicable 'seizures' were simply due to the fact that they were trying to sabotage it. In short, the 'Thing' was forced to use men, but it distrusted, despised and detested them: just as the master does his slaves or the boss his workers. Suspicion, hatred and contempt were the fine sentiments that it sought to inculcate in the relations between men and the relation of each man to himself.

It remains to know whether it succeeded in doing so. Our witnesses reply that there is no doubt that it did. At least in certain cases and up to a certain point. Who, then, lent himself to the system? The corrupt, the cowardly, the ambitious? On the contrary, the best men; the most sincere, the most devoted, the most scrupulous communists. Kundera tells us why. The mechanist vision of man is not, as Kosik seems to think, the cause of bureaucratic socialism; it is its product or, if you like, its ideology. The Revolution of 1917 bore with it immense hopes. Marxist optimism mingled with old dreams of 1848, with Romantic ideals, with Babeuf's egalitarianism, with Utopias of Christian origin. When 'scientific socialism' triumphed, it did not jettison this humanist bric-à-brac; it claimed to be the heir and executor of its deep, if idealist ambitions. Its goal was to liberate the workers from their chains, to put an end to exploitation, to replace the dictatorship of profit, where men are the products of their products, by a free and classless society where they are their own product. When the Party, now bureaucratized, eventually merged with the State, these principles, these ideals, these great objectives did not disappear for all that. On the contrary, government spokesmen made frequent allusions to them in their speeches, at a time when numerous Muscovites had acquired the habit of not going to sleep until the first light of dawn, after having assured themselves that the milkman had already passed their door.

The bureaucratic system had, of course, long since given rise to its own ideology. But this ideology was never explicit; present everywhere in practical acts, it could only be glimpsed in the turn of a phrase, a fleeting passage in official speeches; for it was masked by another ideology, proclaimed *ad usum populi*, a vaguely Marxian humanism. It was this that bemused the young Slovaks and young Czechs of the time. In 1945, galvanized by words, they fell into the trap. Is it not striking that Vaculik, one of the most implacable accusers of the system, joined the Party enthusiastically – he was twenty years old – because he had read Stalin's tract *Dialectical and Historical Materialism*? It is with this in mind that Kundera, without pretending to compare German society to Soviet society, declares that Hitlerism was in one respect much less dangerous than what he calls Stalinism. One at least knew what to expect from Nazism. It spoke out loud and clear; a Manichean vision of the world has rarely been more starkly expressed. But Stalinism was something very different; it was designed to confuse its victims. There were two axes of reference in it, two visions of the world, two ideologies, two types of reason – one dialectical, the other mechanist. Official culture repeated Gorki's egregious slogan: 'Man – that sounds proud', while its functionaries were sending actual men, weak and sinful by nature, to prison camps. How could the contrasts be reconciled? The very idea of socialism seemed to have gone mad.

Of course, it had not. But the servants of the 'Thing' demanded, apparently without cynicism, that their fellow citizens and themselves accept the system in the name of socialist humanism. They presented – perhaps in good faith – the man of the future as the ultimate term of a bold and sublime enterprise in the name of which his ancestor, the man of the present, was called upon to let himself be treated, and to treat himself, as reified and culpable. This was not wholly their fault; their brains were suffering from a malady ordinarily located in the bladder: an affliction of stones. But all those who tried – out of loyalty to the principles of socialism – to look at themselves with the Medusa's gaze of these men, experienced a generalized distortion of thought. The result was the apparent paradoxes that Kundera bitterly enumerates: 'In art, the official doctrine was realism. But it was forbidden to speak of the real. A cult of youth was publicly celebrated, but our own youth was denied us. In those merciless times, films showed nothing but the timid approaches of gentle and enraptured lovers. We were supposed to demonstrate our joy everywhere, yet the slightest sign of gaiety exposed us to the gravest penalties.' He would have defined the situation better, perhaps, if he had written: *in the name of realism*, we were forbidden to depict reality; *in the name of youth*, we were prevented from being young; *in the name of socialist joy*, gaiety was repressed. Worst of all, these gross deceptions met with complicity in themselves. So long as they still believed in bureaucratic socialism – at least as the thankless and painful road that leads to true socialism – these men used their living and dialectical reason to justify the reign of petrified reason, which necessarily led them to ratify the condemnation of the former by the latter. Convinced by propaganda that, as Mirabeau said, 'The road that leads from Evil to Good is Worse than Evil', they first resigned themselves to Evil because they believed it to be the sole means of attaining Good, then driven by what one of them calls 'the demon of consent', they came to see it as Good itself, and assumed their own resistance to petrification to be Evil. Cement poured into them through their eyes and through their ears, and they considered the protests of their simple good sense to be the residue of a bourgeois ideology that divorced them from the people.

All the witnesses who are in their forties admit that they felt a need to disqualify in advance every temptation to criticize, for fear that it might reveal the rebirth of individualism in them. They recount the care with which they buried the smallest surprise or unexpected malaise in the darkest corner of their memory, the effort which they made not to see what might have shocked them. For, in effect, they ran a great risk: a single doubt would have been enough to put the whole system in question, and they were certain that criticism would have reduced them to an ignoble solitude. Born during the First Republic, they bore the indelible marks of a culture which they had at all costs to discard, if they wanted to achieve harmony with the masses. In point of fact, the discourse of the 'Thing' proclaimed itself the thought of the working class itself, and the claim was self-evident since the 'Thing' exercised its dictatorship in the name of the proletariat and was the consciousness of the class. In practice no one actually *thought* the declarations of the 'Thing', for they were precisely *unthinkable*. But each took them to be certified expressions of the Objective Spirit at the time, and while waiting to understand them learnt them by heart and installed them like mysterious icons, within their personal inner shrine. All – workers, peasants or intellectuals – were unaware that they were the victims of a new alienation and atomization. Every man, reproaching himself with subjectivism, sought to break out of his molecular isolation and rediscover the ardent unity of partisan and revolutionary action, in which each comes to each not as another but as the *same* as himself; none dared realize that he was being summoned to erase his suspect anomaly by denying himself, by making himself *other than himself* in order to rejoin others, in so far as they tried to make themselves other than themselves. These serialized men could only communicate among themselves by the intermediary of the *Other-than-man*. They thus plunged ever deeper into solitude by the very efforts they made to escape it, and distrusted each other to the very extent that they mistrusted themselves. Liehm has graphically described here the ultimate hysterical temptation, the logical conclusion of the whole process: falling on one's knees to believe, and replacing reason by faith – *credo quia absurdum*. Which amounts to saying that under the reign of fetichized production every real man appears to himself, in his simple daily existence, as an obstacle to the construction of socialism and can evade the crime of living only by suppressing himself altogether.

Such attitudes, obviously, occurred only in extreme cases. For many workers the system essentially meant a growing disinterest in public affairs, night, numbness. To compensate them, they were granted a title; every worker was deemed a functionary. Many intellectuals, by contrast, were frenetic exponents of self-destruction. It must be said that they were accustomed to the role. In bourgeois democracies as in people's democracies, these specialists of the universal often feel encumbered by their singularity. But, as Kundera remarks, their masochism is completely innocuous in the West; nobody pays any attention to it. But in the socialist countries, they are never trusted and the powers that be are always ready to help them to destroy themselves. In Czechoslovakia they hastened to plead guilty to the slightest reproach, using their intelligence only to recast absurd accusations until they had made them acceptable, and to recast themselves until they could accept them. In the Party, moreover, the best leaders – who were by no means all intellectuals – also recast themselves: from loyalty.

It is only when seen in this light that the famous confessions during the trials of the 1950s can be understood. To secure them, the process of self-destruction had to be driven to extremes. It was no longer a question of tacitly refining improbable imputations to give them a semblance of truth. The 'interrogators' were charged with the task of blunting the critical faculties of the accused by threats, blows, deprivation of sleep and other techniques, to make them accept accusations that were inherently unacceptable. But if the percentage of failures was negligible, it was because Czechoslovak man had long been prepared for confession. Essentially suspect to his leaders, to his neighbours, to himself, a separatist in spite of himself by the simple fact of his molecular existence, potentially guilty in the best of cases, in the worst a criminal without knowledge of his crime, devoted despite everything to the party which crushed him – to such a man, a forced confession could appear to hold out the promise of an end to his insupportable malaise. Even if he kept an inner certainty that he had not committed the faults attributed to him, he could confess to them out of self-punishment. Thus the victims of certain anxiety neuroses, tortured by an inexplicable sentiment of guilt, steal in order to be caught, and recover their tranquillity in prison; in condemning them for a minor felony, society has punished their original sin; once they have paid, they are at peace. There was another psychological mechanism at work too. Goldstücker reports that after his release from prison, he read the work of a psychoanalyst who saw in confession an 'identification with the aggressor', and he adds that in his own experience this interpretation was not very far from the truth. The aggressor was the Party, his reason for living, which excluded him and barred him like an unscaleable wall, answering every denial with the reply of the police: 'There is only one truth – ours.' When the Truth claims the massive solidity of the Great Wall of China, how can fragile subjective convictions oppose it ('I wasn't in Prague that day; I never saw Slansky')? It is better for the unhappy prisoner secretly to reintegrate the Party again, by identifying with it and the things that represent it, embracing the contempt and hatred that they display towards him in its name. Once he finally succeeds in looking at himself with the petrifying eyes of the Gorgon in power, the miserable and petty incongruity that separates him from it will disappear: his life. The prospect of guilt can induce a kind of vertigo. Confession will at least bring peace, torpor, death.

On this subject, I can add to Goldstücker's testimony a story whose authenticity I guarantee. In another people's democracy, on the occasion of another series of trials, a former woman partisan, who had risen to high positions, was thrown in prison on charges of foreign espionage.

The police claimed that she had worked for the British Intelligence Service and that when her husband had unmasked her during the Resistance, she had arranged for him to be trapped and killed in an ambush. After several weeks of 'treatment', she confessed everything, and an indignant tribunal sentenced her to life imprisonment. Her friends later learnt that she was no longer being tortured, that she spoke little to her fellow prisoners, but appeared to have recovered her calm. The affair had been so crudely fabricated that her statements had not convinced anybody; when the leadership of the regime was reshuffled, the young woman was released and rehabilitated. She disappeared, and it was learnt that she was hiding with her family. The first person who forced the door into her room, at the entreaty of her parents, found her curled up on a sofa, her legs tucked under her, utterly silent. He spoke to her for a long time without getting any reply, and when she finally managed a few strangled words, it was to say in an anguished voice: 'What's the matter with all of you? *After all, I was guilty.*' What the condemned woman could not bear was neither her maltreatment, nor her disgrace, nor her imprisonment, but on the contrary her rehabilitation. In other words, mineralized thought can bring repose. Laid like a gravestone in a tormented head, it rests there, heavy, inert, imposing 'security', crushing doubts, reducing the spontaneous movements of life to an insignificant swarming of insects. Without necessarily going to this extreme, confession is in the logic of the system; one might even say that it is the natural term of it. Firstly, because the 'Thing' – possessed neither of understanding nor reason – in no way demands that its instruments believe what they say, but only that they say it publicly. Secondly, because in this imported socialism, which sought to convince Czech workers of 1950 that in the last resort they were simply Russian peasants of 1920, the truth was defined as an institutionalized lie. Those who installed the system in good faith, or who persuaded themselves that it suited Czechoslovakia, were sooner or later forced to lie desperately without believing in their fictions, to continue to advance towards what they took to be the Truth.

The young woman I spoke of was awakened by electric shock treatment. A somewhat Stalinist method of cure, but not an inappropriate one for de-stalinizing brains. Less seriously ill, a single electric shock sufficed for our fourteen witnesses: 'the Report attributed to Khrushchev', as *L'Humanité* used to call it. As a matter of fact, the report had something in common with the horse medicine that 'restored' the innocent-in-spite-of-herself: it was a thunderbolt and nothing more. Not an idea, not an analysis, not even an attempt at an interpretation. A 'tale told by an idiot, full of sound and fury, signifying nothing'. Naturally Khrushchev's own intelligence was not at issue. He simply spoke in the name of the system: the machine was a good one, its principal servant had not been; fortunately this saboteur had since quitted the world and everything would now proceed smoothly again. In short, the new personnel eliminated the encumbrance of a dead man as the old personnel had eliminated living men. It was *true*, however, that Stalin had ordered massacres and transformed the country of socialist revolution into a police state; he had been *truly* convinced that the Soviet Union could only reach communism by passing through a concentration-camp socialism. But as one of our witnesses acutely remarks, when established power judges it useful to tell the truth, it is because it has no better lie available. Such a truth, issuing from official mouths, becomes no more than a lie corroborated by facts.

Stalin was an evil man? Indeed. But how could Soviet society have raised him to his throne and kept him there for a quarter of a century? To those worried by the question, the new personnel tossed four words: 'the cult of personality'. Let them be content with this bureaucratic formula, a typical example of the *unthinkable*. The Czechs and the Slovaks had the feeling that a mass of rubble had fallen on their heads, breaking into pieces and shattering all their idols with it. It was, I imagine, a painful awakening. An awakening? The word is doubtless not the right one, for as one of them writes, there was no sense of great surprise; it suddenly seemed to them that they had always known what they were being told. Moreover, far from reawakening to a world of daylight, everything seemed unreal to them. Those who attended the rehabilitation trials came back dumbfounded: the dead were acquitted with the same words and speeches that had served to condemn them. Certainly, it was no longer criminal to be alive. But this innovation was merely *felt*, and could not be proved. The institutionalized lie subsisted: inert and intact.

Observers of a huge, distant process of crumbling, they scented from afar something rotten in the kingdom of Russia. However, they were ritatively told that in their own country the model imported from USSR had never functioned better. In fact, the machine was still ṇning at home. Everything had changed, and nothing had changed. Khrushchev gave public notice of this when the Hungarian people made an inopportune attempt to draw conclusions from the Twentieth Congress. Obviously, the Czechoslovaks no longer believed in the institutionalized lie, but they were much afraid that they had now nothing left to believe in. They had hitherto lived in what one of them calls a 'socialist fog'; now that the fog was lifting somewhat, they could survey the damage that it had hidden. A devastated economy was on the point of collapse. Antiquated factories were churning out products of mediocre quality, without the slightest concern for the real needs of the conjuncture. Technical and professional skills were sinking in standard day by day. 'The humanities were declining inexorably' (Kundera). The country had literally no idea of its real situation, for official lies and falsification of statistics had both destroyed previous elements of knowledge and halted all new socio-economic surveys or research. It was not even the case that the leaders of the regime knew the truth and concealed it: in this sense the truth simply did not exist, and no one had the means to ascertain it. The youth of the country were unquestionably the most disarmed of all. 'The knowledge of the young is fragmentary, atomized, disconnected; our secondary schools are incapable of providing their pupils with a coherent vision of anything, including our national history. As for world history, it is better left unmentioned; our pedagogic level is past belief' (Goldstücker).

Our witnesses found themselves in an unknown country, on an unidentified planet, between the secret East and the forbidden West. They suspected that Khrushchev's tragi-comic speech on 'Stalin's crimes' would find its truth if it were integrated into a *Marxist* analysis of Soviet society. But what confidence could they retain in Marxism when the 'Thing' in power never ceased to invoke it? If it was the official lie, how could it at the same time be the truth? And if there were two Marxisms, one false and one genuine, how could they – products of the false – tell which was the genuine? They realized then that they were themselves the least known natives in this sequestered land. It is said that when Joseph le Bon, a Deputy of the Convention, was interrogated by his judges in 1795 about the reasons for his terrorism in the Pas-de-Calais, he replied with a sort of astonishment: 'I don't understand. . . . Everything happened so quickly. . . .' Nothing went very quickly in Czechoslovakia from 1948 to 1956, but doubtless fatigue, habit, resignation, lack of imagination and self-delusion created a mournful probability of the improbable, a normality of the abnormal, a daily life of the unlivable, all shrouded in mist. Now the mist was broken, and as its last wisps drifted across the plain, disabused men were to be found saying, in their turn: 'I don't understand.' Who were they, who had lived the unlivable, tolerated the intolerable, taken the destruction of their economy for the construction of socialism, abandoned reason for faith in the name of scientific socialism, and, finally, admitted faults or confessed crimes they had not committed? They were unable to remember their past lives, to measure 'the weight of things said and done', to evoke their most intimate memories, without falling into the slight daze that Freud calls 'estrangement'. At first, their reactions differed widely – from disgust to shame, from anger to scorn.

Kundera chose black humour. 'I was born on the first of April, which was not without its metaphysical consequences. . . . People of my generation are bad company for themselves. I have no great liking for myself.' What he calls 'the ebb of Stalinism' led him to absolute scepticism: 'Stalinism was based on lofty ideals which it gradually transformed into their opposite: love of humanity into cruelty to men, love of truth into delation. . . . In my first book, at the height of Stalinism, I tried to react against it by appealing to an integral humanism. . . . But when the ebb of Stalinism came . . . I asked myself the question: Why in fact should one love man, anyway? Today, when I hear talk of the innocence of a child or the self-sacrifice of a mother, of our sacred duty to increase and multiply, I know the litany all too well. I've learnt my lessons.' This lyricist abandoned poetry to recapture lost categories: the comic, the grotesque. He wrote *The Joke* – whose title alludes not only to the innocent jest of its hero, but to the whole system in which a childish lark inevitably leads to the deportation of its author. Havel, for his part, simultaneously discovered the absurdity of the world and his own absurdity. Born into a bourgeois family, uneasy from the outset at finding himself a rich child among poor children, rootless and disoriented, Havel became a victim after the war of the discrimination against Jews and sons of bourgeois families. Numerous professions were closed to him and he could not enter a university – with the admirably logical result that for years he vainly requested authorization to take a course in drama at the University of Prague, and only obtained it after having made his name as a playwright. He too was alienated, however, to the sovereign 'Thing'. A little less than the others, perhaps. Many of them sought integration, while he knew it to be impossible because he was not wanted. The result was that he very soon tended to feel absurd in a world that was absurd. The 'revelations' of 1956 only increased his feeling of homelessness, which is why his theatre has been compared to the 'drama of the absurd' in the West.[4]

In short, whether they felt themselves unreal in a sadly ceremonious and unreal society – victims, witnesses, and accomplices of a monumental and nightmarish farce, or whether they floated like absurd imps in a milieu governed by such a fundamental absurdity that any attempt either to adapt to it or to change it was itself rendered absurd from the outset, all the men who speak here suffered what psychiatrists call 'a crisis of identity' in the first years after the Twentieth Congress. They were not the only ones – a silent, dumb malaise was spreading among the masses. But they were probably the worst affected in this respect. What were they to do? They could kill themselves or try to live. From certain allusions that the reader will find in the interviews, it can be guessed that some of them chose the first. The others sought to make use of the right to exist that had just been officially granted to them. They then had little option: to live was first of all to wrest oneself away from a depersonalization that risked becoming an alibi, to learn to know oneself in order to remake oneself. And how could they recount their own history to themselves without seeking it out where it belonged, in the last fifty years of their national history? For their individual adventures and the great collective adventure of the Czechoslovak people reflected each other: in the situation of extreme urgency in which they found themselves, without categories or concepts to think reality, or to think them-

4. With this difference, however, that his plays have an unmistakable political content for his compatriots. In *A Report about You*, he made it clear that nothing could change so long as the system remained intact and secreted its bureaucracy.

selves, they realized that each of these two histories could only be reconstructed through the other. Subjectivism? No, modesty. They had to find the truth or perish. Not the truth of the system: they were not yet armed to attack it – that would come later. The truth, for this moment, of their own life, of all Czech and Slovak lives in this brute reality. They sought it with nothing in their hands and nothing in their pockets, abstaining from any ideological interpretation. They started by returning to the facts, to the concealed and travestied facts which Novotny had candidly said should not be treated with too much servility.[5]

Slowly and stubbornly, amidst their own uncertainty, and despite the threats and censorship of the regime, these men had the great merit of publicly undertaking this Oedipal search. We shall see, for example, how Putik left journalism for literature. Formerly, no doubt to avoid questioning the great syntheses of Stalinism, Putik immersed himself in external facts, as they were reported by the radio and the press throughout the world, fruits disguised in the East by a leaden pedantry, and in the West by a sly 'objectivism'. 'The need to write down my own thoughts, to express myself in my own way, developed only after 1956. That year, like the war, left its mark on many people. Brutally so. In my case, I had already guessed many things and asked myself others. Nevertheless, it was the decisive . . . jolt. It was then that I became acutely aware that I was not doing what I really wanted to do.' What he wanted to do was write in order to know himself, and as most of the novelists represented here put it, to 'know men', to rediscover them in 'their existential dimensions'. 'From 1956 to 1958,' Kosik says, 'Czech culture was polarized on existential problems and the question – "What is man?" – became its common denominator.'

Have no fear: Czechoslovak intellectuals were not interested in patching up another humanism. They had known two sorts of humanism – that of Beneš and that of Stalin – both of which, as one of our witnesses aptly comments, 'hid men from them'. Both had crumbled, and no one dreamt of reassembling the debris. The hard and exhilarating task before them was the only possible one, the only necessary one – to approach their

---

5. An idea which in a certain sense is perfectly correct, since it seems to criticize *Realpolitik*. But coming from Novotny, it simply meant that facts should be disregarded when they contradicted the decisions of the leadership.

low men without any philanthropic prejudice. From this point of view, ie question posed by Kundera was the sign of a salutary radicalism: 'Why should one love men?' Yes, why? Some day they would know the answer, or perhaps never. For the moment it mattered little. Kundera's scepticism was certainly no soft pillow for the mind, but it would be a mistake to believe that it led to despair. Kundera expressly tells us that he saw in it the renaissance of thought: 'Scepticism does not abolish the world, it turns it into questions.' Profiting from their estrangement, they decided that nothing shall be taken for granted, no truth be sanctified. For them as for Plato, astonishment was the beginning of philosophy and for the moment they had no wish to go beyond it. The affirmations of officialdom were replies that pre-empted questions to prevent them being asked; they preferred questions that had no answers. Thought could not rid itself of the chalky concretions which had so long damaged or distorted it, by countering them with other concretions, but only by dissolving them in fluid problems. This did not prevent research; on the contrary, it stimulated it, assigning new tasks and provisional limits to it. In April 1968, Havel foresaw 'a social art of a profoundly realist temper', which would show 'the individual in his social context, with his private life, his family, his children, his material situation. All this will be on the agenda once it becomes possible to tell the truth about things. . . . We can expect a new type of social realism, and even in the novel a new direction of psychological research, sounding out the unexplored.'[6] Goldstücker concurs when – to show that the quest of these new Oedipuses seeks to be exhaustive – he declares (Marx and Freud said it before him): 'It is impossible to attain the depths of reality by describing its surface manifestation.'

This zeal will make more than one Western reader smile: we in the 'free' world have advanced beyond that! We have long been familiar with introspection, metapsychology, psychoanalysis. It is true: we have another way of not knowing ourselves, and we speak more freely of our emotional complexes than of our material condition or of our socio-professional milieu; we prefer to ask ourselves about the homosexual

6. It will be noted that the art which Havel envisaged here had nothing in common with his previous 'absurdism'. He hoped at the time that the new society in gestation would at last be able to integrate the outlaws on the margins of the dying system.

component of our characters than about the history which has made us and which we have made. We too are victims and accomplices of alienation, reification, mystification. We too stagger beneath 'the weight of things said and done', of lies accepted and transmitted without belief. But we have no wish to know it. We are like sleepwalkers treading in a gutter, dreaming of our genitals rather than looking at our feet. The Czechs too, of course, have to rethink these problems which the puritanism of the fifties had masked from them.[7] But as one of them said to Liehm: 'How lucky we would be if all we had to think about was that!' For these men must say *everything* or disappear. The questions that we ask ourselves casually, abstractly, and a thousand others that we would never think of asking ourselves, they ask passionately and concretely. If they do not yet know themselves completely, it is because their experience is too rich; it will take them time to put it in order.

This is not the only reason. I remember a conversation with a Latin American writer in 1960: he was tired, more lucid than disappointed, still a militant. I knew that his life was full of battles, of victories and failures, that he had known exile and prison, that he had been expelled from the Party by his comrades and then reintegrated, and that in the course of this incessant struggle he had kept his loyalties while losing his illusions. 'You ought to write this history – your history,' I said to him. He shook his head – it was the only time he showed any bitterness – and replied: 'We Communists have no history.' I realized then that the autobiography of which I had spoken, his own or that of one of his comrades there or elsewhere, had little chance of seeing the light. No history, and no memory. The Party of course, possesses the one and the other, but both are counterfeit. He who writes the history of a Communist Party from the outside, using public materials, documents, and testimonies, is always liable to be misled by his prejudices, and in any event necessarily lacks the irreplaceable experience of having known it from within. He who has left the Party tends to choke on his rancour and dip his pen in bile. He who writes from inside the Party, with the assent of its leadership, becomes an official historiographer, eluding questions of the past according to the positions of the present. To what

7. Several of them in these interviews explicitly refer to psychoanalysis as a means of access to a 'deeper reality'.

can a militant who seeks to understand his life turn, since the organization that has surrounded and produced him discourages such subjective ventures in principle, at best inclining him to bear false witness against himself even in his innermost thoughts? What does he have at his disposal? Reconstructed memories, desiccated or cancelled by a succession of self-criticisms, or other remembrances still vivid but insignificant or incomprehensible. After having 'negotiated' so many twists and turns in the party line, how is he to remember the direction he thought he was taking at the start, or even to know where he is heading at present? Who in the party can claim that the key he uses to interpret its actions today will still be the same a year hence? Dissemblers arrange to keep secret dimensions to themselves, like the Russian whose friends told me: he has twelve storeys of sincerity, you have only reached the fourth. This type is always silent. Others have given their lives to their party twice over; they have often risked their life on its orders in emergencies, while in day-to-day discipline they have let it sink into sand behind them, in dunes where the slightest gust of wind suffices to erase their footprints.

The Czechs and the Slovaks who speak here are for the most part members of the Communist Party. They, too, gave their lives in enthusiasm and then lost sight of them for several years. It is they, however, who have undertaken in these interviews, in novels, in a hundred different essays,[8] the task of recovering them, which seemed impossible in 1960 and which encounters the same difficulties today. For this reason, they had to proceed step by step, to overcome their inner resistances, to scan virtually invisible traces, to raise tombstones to see what was buried beneath. Above all – this was the fundamental problem – they had to find the right *lighting*. Fortunately, their memories were still fresh: in 1956 the 'socialist fog' was only eight years old. Khrushchev's report, however absurd it may have been, gave them the 'final shock' which allowed them to speak of themselves and the Party in the necessary way. They did not attempt to plane above this great body of which they were an integral part; it was their anchorage. If they had suffered the system, they also knew that they had made it – for although it was prefabricated, it had at least to be installed – and that their very struggle to limit some

8. In this respect I know no document so considered, so stubborn, and so lucid as Artur London's admirable record of his imprisonment, *The Confession*.

of its excesses had merely been a certain way of accepting it. therefore spoke of it *from the inside*, since that is where they still are with an incontestable solidarity, without ever condemning it in hatred and rage the better to proclaim their innocence. They took their distance *within it*, by virtue of the dislocation induced by their estrangement, which suddenly illuminated practices that had been so routine that they had performed them without noticing it. It was as if they could only recover their lives, in the name of norms to be fixed, of fidelities to be regained, by an internal critique of the Party, and as if they could contest the role of the Party only by a radical contestation of themselves, interrogating their actions and results, their omissions, their abdications and their compromises. What might seem a vicious circle emerges in these interviews as in fact a dialectical movement to permit both their readers and themselves to find their lost truth – a concrete totalization, continually detotalized, contradictory and problematic, never closed back on itself, never completed, yet nevertheless one single experience. It is this totalization that is the necessary point of departure for any theoretical research, the point from which Marxism started with Marx and then restarted again with Lenin, with Luxemburg, with Gramsci, but to which it has never since returned.

What could they base themselves on to maintain the *distanciation* necessary to the pursuit of their inquiry? The answer is clear: their national culture. Is this any reason to tax them with nationalism as the old guard of mummified Stalinists did? No. Read them and you will see. Is it their fault if the tide of pseudo-Marxism revealed, as it ebbed, that their historical traditions remained intact because they had never been developed and surpassed towards a genuine socialism? Who is responsible if they discover that a recourse to their own history, however insufficient it may be, is temporarily more useful for understanding their present than the empty concepts hitherto imposed on them? They do not deny that at a later stage there must be a return to a Marxist interpretation of their national experience; quite the contrary. But to meet the urgent needs of the moment it was necessary to start with simple, known facts: the configuration of the soil, the geo-political situation of the country, its small size, all of which made Bohemia and Slovakia battlefields for their powerful neighbours; its incorporation in the

Austro-Hungarian Empire which then 're-Catholicized' them by force, as the Russian State is now trying to 're-Stalinize' them. Such elements of the past were so many mortgages on their future and explanations of the present. The two peoples have always struggled against occupying powers, of whatever provenance, and against their lumbering invincible armies, by a constant reaffirmation of their cultural identity. 'The Czechs,' Liehm says, 'are the only people in Europe to have traversed most of the 17th century and the whole of the 18th century without possessing a national aristocracy, the normal fount of education, culture, and politics at the time. The result of coercive germanization and re-catholicization . . . was that the birth of Czech politics was necessarily an effort to revive national language and civilization. . . . Thus there has long been a close and organic unity between culture and politics in our country.'

In the epoch of Stalinization, the problems were different, but the weapons of the Czechs remained the same: against the glacial socialism imposed on them, they asserted their own cultural character. Czech intellectuals rediscovered in the 1960s a duty: to protect their national culture, not in order to preserve it as it was, but in order to construct beyond it a socialism that would change it, and yet retain its imprint. This perspective allowed them to feel more at home on the planet; they were not, as they had once thought, strangers among strangers. If they had temporarily believed otherwise, it was because the reign of the 'Thing' had atomized them. To overthrow it without lapsing into 'subjectivism', each of them had to recognize in each of his neighbours his *fellow* – that is to say, the product of the same cultural history. The struggle involved here is hard, and its outcome uncertain. Our witnesses know that they are 'living in a century of incorporation of smaller units by larger units'. One of them even declares that 'the process of integration threatens sooner or later to absorb all small nations'. What is then to be done? They have no ready answer; since they closed their catechisms, they ceased to want to be sure of anything. All they know is that at present the struggle of Czechoslovakia for its cultural autonomy is part of a much wider struggle, waged by many nations – large and small – against the policy of blocs and for the achievement of peace.

The regime, already uncertain and divided by inner conflicts, now deemed it prudent to unload some ballast. For fear that the new cultural commitment of intellectuals might lead them to abandon 'socialist realism' for 'critical realism' – two equally *unthinkable* concepts, but the servants of the 'Thing' can only react to dangers that threaten it if they can find a definition of them in their catalogues – it invited them to become non-committed. 'If you lack the means to declare your confidence in the system, you have permission to talk without saying anything.' Such concessions were too late. Those who express themselves here – and many others whom they represent – rejected this tolerance. Goldstücker's comment is admirable: 'The notions of "realism" and "non-realism" merely obscure the true problem – which is how far the commitment of the artist is allowed to go when he seeks to depict the historical conditions of life created by the social processes of the last years.' They were not calling for a return to bourgeois liberalism but, since truth is revolutionary, were claiming the revolutionary right to tell the truth.

The Party leadership of the time could not even understand this demand. For them the truth had already been spoken, everyone knew it by heart, and the duty of the artist was simply to repeat it. A dialogue of the deaf appeared to be occurring. But suddenly the masses caught fire: what might have seemed, at the outset, the professional concern of a privileged caste, became the passionate demand of an entire people. We must now explain how that which was so acutely lacking in France a month later came to be realized in Czechoslovakia in April 1968: the unity of intellectuals and working class.

The economic situation in the sixties had become more and more disquieting: there was no lack of Cassandras among economists. Their cries of alarm had not yet reached the general public. Everything happened inside the Party, or rather inside its permanent apparatus: in other words, the struggle to repair the machine merged with the struggle for power within it. In the leadership, conflict sharpened between the bureaucrats of yesterday and those of today. The former, whom Liehm calls 'amateurs', justified their universal incompetence by the Stalinist principle of the autonomy of politics. The latter were younger and almost all belonged to the generation of 'eternal dauphins'; without questioning the system, they advocated the primacy of economics, at least in the current conjuncture.[9] In short, they were reformists. The nature of the regime was not at stake in this conflict. The old men in power legitimized their authority under the ancient slogan of the intensification of the class struggle during the building of socialism. The young men seeking power justified their claims by invoking their skills and the urgent need to redress the economy. These authoritarian reformists saw no contradiction in basing an unmodified autonomy of politics on immediate imperatives of the economic infrastructure. They promised to abolish the fetishism of production from above, readjusting output to the resources and the needs of the country and adapting it to some extent to the demands of consumption. The conflict of these two despotisms, one obscurantist and the other enlightened, led both of them to turn toward the working class. The proletariat would arbitrate between them.

Now initially, the working class seemed to lean towards the old leadership. Depoliticized by the dreary routine to which they were confined, many workers were apprehensive of changes that appeared to threaten the security of their jobs. To win them to its side, the other clan had to concede the workers a certain control over production, and to promise them a 'law on the socialist enterprise'. The reforms envisaged necessarily involved a certain *liberalization* of the regime: there was talk of decentralization, of self-management. There was *talk*, but so long as the system subsisted, such words were void of meaning. The Yugoslav experience has shown that self-management remains a dead letter when political power is monopolized by a privileged group based on a centralized apparatus. It was now the merit of Slovak intellectuals to exploit the paralysis of a regime blocked by its own internal contradictions, and to incite the workers to respond to the offers of reformist liberalism by the revolutionary demand for socialist *democratization*. In reality, no one on either side had a clear awareness at first of what was happening. The intellectuals, attracted towards reformism, essentially wanted their articles to help swing the masses over to the side of the reformers. But their writings – those the reader will find here and many others too,

9. It is striking that the Party leadership in East Germany had simultaneously defused conflicts at the top and dynamized the East German economy, by associating technocrats with it in the exercise of power. The result is that its domination of the masses is more rigorous than in any other people's democracy.

products of the long process of meditation that had begun in 1956 – had a wider and deeper effect than they themselves suspected. By seeking and setting out the truth, they laid bare the system, and by explaining their own experience they demonstrated to their readers that the Czechoslovak people needed, not to put an end to the 'abuses' of the regime, but to liquidate the system as a whole.

The trials, the confessions, the deformation of thought, the institutionalized mendacity, the atomization, the universal mistrust – these were not abuses; they were the inescapable consequences of a prefabricated socialism. No improvement, no patching could make them disappear. No matter what team was in power, even if it revealed goodwill, it would be petrified or crushed, unless both Czechs and Slovaks fell upon the machine with hammer-blows and pounded with all their might until it collapsed, demolished beyond repair. The intellectuals learnt the real dynamic content of their thought at the end of 1967, when their writings were honoured with the wrath of a now weary regime. Gagged for a brief interval, they saw their ideas descend into the streets. Student youth – the generation they so doubted – had appropriated them and were brandishing them like banners. The victory of reformism in January 1968 was no longer their victory, in spite of the temporary alliance of the masses and the technocrats. Their real triumph came a little later, when the working class, roused from its torpor if not yet fully conscious of itself, remembered its old maximalist demand, the only one that truly sprang from this class: power to soviets. There were discussions in every enterprise, experiments in direct democracy. In some factories the workers did not even wait for the passage of the new law to evict the manager and place his *elected* successor under the control of a workers' council. The new Party leadership, overtaken by mass initiatives, had to revise its draft law to take account of this popular upsurge. But it was too late; for it was becoming clear that the process of democratization could not be halted. The intellectuals realized that this great popular movement represented a radicalization of their own thought, and now radicalized themselves, intensified their struggle against the system, without turning against the new team of leaders.

No press or radio has ever been freer than in Czechoslovakia during the spring of 1968. What was most striking to a Westerner was that the

battle of the intellectuals for complete freedom of expression and information was supported by the workers, who very quickly decided that the
right to unrestricted information was one of their basic demands. It was
on this common foundation that the union of workers and intellectuals
was sealed.[10] The fact reveals the extent to which the problems of a
'people's democracy' differ from our own. French workers will not
launch a strike if the Government infringes the freedom of the press,
and under present conditions their attitude is understandable. Power
rarely needs to muzzle the newspapers; profit takes care of that. Workers
read *Le Parisien Libéré* without believing a word of it and reason that the
problems of the press will find their solution with the pure and simple
abolition of profit. They know, perhaps, that censorship exists in the
USSR or in Poland, but this doesn't stop them sleeping. They have been
told that in those countries the proletariat exercises its dictatorship;
and that therefore it would be a crime to permit counter-revolutionary
gazettes, in the name of abstract bourgeois principles, to continue to
poison the air with their lies.

But in 1968, after twenty years of Stalinism, the situation was very
different for Czech and Slovak workers. To start with, they too had been
sated with lies, though just how sick of them they had been they were
only now becoming fully aware. The dictatorship of the proletariat was
the dictatorship of a party that had lost all contact with the masses. As
for class struggle, how could they believe that it intensified with the
progress of socialism? They were perfectly well aware that ever since
its installation socialism had done nothing but regress. Censorship in
their eyes was not even a lesser evil, since it was lies that censored truth.
On the contrary, to the very extent that they became conscious of their
maximalist demand for councils, the full truth – as theoretical and practical knowledge – became indispensable to them, for the simple reason

10. This union still existed when I returned to Prague in November 1969. The students
had occupied certain faculties to protest against the *de facto* re-establishment of
censorship. It was still possible to speak with a certain freedom about the occupying
power. For example, at the request of a student, I could say in front of a crowded
auditorium that I considered the intervention of the Five to be a war crime; while the
students could demand freedom of information within the perspective of the maximalist
demand outlined above. The government was contemplating repression of them, without much confidence, when the workers in key Czech factories halted its plans by
announcing that they would immediately strike if action was taken against the students.

that workers' power cannot be exercised even in the workplace if it is not constantly well informed at all levels. Naturally, this demand affected not only the daily diffusion of national and international news by the mass media. It acquired its real meaning at a deeper level. To be able to orient, correct, and control production, to situate their own activities within the country and within the world, to remain across geographical distances in permanent contact with each other, the Czech and Slovak workers demanded full participation in the scientific and cultural life of the nation. This claim, which only just started to become conscious of itself during the Prague spring, would sooner or later have set off a revolution in culture and education. Thus within a vast revolutionary movement, workers and intellectuals constantly radicalized each other. Intellectuals became convinced that they could perform their office – the search for truth – only in a socialist society in which power was shared by all. Workers, fascinated by the polemics unleashed in the newspapers, became convinced that they could never achieve socialism without breaking the monopoly of knowledge (which exists in the East as in the West) and guaranteeing the widest social diffusion of truth. The full development of this truth as both theory and practice would be the fruit of the dialectical unity of these two aspirations. There is no doubt that all the agents of this process were far from knowing where they were going and what they were doing. But neither can there be any doubt that they were trying to *achieve socialism* by liquidating the system and establishing new relations of production. The new ruling group, out-paced but unbemused, saw this quite clearly, as can be seen from the timid project for 'revisions of the party statutes' published in *Rude Pravo* on 19 August 1968, which forbade 'occupancy of a plurality of public offices in the Party and in the State'.[11] It was the bureaucracy itself that was finally obliged to administer the first hammer-blows to break the machine.

Everyone knows the sequel. Before it was even full-born, this socialism was smothered by counter-revolution. This is what *Pravda* claims, and I

11. The idea in itself, of course, was neither new nor revisionist. It is even formally inscribed in the statutes of the CPSU. I have shown elsewhere why it never received the slightest shadow of application in the USSR. What mattered in Czechoslovakia was the willingness the new rule revealed to return to original ideals, to give life to a forgotten principle, to restore some revolutionary role to the Party.

am in complete agreement with the Russian newspaper except on the minor question of cardinal points: the counter-revolutionary forces did not come from the West. For once it was not Western imperialism that crushed a movement towards democratization and restored the reign of the 'Thing' by constraint and violence. The leaders of the USSR, terrified to see socialism on the march again, sent their tanks to Prague to stop it. The system was saved just in time, another set of leaders was rapidly installed. Public congratulations on the Soviet intervention renewed the institutionalized lie. Nothing had changed, except that a prefabricated socialism, now become an oppressor socialism, had been unmasked. Official propaganda resounds amid the silence of fourteen million people who no longer believe a word of it. Those who repeat it at the top are as lonely as the French collaborators during the German occupation. They know that they are lying, that the 'Thing' is the enemy of Man; but the lie has taken hold of them and will no longer let them go. Their incitement to delation is within the logic of the system, whose survival depends on every citizen mistrusting others and himself. But self-distrust is now finished: after the Twentieth Congress and the invasion of 1968, Czechs and Slovaks can no longer be tricked into it. The regime can now only try to make everyone, in spite of this, a potential informer and therefore a suspect to his neighbours. Despite a few token precautions, the five invading powers scarcely troubled to conceal the eminently *conservative* nature of their intervention. Our Western bourgeoisie was not in error: the entry of tanks into Prague *reassured* it. Why not end the Cold War and conclude a new Holy Alliance with Russia to maintain order everywhere? This is the perspective at which we have now arrived. The cards are on the table and it is no longer possible to cheat.

Yet we still do cheat. The Left *protests*, denounces, blames, or 'regrets'. *Le Monde* often publishes texts inspired by a virtuous anger, followed by a long list of signatures that always include the same names – mine for example. Let us sign indeed! Anything is better than a mutism that might appear acceptance. Provided that moralism does not serve as an alibi. It is true, of course, that what the Five have done is ugly and shameful. But how little they care! Even if they were concerned about the reactions of the European Left, they would be gratified if it merely stamped its foot and shouted. So long as we restrict ourselves to deontology,* the system can rest easy. The Soviet leaders are guilty, they did not act as *socialists*! The accusation implies that they could have done. They alone are charged; the regime itself is not questioned. But if we will read these interviews and decipher the Czech experience through them, we will soon understand that these leaders, recruited and formed by the system, exercising power in the name of the 'Thing', could not have acted otherwise than they did. It is the whole regime that must be assailed, and the relations of production which generated it and have in turn been reinforced and petrified by it. After the month of August 1968, it is necessary to forsake the comforts of moralism and to abandon reformist illusions about this type of regime. The machine cannot be repaired; the peoples of Eastern Europe must seize hold of it and destroy it.

The revolutionary forces of the West now have only one way of helping Czechoslovakia effectively in the long run. That is, to listen to the voices that speak to us of its fate, to assemble documents about it, to try to reconstruct and analyse events there in depth, beyond the present conjuncture, for the light they cast on the structures of Soviet society, the nature of the people's democracies, and the interconnections between the two. The duty of the Left in Western Europe is to profit from this analysis, to rethink, without preconceptions or prejudices, its own objectives, tasks, possibilities and types of organization, in order to be able to answer the fundamental question of our time: how to unite all the exploited to overthrow the old ossified structures of our own society, how to produce new structures which will ensure that the next revolution does not give birth to *that sort of socialism*.

*Translator's note: Deontology = Science of moral duty or obligation.

France: Masses, Spontaneity, Party

During the May events in France, and in the course of the working-class struggle of 1968 generally, movements at the base attacked the Communist parties not only for their bureaucratic degeneration or for their reformist options; they also criticized the very notion of the party as the political, structured organization of the class. When these movements suffered setbacks, a number of 'leftist' groups came to emphasize organization against spontaneity, and advocated a return to 'pure' Leninism. Neither of these attitudes seems to us satisfactory. It seems to us that one can only properly criticize spontaneity – and this was the lesson of 1968 – if it is realized that the subjective maturity of the working class requires today a new form of organization, adapted to the conditions of struggle in the societies of advanced capitalism.

We should like to focus this conversation on the theoretical bases of this problem. You have been concerned with this ever since the now classic discussion of 1952 (Communists and Peace) *and the polemic which followed with Lefort and Merleau-Ponty, by way of* The Ghost of Stalin *of 1956 to the* Critique de la Raison Dialectique. *In 1952, you were charged with hyper-subjectivism and you were reproached with a failure to recognize any existence of the working class other than in the party. In 1956, it was the reverse accusation that was directed at you, namely that you were guilty of an objectivism which tended to explain Stalinism as the inevitable product of a particular historical situation. In actual fact, it seems to us that both positions had a common basis in the concept of 'scarcity', in the structural backwardness of the country in which the October Revolution occurred, in the 'necessities' imposed by the fact that the revolution was not 'ripe' and that socialism had to be built in a context of primitive accumulation. In this specific situation, you considered that the party was bound to superimpose itself upon a mass which had not reached the required level of consciousness. Do you believe that this image of the party – which we shared with you in the fifties – must be revised because the situation has changed; or, on the contrary, that it must be revised because the earlier formulations were vitiated by theoretical inadequacies which have since then been more clearly revealed?*

There was certainly inadequacy. But this must be situated historically. In 1952, when I wrote *Communists and Peace*, the essential political choice was the defence of the French Communist Party, and particularly of the Soviet Union, accused as it was of imperialism. It was essential to reject this accusation if one did not wish to find oneself on the side of the Americans. Afterwards, it was shown that the USSR, by behaving in Budapest as Stalin (whether because of political intelligence or for other reasons) did not behave in 1948 in relation to Yugoslavia, and then by repeating the operation in Czechoslovakia, was acting in the manner of an imperialist power. In saying this, I do not intend to express a moral judgement. I am only stating that the external policy of the USSR seems essentially inspired by its antagonistic relations with the United States, and not by a principle of respect, of equality, vis-à-vis other socialist states. I tried to explain the point in the *Critique de la Raison Dialectique*. This of course was still an attempt at a formal solution, which should have been followed by an historical analysis of the USSR in Stalin's time – an analysis which I have already sketched out and which forms part of a second volume of the *Critique*, but which will probably never appear.

In short, what I tried to show in relation to concepts like *mass*, *party*, *spontaneity*, *seriality*, *channels*, *groups*, represents the embryo of an answer to this problem. In effect, I tried to show that the party, in relation to the mass, is a *necessary* reality because the mass, by itself, does not possess *spontaneity*. By itself, the mass remains serialized. But conversely, as soon as the party becomes an institution, so does it also – save in exceptional circumstances – become reactionary in relation to what it has itself brought into being, namely the *fused group*. In other words, the dilemma spontaneity/party is a false problem. In terms of its self-consciousness, the class does not appear homogeneous; but rather as an ensemble of elements, of groups, which I define as 'fused'. Among the workers, we always find fused groups in this or that factory where a struggle occurs, in the course of which individuals establish relations of reciprocity, enjoy in regard to the totality of groups what I have called a 'wild freedom', and acquire a definite consciousness of their class position.

But besides these fused groups, there are other workers who are not united by struggle, who remain serialized, and who are therefore incapable of spontaneity because they are not linked to the rest, except in a reified relation, in a serialized connection. Even a fused group – for instance a factory which is on strike – is continually subjected to and weighed down by serialized relations (massification, etc). The same worker who finds himself in a fused group at his place of work may be completely serialized when he is at home or at other moments of his life. We are therefore in the presence of very different forms of class consciousness: on the one hand, an advanced consciousness, on the other an almost non-existent consciousness, with a series of mediations in between. This is why it does not seem to me that one can speak of class *spontaneity*; it is only appropriate to speak of *groups*, produced by circumstances, and which create themselves in the course of particular situations; in thus creating themselves, they do not rediscover some kind of underlying spontaneity, bur rather experience a specific condition on the basis of specific situations of exploitation and of particular demands; and it is in the course of their experience that they achieve a more or less accurate consciousness of themselves.

This said, what does the party represent in relation to the series? Surely a positive factor, since it prevents a collapse into complete seriality. The members of a Communist Party would themselves remain isolated and serialized individuals if the party did not turn them into a group through an organic link which enables a Communist in Milan to communicate with another Communist worker from any other region. Moreover, it is thanks to the party that many groups are formed in the course of struggle, because the party makes communication easier. However, the party finds itself as a general rule compelled either to absorb or to reject the fused group which it has itself helped to create. In comparison with the group, whose organization never goes beyond a kind of reciprocal pact, the party is much more strongly structured. A group forms itself under stress, for instance to achieve some goal ('We must take the Bastille'); as soon as the action is over, the individuals who compose the group anxiously face each other and try to establish a link which might replace the link forged in action, a kind of pact or oath, which in turn tends to constitute the beginning of a series and to establish between them a relationship of reified contiguity. This is what I have called *'Fraternity-terror'*. The party, on the contrary, develops as an ensemble of institutions, and therefore as a closed, static system, which has a tendency to sclerosis. This is why the party is always behind in relation to the fused mass, even when it tries to guide that mass: this is so because it tries to weaken it, to subordinate it, and may even reject it and deny any solidarity with it.

The thought and action of each group necessarily reflect its structure. What occurs is therefore the following: the thought of a fused group – by virtue of the fact that it is born in the stress of a particular situation and not because of some kind of 'spontaneity' – has a stronger, fresher, more critical charge than that of a structured group. As an institution, a party has an institutionalized mode of thought – meaning something which deviates from *reality* – and comes essentially to reflect no more than its own organization, in effect ideological thought. It is upon its own schema that is modelled, and deformed, the experience of the struggle itself; while the fused group thinks its experience as it presents itself, without institutional mediation. This is why the thought of a group may be vague, incapable of being theorized, awkward – as were the ideas of the students in May 1968 – but nevertheless represents a *truer* kind of thought because no institution is interposed between experience and the reflection upon existence.

No doubt, we are dealing with a contradiction which is inherent in the very function of the party. The latter comes into being to liberate the working class from seriality; but at the same time, it is a reflection – a reflection of a certain type, since the party is intended to abolish that condition – of the seriality and massification of the masses upon which it operates. This seriality of the masses finds expression in the party's institutional character. Compelled as it is to deal with what is serialized, it is itself partly inert and serialized. In order to protect itself, it thus ends up by opposing the fused groups, even though these groups are an aspect of a working class which it wants to represent and which it has itself very often brought into movement.

Here is the underlying contradiction of the party, which has emerged to liberate the masses from seriality and which has itself become an institution. As such, it harbours so many negative features (I don't mean here bureaucracy or other forms of degeneration, but rather the institutional structure itself, which is not necessarily bureaucratic) that it finds itself compelled, fundamentally and in all cases, to oppose all the new forces, whether it tries to use them or whether it rejects them. We have seen these two different attitudes adopted by the French and the Italian Communist parties *vis-à-vis* the students: the French party rejected them; more subtly, the PCI tried to attract them and to direct their experience by means of contact and discussion. A party can only choose between these two attitudes: this is its underlying limitation.

Let me give you another classic example, namely the question of democratic centralism. As long as democratic centralism operated in a dynamic situation, for instance during clandestinity and the organization of the struggle in Russia, that is precisely at the time when Lenin elaborated its theory, it remained a living thing. There was a moment of centralism, because it was necessary, and a moment of real democracy, because people could argue and decisions were taken in common. As soon as it was institutionalized, as was the case in all Communist countries, centralism took precedence over democracy, and democracy itself became an 'institution', subjected to its own inertia: there exists, for instance, a right to speak, but the fact alone that it should be a right – and only that – empties it so much of its substance that, in reality, it becomes a non-right. The real question is therefore to know how to overcome the contradiction which is inherent in the very nature of the party, so that (not only in its relations with opponents and in its tasks as a fighting organization, but also in relation to the class which it represents) the party may constitute an active mediation between serialized and massified elements for the purpose of their unification; in other words, how the party may be able to receive the impulses which emanate from movements and, rather than claim to direct them, may be able to generalize experience for the movement and for itself.

The real location of revolutionary consciousness is therefore neither in the immediate class, nor in the party, but in the struggle. On this view, the party remains alive as long as it is an instrument of struggle, but exchanges the end for the means as soon as it becomes an institution, and becomes its own end. The contradiction which is inherent in the party, and which you emphasize, can perhaps be resolved to the extent that one tries to approach the problem of the political organization of the class not in general terms, but in the immediacy of specific situations. What seems impossible is a meta-historical solution. It therefore seems necessary to envisage the objective conditions in which this dilemma can be resolved on each occasion. In our view, this implies two conditions: first of all that the class should transcend the level of seriality to become effectively and totally the subject of collective action.

This is an impossible condition; the working class can never express itself completely as an active political subject: there will always be zones or regions or sectors which, because of historical reasons of development, will remain serialized, massified, alien to the achievement of consciousness. There is always a residue. There is a strong tendency today to generalize the concept of *class consciousness* and of *class struggle* as pre-existing elements antecedent to the struggle. The only *a priori* is the objective situation of class exploitation. Consciousness is only born in struggle: the class struggle only exists insofar as there exist places where an actual struggle is going on. It is true that the proletariat carries within itself the death of the bourgeoisie; it is equally true that the capitalist system is mined by structural contradictions. But this does not necessarily imply the existence of class consciousness or of class struggle. In order that there should be *consciousness* and *struggle*, it is necessary that somebody should be fighting.

In other words, the class struggle is virtually possible everywhere in the capitalist system, but really exists only where the struggle is actually being carried on. On the other hand, the struggle, even while it is being carried on, differs in terms of each situation. In France, for instance, the conditions and forms of struggle are extremely diverse: in Saint-Nazaire, the workers' struggles, which are very violent, retain the characteristics of the last century; in other, more 'advanced', capitalist zones, they assume a different character, with an articulation of demands which may be greater, but in a more moderate context. This is why it is impossible, even for that part of the working class which is actually struggling, to speak of *unification*, save theoretically. The twenty-four-hour general strikes organized by the CGT are no more, at best, than the symbol of a unified struggle.

But are we not in a phase of capitalist unification of society, as much in terms of the infrastructure as of the superstructures (types of consumption and styles of life, language, massification)? Is it not true that the fragmentation of individual situations is accompanied by the ever more obvious 'totalization' of the system? And should not this have as its consequence the formation of an objective material base for the growing unification of the class and of its class consciousness?

In actual fact, the structure remains extremely diversified and unstable.

But is there a tendency towards unification or not?

Yes and no. In France, for instance, capitalism artificially maintains alive thousands of small enterprises, for whose existence there is no reason from the point of view of economic rationality; but they are useful to capitalism, either because they represent a conservative political sector (these are the social strata which vote for de Gaulle or Pompidou), or because they provide a norm for capitalist costs of production, despite the increase in productivity. In effect, the tendencies to integration do not cancel out the profound diversities of structural situations.

Add to this that advanced capitalism, in relation to its awareness of its own condition, and despite the enormous disparities in the distribution of income, manages to satisfy the elementary needs of the majority of the working class – there remain of course the marginal zones, 15 per cent of workers in the United States, the blacks and the immigrants; there remain the elderly; there remains, on a global scale, the third world. But capitalism satisfies certain primary needs, and also satisfies certain needs which it has artificially created: for instance the need of a car. It is this situation which has caused me to revise my 'theory of needs', since these needs are no longer, in a situation of advanced capitalism, in systematic opposition to the system. On the contrary, they partly become, under the control of that system, an instrument of integration of the proletariat into certain processes engendered and directed by profit. The worker exhausts himself in producing a car and in earning enough to buy one; this acquisition gives him the impression of having satisfied a 'need'. The system which exploits him provides him simultaneously with a goal and with the possibility of reaching it. The consciousness of the intolerable character of the system must therefore no longer be sought in the impossibility of satisfying elementary needs but, above all else, in the consciousness of *alienation* – in other words, in the fact that *this life* is not worth living and has no meaning, that this mechanism is a deceptive mechanism, that these needs are artificially created, that they are false, that they are exhausting and only serve profit. But to unite the class on this basis is even more difficult. This is why I do not agree with any of the optimistic visions presented by Communist parties or by left movements, who seem to believe that capitalism is henceforth at bay. Capitalism's means of control over classes are still powerful; and it is far from being on the defensive. As for bringing about a revolutionary élan, this requires a long patient labour in the construction of consciousness.

Even so, this unification appeared immediate and obvious in May 1968.

Absolutely obvious. It is one of the rare instances where everyone saw in the struggles of the local factory a model of his own struggles. A phenomenon of the same order, but of far greater dimension, occurred in 1936. But at that time the working-class institutions played a determinant role. The movement started when socialists and communists were already in power, and offering, up to a certain point, a model which allowed the class a rapid achievement of consciousness, the fusion of groups, and unification.

In May, not only were parties and unions not in power, but they were also a long way from playing a comparable role. The element which unified the struggle was something which, in my opinion, came from afar; it was an idea which came to us from Vietnam and which the students expressed in the formula: '*L'imagination au pouvoir.*' In other words, the area of the possible is much more vast than the dominant classes have accustomed us to believe. Who would have thought that fourteen million peasants would be able to resist the greatest industrial and military power in the world? And yet, this is what happened. Vietnam taught us that the area of the possible is immense, and that one need not be resigned. It is this which was the lever of the students' revolt, and the workers understood it. In the united demonstration of the 13th of May, this idea suddenly became dominant. 'If a few thousand youngsters can occupy the universities and defy the government, why should we not be able to do the same?' Thus it was that from the 13th of May onwards, and following a model which at that moment came to them from outside, the workers went on strike and occupied the factories. The element which mobilized and united them was not a programme of demands: this came later, to justify the strike, and of course there was no lack of motives for strike action. But it is interesting to note that the demands came later, after the factories had already been occupied.

It would therefore seem that, at the origin of May, there was no immediately material element, no particularly explosive structural contradiction?

The preceding autumn, something had provoked a generalized discontent among the workers, namely the reactionary measures of the government in the field of social security. These measures had hit the whole working population, whatever their occupation. The unions, either because they were taken by surprise or because they did not want to expose themselves too much, did not manage to offer adequate opposition to the measures. There was, if my memory serves, a day of general strike, but that is as far as it went. However, a deep and unexpressed discontent endured; and it broke out again in strength in the May demonstrations. There is today a possible new element of unification: this is the absolutely futile character which the rise in prices, and then devaluation, have given to the increases in wages which were obtained at the time. But it is not easy to know in advance whether these unifying elements of discontent will lead to a united revolt. In May, on the other hand, this revolt occurred and in my opinion, the detonator was not so much that the workers became conscious of exploitation but that they became conscious of their own strength and of their own possibilities.

Yet, this revolt of May was a failure and was followed by a victory of reaction. Is that because it did not contain the elements capable of pushing the revolution to a conclusion or because it lacked political direction?

It lacked political direction, of a kind capable of giving it the political and theoretical dimension without which the movement could not but subside, as indeed happened. It lacked a party capable of taking up completely the movement and its potentialities. As a matter of fact, how could an institutionalized structure, as in the case of the Communist parties, place itself in the service of something which took it by surprise? How could it be sufficiently receptive to react, not by saying 'Let us see what we can get out of this?' or 'Let us try to attract the movement to ourselves so that it does not escape from us', but by saying 'Here is reality and we must serve it by trying to give it theoretical and practical generality so that it may grow and be further advanced? Naturally, a communist party which is unable to adopt this attitude becomes what the French Communist Party has been in practice for twenty-five years: a brake on any revolutionary movement in France. Everything which does not emanate from it alone, the party either rejects or suppresses.

In fact, while you criticize the Communist parties as they are, you affirm the need for a moment of unification and of organization of the movement?

Certainly, and this is where the problem lies. We are confronted with reaction, with strong and complex capitalist rule, which has an ample capacity of repression and integration. This demands a counter-organization of the class. The problem is to know how to prevent that counter-organization from deteriorating by becoming an 'institution'.

Agreed. But it is interesting to note that the need for a political organization of the class seems to contradict a forecast of Marx, according to which the proletariat, with the growth of capitalism, would express itself immediately in a revolutionary movement, without the help of political mediation. At the origin of this thesis, there was the conviction that the crisis of capitalism would occur fairly early, and that there were growing within capitalism strains which the system could not absorb – for instance, the development of productive forces would enter into contradiction with the mechanism of capitalist development. Later on, Lenin saw in the socialization of productive forces a factor capable, up to a certain point, of laying the ground for the socialist organization of the economy, once the political apparatus of the bourgeois state had been smashed. We are forced today to recognize the inadequacy of such theses. In the first place, the productive forces do not enter directly into contradiction with the system, because they do not represent something neutral and objective, but are the product of the system and are subjected to its priorities and are affected by it. . . .

Yes, these forces are not necessarily fated to come into conflict; they are produced by this type of development, as is shown – for instance – by the choosing of space development in the scientific field. As for the socialization of productive forces, even though it is incorrect to speak here of a 'class', one must recognize that the development of these forces has brought into being a bureaucracy and a certain technocracy which have acquired a dangerous power of control over the masses and the means of integrating them into an authoritarian society.

In effect, the passage of capitalism into socialism does not have the same characteristics as the passage of feudalism into capitalism. Capitalist relations of production developed progressively inside feudal society, so much so that when the latter collapsed, it had become no more than the shell of a different structural reality, which had already ripened within it. This is what cannot happen with the proletariat; it cannot, inside capitalism, express itself through embryonic forms of socialist organization.

The processes are indeed different, whether from the angle of structures, or of relations of production, or of ideas. From the Renaissance onwards, culture was no longer feudal but bourgeois; new social groups, such as the *noblesse de robe*, were bourgeois. This process preceded and accompanied the establishment of capitalist relations of production. The gestation of the bourgeoisie lasted for centuries and expressed itself in an alternative that was *present* in existing society. This cannot happen in relation to the proletariat – not even from the point of view of culture. For the proletariat does not possess a culture which is autonomous: it either uses elements of bourgeois culture, or it expresses a total refusal of any culture, which is a way of affirming the lack of existence of its own culture. It may be objected that the proletariat nevertheless possesses a 'scale of values' which is proper to it. Of course, by wanting a revolution, it wants something different from what now exists. But I am suspicious of expressions such as 'scale of values' which can easily be turned into their opposite. The revolt of the students was a typical expression of the problem of a counter-culture: it was a refusal which, because it lacked its own elaboration, ended up by borrowing, even though it gave them a contrary meaning, a series of ideological trappings from its opponents (conceptual simplification, schematism, violence, etc).

The anti-capitalist revolution is, therefore, both ripe and not ripe. Class antagonism produces the contradiction, but is not, by itself, capable of producing the alternative. Yet, if one is not to reduce the revolution to a pure voluntarism and a pure subjectivity, or, conversely, if one is not to fall back into evolutionism, on what precise bases can one prepare a revolutionary alternative?

I repeat, more on the basis of 'alienation' than of 'needs'. In short, on the reconstruction of the individual and of freedom – the need for which is so pressing that even the most refined techniques of integration cannot afford to discount it. This is why these techniques try to satisfy that need in imaginary form. All of 'human engineering' is based on the idea that the employer must behave towards his subordinate *as if* the latter was his equal, because – this is implicit – no man can renounce this right to equality. And the worker who falls into the trap of the 'human relations' of paternalism becomes its victim, to the very degree that he wants effective equality.

This is true, but then how is one to demonstrate that this need is produced by advanced capitalism and that it is not simply the residue of a 'humanism' which antedates capitalism? It may be that the answer will have to be sought precisely in the contradictions inherent in the development of capital: for instance, in the fragmentation of work as opposed to a level of education much higher than is required by the role which the worker is called upon to assume; in the quantitative and qualitative development of education paralleled by inadequate job opportunities; in an increase of demands and in the obstacles to their satisfaction – in short, in a constant frustration of that productive force which is man.

The fact is that the development of capital increases proletarianization – not in the sense of absolute pauperization, but by the steady worsening of the relation between new needs and the role played by the workers, a worsening provoked not by slump but by development.

The revolutionary political organization of the class therefore requires the elaboration of an alternative. It seems to us that this problem was underestimated during May. Those who took up positions of Marcusian inspiration or of a spontaneist kind in the fashion of Cohn-Bendit relied exclusively on negation; in so doing, they were not even able to ensure that the struggle would be continued, because in complex and advanced societies the majority of people want to know what is being proposed. Even though it is oppressed and alienated, the working class does have access to means of subsistence, and is bound to ask what will replace what is to be destroyed.

On the other hand, those who assumed positions opposed to those of Cohn-Bendit – for instance Alain Touraine and Serge Mallet – did not see the necessity of proposing an alternative because, according to them, the development of productive forces and the subjective maturation of the masses would make immediately possible the self-government of society. This too seems to us mistaken: for while it is true that the development of capitalism ripens the possibility of revolution by creating new needs and new forces, it is also true that these reflect the system which produces them. This is why the sudden breakdown of the system necessarily leads to a fall in production: it is an illusion to believe that socialism is the productive system inherited from capitalism with self-government added to it. What is involved is a system of an altogether different kind, in a national and international context which acts and reacts upon it. This suggests the need for a transitional model, for the construction of an alternative, for a revolutionary project which constitutes the idea of the new society. One is thus driven back to the problem of uni-fication, of political preparation, of the party.

It is undoubtedly true that a theory of the passage to socialism is necessary. Suppose that the situation quickens in France or in Italy and leads to the achievement of power. What ideas do we have as to how a highly industrialized country can reconstruct itself on a socialist basis, while it is subjected to foreign boycott, to the devaluation of its currency and to the blockade of its exports? The USSR found itself in such a situation after the revolution. Despite the terrible sacrifices and the enormous losses inflicted upon it by civil war, despite the political and economic encirclement which was stifling it, the problems which the USSR had to resolve were less complex than those which would today be confronted by an advanced society. From this point of view, none of us – and no Communist party – are prepared. You speak of the necessity of a political perspective of transition. So be it. But what Communist party has ela-

borated a theory of revolutionary transition in a country of advanced
and non-autarchic capitalism?

*Since the twenties, the problem of the passage to socialism has never been
placed on the agenda by Communist parties in regard to advanced capitalist
countries.*

Exactly. Especially not since the war and the Yalta agreements. There
has therefore been no real thinking devoted to alternatives. And this is
not a secondary matter if one wishes to understand what Communist
parties have become. In the book by Annie Kriegel, *Les Communistes
Français*, the judgement passed on the French Communist Party is on the
whole a severe one; but what remains implicit is that, despite all the
errors and failings which Annie Kriegel enumerates, the party, as far as
she is concerned, constitutes a given alternative, notwithstanding its
actual policies. Indeed, it constitutes the proletarian alternative to capitalist society in France. This reasoning makes no sense. At the point where
we reach agreement in insisting on the need for the political organization
of the class, we must also realize that the 'historical' institutions of the
Communist Party are completely inadequate for the achievement of the
tasks which are often assigned to them. We were saying just now that,
without a moment of unification of the struggle, without a cultural
mediation and a positive response, it is impossible to go beyond revolt;
and revolt is always defeated politically. We agree on that. But this does
not change in any way the fact that an institutionalized party is not capable of acting as a mediator between culture and struggles: the reason
being that what is still confused and non-systematized thought in the
masses (though *true* as a reflection of experience), is completely deformed
once it has been translated by the ideological mechanisms of the party,
and presents a totally different relation to what we call culture. In order
that the schema which you propose may operate, it would be necessary
that the party should continually be able to struggle against its own
institutionalization. Without this, the whole schema is falsified. If the
cultural apparatus of the Communist parties is practically null, the
reason is not that they lack good intellectuals, but that the mode of
existence of these parties paralyses their collective effort of thought. Action
and thought are not separable from the organization. One thinks as one

is structured. One acts as one is organized. This is why the thought of Communist parties has come to be progressively ossified.

Historically, Communist parties assumed their particular character in the context of the Third International and of political and ideological events in the Soviet Union and in the socialist camp. These parties constitute a reality which has influenced the configuration of the class and which has produced certain forms of action, certain ideologies, certain changes in existing forces. Today, however, we are witnessing a class movement which, for the first time in Europe, tends to situate itself in a dialectical relation with the Communist parties, and to identify itself with them only in part. This movement weighs upon the parties, which must either reject it or be modified by it. (The hypothesis that the movement can simply be absorbed by the party does not seem realistic to us, as is shown by the students). In either case, the problem which is posed is that of a new manner of being of the party, either through crisis and the renewal of existing parties, or through a new construction of the unitary political expression of the class. Is such a new manner of being possible? Is a party fated to become progressively institutionalized and to detach itself from the movement which gave birth to it, as you suggested at the beginning, or can one conceive of an organization which would be capable of fighting continually against the limitations, the sclerosis and the institutionalization which threaten it from within?

While I recognize the need of an organization, I must confess that I don't see how the problems which confront any stabilized structure could be resolved.

To summarize what you have just said, the political party would need to ensure the growth and the autonomy of mass struggles instead of restraining them; it should also ensure the development of a counter-culture; and it should finally know how to oppose a global, total response to the type of rationality and to the social relations upon which society rests. These are, it seems, specific tasks of the party, in so far as their global character transcends the problems which the specific moment of struggle and the fused group can resolve.

Yes, but these cannot be resolved without the party either.

Agreed. In order to get out of this, one may advance some hypotheses.

Before all else, the revolutionary party must, so that it may escape institution-alization, consider itself as permanently in the service of a struggle which has its own dimensions, its own autonomous political levels. This implies the transcendence of the Leninist or Bolshevik model of the party – from its origins to the Popular Fronts – according to which there is supposed to exist a constant separation between the moment of a mass struggle purely con-cerned with specific demands and the political moment, which is specific to the party. In history, this transcendence has only been sketched out in the 'soviets'. It corresponds to a model of a social revolution rather than a purely political one, a revolution where power is taken by the soviets and not by the party. Moreover, the revolutionary movement must transcend an inadequacy of Leninism: the theory of revolution has until now been a 'theory of the seizure of power' much more than a 'theory of society'. The result has been an inability of Communist parties to analyse advanced capitalist societies and to foreshadow the goals which the revolution must reach; in other words, an inability to understand the new needs expressed by the movement and to say how they are to be satisfied. (This is what happened with the students: there was neither understanding nor solution of the problems which they posed on the role of education, its relation to society, the modes and content of a non-authoritarian type of education.) Thirdly, there is need of permanent probing so that theory should be able to encompass all features of the move-ment. A political organization of the class which claims to be Marxist does not merely think a posteriori; it interprets experience through a methodology, a grid – in regard to such categories as 'capital', 'class', 'imperialism', etc. Thus, in so far as the relation between party and class remains open – and this alone is capable of preventing both the particularism of a fragmented experience and the institutionalization of the unifying political moment – one needs to find a solution to these three problems.

I agree, on condition that this dialectic manifests itself as a dual power, and that one does not claim to solve it within a purely political schema. Even then, there are many problems which remain. You speak of a methodological or a theoretical 'grid', provided as it were in advance and through which experience may be interpreted. But is it not the case that the concept of *capital* remains a thin and abstract notion if one does not constantly elaborate anew the analysis of modern capitalism by research and by the permanent critique of the results of research and of struggle? *True* thought is certainly *one:* but its unity is dialectical – it is a living reality in the process of formation. What is required is the construction of a relationship between men which guarantees not only freedom, but *revolutionary* freedom of thought – a relationship which enables men to appropriate knowledge completely and to criticize it. This, in any case, is how knowledge has always proceeded, but it is never how the 'Marxism' of Communist parties has proceeded. So that the creative culture of its members may grow and in order to enable them to acquire a maximum of true knowledge, the party – the political organization of the class – must make it possible for them to innovate and to engage in mutual argument, instead of presenting itself as the administrator of acquired knowledge. If one looks outside the party, the debate on Marxism has never been richer than it is now because, particularly since the break-up of mono-lithism and the posing of the problem of the diversity of socialism, there exists a plurality of Marxist inquiries and open disagreements between them.

But these are disagreements on the exegesis of sacred texts, quarrels of inter-pretation, rather than a renewal of inventiveness and of a creative interpre-tation of reality.

That is not altogether true. Of course, the discussion on the texts pre-dominates. But take the example of Althusser: he is not simply involved in exegesis. One finds in him a theory of the concept, of autonomous theoretical knowledge, of the study of contradictions from the angle of the dominant contradiction, or 'over-determination'. These are original inquiries, which cannot be criticized without a new theoretical elabor-ation. Personally, I have been compelled, in order to criticize Althusser, to look again at the idea of 'notion' and to draw a series of conclusions in the process. The same may be said about the concept of 'structure' introduced by Lévi-Strauss which some Marxists, whether fruitfully or not, have tried to use. In other words, a real discussion always demands an effort and leads to new theoretical results. If what is wanted is genuine inquiry, one must therefore set up a structure which guarantees dis-cussion; without this, even the theoretical model which the political organization would wish to place before the experience of the class remains inoperative. This is a permanent contradiction in the party: in fact, it is a limitation of all Communist parties.

Just as complex is the hypothesis of an 'open' relation between a unifying political organization of the class, i.e. the party, and the self-government of the masses in councils or soviets. We must not forget that when this was attempted, in post-revolutionary Russia, the unitary organizations of the masses rapidly disappeared, and only the party remained. Thus a dialectically necessary process resulted, in the USSR, in the party taking the power which should have been taken and kept by the soviets. It may be that it could be otherwise today, but in the years of encirclement of the USSR by capitalist countries, in conditions of civil war and dreadful internal shortages, it is not too difficult to understand the process whereby the soviets completely disappeared. This is the reason why I have occasionally written that in the USSR, it is of a dictatorship *for* the proletariat rather than *of* the proletariat that one should speak, in the sense that the party assumed the task of destroying the bourgeoisie on behalf of the proletariat. It was, moreover, unavoidable that, in order that the USSR should survive, the proletariat, as has happened wherever there has been a revolution, should find itself asked to renounce what were, before the revolution, the most specific objectives of its struggle, namely an increase in its wages and the reduction in the hours of work. It could not have been otherwise, for it would have been difficult for the workers themselves to give up these objectives, even if they had experienced self-government at their place of work. Finally, to speak of what is relevant today, it seems to me difficult for an organization of soviets or councils to be created when there exists a strong 'historical' articulation of the working class, in the form of trade unions or the party. In France, we have had the experience of committees of action. But these were quickly dissolved, not because they were prohibited but because the trade unions soon resumed control of the situation.

This last contradiction does not seem insurmountable. Every trade union struggle which involves not only negotiations about wages but also about rhythms of work, hours, the organization of work and its control, shows the need for direct forms of organization of the workers. Without a unitary assembly at the base, possessed of an autonomous character and a high political level, negotiations on this scale cannot be undertaken. It is in this sense the trade union struggle which compels the rediscovery of the problem of the direct institutions of the class. This is a matter of experience, not an intellectual invention. Of course, these new forms come up against conservatism and bureaucracy. But one must also take into account certain limitations which are part of their being. From this point of view, the Italian experience is interesting: between the party or the union on the one hand and the movement on the other, the alternative is not always, as you were suggesting, either rejection or reduction to the role of a transmission belt. We are here confronted with social tension, which assumes its own forms and which, at the same time, weighs upon the traditional institutions of the class, without finding a point of equilibrium either in the first or in the second. In fact, while the limitations of the union exist and are known, the institutions of direct democracy also have their limitations: though they do, in general, function perfectly well during a period of agitation, as happened at Fiat during the recent struggles, they run the risk of subsequently becoming, unconsciously, the instruments of a separation between one group and another, one enterprise and another, and therefore of being useful to the management. And does not the union, at that point and despite all its limitations, constitute a defence against the fragility of the new institutions? In effect, the movement appears today richer and more complex than its political expression.

At any rate, what seems to me interesting in your schema is the duality of power which it foreshadows. This means an open and irreducible relation between the *unitary* moment, which falls to the political organization of the class, and the moments of self-government, the councils, the fused groups. I insist on that word 'irreducible' because there can only be a permanent tension between the two moments. The party will always try, to the degree that it wants to see itself as 'in the service' of the movement, to reduce it to its own schema of interpretation and development; while the moments of self-government will always try to project their living partiality upon the contradictory complex of the social tissue. It is in this struggle, maybe, that can be expressed the beginning of a reciprocal transformation; however, that transformation – if it is to remain revolutionary – cannot but go in the direction of a progressive dissolution of the political element in a society which not only tends towards uni-

fication but also towards self-government, that is to say, which seek
accomplish a social revolution that abolishes, together with the state
other specifically *political* moments. In short, this is a dialectic so oriented
as to bring us back to the schema of development of Marx. Up to now,
it has not happened; but it may be that the conditions for it are beginning
to exist in the societies of advanced capitalism. This is in any case a
hypothesis on which to work.

3. Philosophy / Poetry / Painting

Kierkegaard: The Singular Universal was a paper delivered to a UNESCO colloquium on Kierkegaard, entitled 'The Living Kierkegaard', in April 1964.

Mallarmé: The Poetry of Suicide was first published as an introduction to a new Gallimard edition of Mallarmé's poems in 1966.

Tintoretto: St George and the Dragon is part of Sartre's uncompleted study of Tintoretto (Jacopo Robusti), and was probably written towards 1957. It was first published in *L'Arc* No 30, 1966. Another major section of this projected study was published in *Les Temps Modernes* in 1957 as *Le Sequestré de Venise*, of which an English translation can be found in *Essays on Aesthetics* (London 1964): it is essentially biographical in focus. The present essay provides a complementary formal analysis of one of Tintoretto's major works, *St George and the Dragon*, which is in the National Gallery. The painting of the same theme by Carpaccio, to which Sartre refers, is in the oratory of the Church of San Giorgio dei Schiavoni in Venice, and was painted shortly after 1500.

Kierkegaard: The Singular Universal

The title of our colloquium is 'The Living Kierkegaard'. It has the merit of plunging us to the very heart of *paradox*, and Soeren himself would have appreciated this. For if we had gathered here today to discuss Heidegger, for example, no one would have dreamed of entitling our debate 'The Living Heidegger'. The living Kierkegaard, in other words, turns out to mean 'the dead Kierkegaard'. But not just this. It means that for us he exists, that he forms the object of our discussions, that he was an instrument of our thought. But, from this point of view, one could use the same expression to designate anyone who became part of our culture after he died. One could say, for example, 'The Living Arcimboldo',* since surrealism has allowed us to reappropriate this painter and cast him in a new light; but this would amount to making an *object* of him within what Kierkegaard called the *world-historical*. But, precisely, if Soeren is in our eyes a sort of radioactive object, of whatever potency and virulence, then he can no longer be this living being whose subjectivity necessarily appears – in so far as it is lived – as other than what we know of it. In short, he sinks into death. The abolition of the subjective in a subject of History – the reduction of one who was an agent to an object – is an explosive historical scandal in the case of all who disappear from amongst us. History is full of holes. But nowhere is this more obvious than in the case of the 'knight of subjectivity'. Kierkegaard was a man who set out to pose the problem of the historical absolute, who emphasized the scandalous paradox of the appearance and disappearance of this absolute in the course of History. If we cannot revive this martyr of interiority other than in the form of an object of knowledge, a determination of his *praxis* will forever escape us: his living effort to elude knowledge through reflective life, his claim to be,

* Translator's note: Giuseppe Arcimboldo (*c.* 1530–1593), painter of fantastic faces and figures.

in his very singularity and at the heart of his finitude, the absolute subject, defined in interiority by his absolute relationship with being. In other words, if death is historically no more than the passage of an interior to exteriority, then the title 'The Living Kierkegaard' cannot be justified.

If we retain something of this life which, in its time and place, removed all traces of itself, then Kierkegaard himself is the scandal and the paradox. Unable to be understood as anything other than this immanence which for forty years never stopped designating *itself* as such, either he eludes us forever and the world rid itself, in 1856, of *nothing*; or else the paradox exposed by this dead man is that a historical being, beyond his own abolition, can still communicate as a non-object, as an absolute subject, with succeeding generations. What will attract our attention then will not be the religious problem of Christ incarnate nor the metaphysical problem of death, but the strictly historical paradox of survival: we shall plumb our knowledge of Kierkegaard in order to locate what in a dead man eludes knowledge and survives *for us* beyond his destruction. We shall ask ourselves whether the presence, that is the subjectivity of someone else, always inaccessible to cognition in its strict sense, can nevertheless be given to us by some other means. Either History closes back over our knowledge of this death, or the historical survival of the subjective ought to change our conception of History. In other words either Kierkegaard today, 24 April 1964, is dissolved by the enzymes of knowledge or he persists in demonstrating to us the still virulent scandal of what one might call the transhistoricity of a historical man.

He posed the fundamental question in these terms: 'Can History act as the point of departure for an eternal certitude? Can one find in such a point of departure anything other than an historical interest? Can one base eternal happiness on a merely historical knowledge?'

And of course what he has in mind here is the scandalous paradox of the birth and death of God, of the historicity of Jesus. But we must go further; for if the answer is yes, then this transhistoricity belongs to Soeren, Jesus' witness, just as much as to Jesus himself; and to us as well, Soeren's grand-nephews. As he says himself, we are all contemporaries.* In a sense, this is to explode History. Yet History exists and

* Translator's note: Epigraph to *Philosophical Fragments.*

it is man who makes it. Thus posteriority and contemporaneity mutually imply and contradict each other. For the moment we cannot proceed further. We must go back to Kierkegaard and question him as a privileged witness. Why privileged? I am thinking of the Cartesian proof of the existence of God through the fact that *I exist with the idea of God.* Kierkegaard is a singular witness – or, as he says, the Exception – by virtue of a *redoubling* in himself of the subjective attitude: in our eyes he is an object of knowledge in so far as he is a subjective witness of his own subjectivity, that is to say, in so far as he is an existent announcer of existence by virtue of his own existential attitude. Thus he becomes both object and subject of our study. We should take this subject-object in so far as it demonstrates a historical paradox that transcends it; we shall question its testimony in so far in its historicity – he said such-and-such on such-and-such a date – transcends itself and makes the paradox of the object-subject burst within History. By integrating *his* words into our language, in translating him with *our* words, will the limits of knowledge be revealed? And by virtue of a paradoxical reversal of meaning, will this knowledge point to the signifier as its silent foundation?

In principle everything about him can be *known* (*connu*). Doubtless he kept his secrets well. But one can press him hard and extract statements from him and interpret them. The problem can now be formulated: when everything is *known* (*su*) about the life of a man who refuses to be an object of knowledge and whose originality rests precisely in this refusal, is there an irreducible beyond this? How are we to seize it and think it?* The question has two sides to it – prospective and retrospective. One can ask what it means to have lived when all the determinations of a life are *known*. But one can also ask what it means to live when the essential core of these determinations has been foreseen? For the singularity of the Kierkegaardian adventure is that, as it unfolded, it revealed itself to itself as known in advance. Thus it lived within and in spite of knowledge. It must be borne in mind that this opposition between foreseen and lived experience was made manifest around 1850 in the opposition between Hegel and Kierkegaard. Hegel had gone, but his system lived on. Soeren, whatever he did, acted within the limits of what Hegel

* Translator's note: Sartre uses 'think' transitively.

had called the unhappy consciousness – that is to say he could only realize the complex dialectic of the finite and the infinite. He would never be able to surpass it. Kierkegaard knew that he already had his place within the system. He was familiar with Hegel's thought, and he was aware of the interpretation it conferred *in advance* on the movements of his life. He was trapped and held in the beam of the Hegelian projector; he either had to vanish into objective knowledge or demonstrate his irreducibility. But, precisely, Hegel was dead and this death pronounced his knowledge as dead knowledge, or as knowledge of death. While Kierkegaard showed by the simple fact of his life that all knowledge concerning the subjective is in a certain sense false knowledge. Foreseen by the system, he disqualified its legitimacy by not appearing *in it* as a moment to be surpassed and at the site assigned to him by the master, but on the contrary, emerging quite simply as a survivor of the system and its prophet, as one who, despite the dead determinations of an anterior prophecy, had to live this foreseen life as if it were indeterminate at the outset and as if its determinations had arisen of their own accord within free 'non-knowledge'.

The new aspect of the problematic that Kierkegaard reveals to us is the fact that in his personal life he did not contradict the content of knowledge but illegitimized knowledge of any content. By negating the concept through the very fashion in which he realized its prescriptions in another dimension, he was traversed through and through by the light of knowledge – for others and also for himself, as he was acquainted with Hegelianism – but at the same time remained utterly opaque. In other words, this pre-existent knowledge revealed a being at the heart of future existence. Thirty years ago, the contradictions of colonialism constituted, in the eyes of the generation of colonized born into it, a being of misery, anger, blood, revolt and struggle; a few amongst the best-informed of the oppressed and of the colonialists themselves were aware of this. Or to take a quite different example, a vacancy created high up or low down on the social scale creates a destiny, that is to say a future but foreseeable being for the person who will fill it, even though this destiny remains for each candidate, if there is more than one, no more than a *possible being*. Or, in the narrow particularity of private life, the structures of a specific family (seen as a local example of an institution produced by the movement of History) permit the psychoanalyst, in theory at least, to foresee the future destiny (to be lived and undergone) that will be a particular neurosis for a child born into this milieu. Kierkegaard *foreseen* by Hegel is but a privileged example of such ontological determinations which pre-date birth and allow themselves to be *conceptualized*.

Soeren identified with the problem because he was conscious of it. He knew that Hegel, in pointing to him as a moment of universal History vainly posed for itself, attained him in the being which he suffered as a schema to be accomplished in the course of his life, and which he called his Untruth, or the error that he was at the start of his life, as a truncated determination. But this was the point: Hegel's designation attained him like the light from a dead star. The untruth *had to be lived*; it too belonged to his subjective subjectivity. And so he could write, in the *Fragments*: 'My own Untruth is something I can discover only by myself, since it is only when I have discovered it that it is discovered, even if the whole world knew of it before.'* But when it is discovered, my Untruth becomes, at least in the immediate, my Truth. So subjective truth exists. It is not knowledge (*savoir*) but self-determination; it can be defined neither as an extrinsic relation of knowledge (*connaissance*) to being, nor as the internal imprint of a correspondence, nor as the indissoluble unity of a system. 'Truth,' he said, 'is the act of freedom.' I would not know how to *be* my own Truth even if its premises were given in me in advance: to reveal it means to produce it or to produce myself as I am; to be for myself what I have to be.

What Kierkegaard highlighted was the fact that the opposition between non-knowledge and knowledge is an opposition between two ontological structures. The subjective has to be what it is – a singular realization of each singularity. One would have to go to Freud for the most illuminating commentary on this remark. In fact psychoanalysis is not knowledge nor does it claim to be, save when it hazards hypotheses on the dead and thus allows death to make it a science of death. It is a movement, an internal labour, that at one and the same time uncovers a neurosis and gradually makes the subject capable of supporting it. With the result that at the term

* Translator's note: Kierkegaard, *Philosophical Fragments*, trans. David Swenson, Princeton University Press, 1962, p. 17.

(actually an ideal) of this process, there is a correspondence between the being that has developed and the truth it once was. The truth in this case is the unity of the conquest and the object conquered. It transforms without teaching anything and does not appear until the end of a transformation. It is a non-knowledge, an effectivity, a placing in perspective that is present to itself in so far as it is realized. Kierkegaard would add that it is a decision of authenticity: the rejection of flight and the will to return to oneself. In this sense *knowledge* cannot register this obscure and inflexible *movement* by which scattered determinations are elevated to the status of being and are gathered together into a tension which confers on them not a signification but a synthetic meaning: what happens is that the ontological structure of subjectivity escapes to the extent that the subjective being is, as Heidegger has put it so well, in question in its being, to the extent that it never *is* except in the mode of having to be its being.

From this point of view, the moment of subjective truth is a temporalized but transhistorical absolute. And subjectivity is temporalization itself: it is *what happens to me*, what cannot be but in happening. It is myself in so far as I can only be a random birth – and, as Merleau-Ponty said, in so far as I must, no matter how short my life, *at least* experience the occurrence of death; but it is also myself in so far as I try to regain control of my own adventure by assuming – we shall come back to this point – its original contingency in order to establish it in necessity. In short, in so far as *I* happen to myself. Dealt with in advance by Hegel, subjectivity becomes a moment of the objective spirit, a determination of culture. But if nothing of lived experience can elude knowledge, its *reality* remains irreducible. In this sense, lived experience as concrete reality is posed as *non-knowledge*. But this negation of knowledge implies the affirmation of itself. Lived experience recognizes itself as a projection into the milieu of meaning, but at the same time it fails to recognize itself there since, in this milieu, an ensemble is constituted which aims randomly at objects and since, precisely, it is itself not an object. Doubtless, one of the principal concerns of the nineteenth century was to distinguish the being of an object from one's knowledge of it, in other words to reject idealism. Marx attacked Hegel not so much for his point of departure, as his reduction of being to knowledge. But for Kierkegaard, as for ourselves today when we consider the Kierkegaardian scandal, the question is one of a certain ontological region in which being claims at once to elude knowledge and to attain itself. Waelhens has rightly written: 'With the advent of Kierkegaard, Nietzsche and Bergson, philosophy ceased to be *explanation at a distance*, and claimed to be henceforth *at one* with experience itself; it was no longer content to throw light on man and his life, but aspired to become this life in its full consciousness of itself. It seemed that for the philosopher this ambition involved an obligation to renounce the ideal of philosophy as a rigorous science, since the basis of this ideal was inseparable from the idea of a detached . . . spectator.'

In short, the determinations of lived experience are not simply hetero-geneous to knowledge, as the existence of thalers was heterogeneous for Kant to the concept of thaler and to the judgement that combined the two. It is the very way in which these determinations attain themselves in the redoubling of their presence to themselves that reduces knowledge to the pure abstraction of the concept and, in the first moment at least (the only one Kierkegaard described) turns an object-subjectivity into an objective *nothing* in relation to a subjective subjectivity. Knowledge (*savoir*) itself has a being; bodies of knowledge (*connaissances*) are realities. For Kierkegaard, even in his lifetime, the being of knowledge was obviously radically heterogeneous to that of the living subject. Thus we can designate the determinations of existence with words. But *either* this designation is nothing but a place-marker, a set of references without conceptualization, *or else* the ontological structure of the concept and of its links – i.e. objective being, being in exteriority – is such that these references, grasped as notions, cannot but yield a false knowledge when they present themselves as insights into being in interiority.

In his life, Kierkegaard lived this paradox in passion: he desperately wanted to designate himself as a transhistorical absolute. In humour and in irony, he revealed himself and concealed himself at the same time. He did not refuse to communicate, but simply held on to his *secrecy* in the act of communication. His mania for pseudonyms was a systematic disqualification of *proper names*: even to *assign* him as an individual before the tribunal of others, a welter of mutually contradictory appellations was necessary. The more he becomes Climacus or Virgelin Hufnensis, the less he is *Kierkegaard*, this Danish citizen, this entry in the registers of the civil authorities.

This was all very well so long as he was alive: by his life he gave the lie to a dead man's predictions which were a knowledge of death. That is to say he ceaselessly fabricated himself by writing. But on the 11th of November 1855 he died, and the paradox turned against him without ceasing to be scandalous *in our eyes*. The prophecy of a dead man condemning a living being to exist as an unhappy consciousness, and our knowledge of this living being once he has died, reveal their homogeneity. In fact in our own time Käte Nadler – to cite but one example – has applied to the late Kierkegaard the prediction of the late Hegel. A dialectical pair is formed, in which each term denounces the other: Hegel foresaw Kierkegaard in the past, as a superseded moment; Kierkegaard gave the lie to the internal organization of Hegel's system by showing that superseded moments are conserved, not only in the *Aufhebung* that maintains them as it transforms them, but in themselves, without any transformation whatever; and by proving that even if they arise anew, they create, merely through their appearance, an anti-dialectic. But, once Kierkegaard died, Hegel regained possession of him. Not *within the System*, which visibly crumbled in so far as it was a finished totality of Knowledge which, as a system, was subsequently totalized by the onward movement of History itself – but simply by virtue of the fact that the late Kierkegaard has become *in our eyes* homogeneous with the descriptions that Hegelian knowledge gives of him. The fact remains, of course, that he contested the whole system by appearing in a place that was not assigned to him: but since the system itself is an object of knowledge and as such is contested, this anachronism provides us with nothing really new. By contrast, the Knowledge that *we* have of him is knowledge of a dead man and thus knowledge of death; as such it rejoins the Hegelian intuition which produced and conceptualized a future death. In ontological terms, Kierkegaard's pre-natal being was homogeneous with his post-mortem being and his existence seemed merely to be a way of enriching the first so that it could equal the second: it was no more than a provisional *malaise*, an essential means of getting from one to the other, but, in itself, an inessential fever of being. The notion of the unhappy consciousness became Soeren's insurpassable destiny as well as the generality enveloping our most particularized items of knowledge concerning his dead life. Or if you like, to die meant to be restored to being and to become an object of knowledge. That at least is the recurrent lazy conception whose aim is to close a breach. Is it true? Should we say that death terminates the paradox by revealing that it is nothing more than a provisional appearance, or on the contrary, that it pushes it to the extreme and consequently, since we die, the whole of History becomes paradoxical – an insurmountable conflict between being and existence, between non-knowledge and knowledge? It was Kierkegaard's merit that he formulated this problem *in the very terms of his life*. Let us come back to him.

Let us note at the outset that between him and us, History has *taken place*. No doubt it is still going on. But its richness puts a distance, *an obscure density* between him and us. The unhappy consciousness will find other incarnations, and each of them will contest this consciousness by his life and confirm it by his death, but none of them will reproduce Kierkegaard by virtue of a kind of resurrection. Knowledge has its foundations in this instance in non-coincidence. The poet of faith left texts behind. These writings are dead unless we breathe our life into them; but if revived they bear the stamp of thoughts committed to paper long ago, somewhere else, with the means to hand – they only partially answer to our present requirements. Unbelievers will pronounce *the Kierkegaardian proof to be unconvincing*. Theologians, in the name of dogma itself, may declare themselves unsatisfied and find the attitude and declarations of the 'poet of Christianity' insufficient and dangerous. They may reproach him in the name of his own admission, through the very title of *poet* that he gave himself, with not having got beyond what he himself called the 'aesthetic stage'. Atheists will *either* – a formula dear to him – reject any relationship with this absolute and opt firmly for a relativism, *or else* define the absolute in History *in other terms* – and regard Kierkegaard as the witness of a false absolute or a false witness of the absolute. Believers, on the other hand, will declare that the absolute Kierkegaard aimed at is certainly that which exists, but that the relation of historical man to transhistoricity which he tried to establish, was involuntarily deflected and lost by him in the night of atheism. In each case, his attempt is pronounced a *failure*.

There is more: the failure is *explained*. In different ways, it is true, but by convergent approximations. Mesnard, Bohlen, Chestov and Jean Wahl are all agreed in stressing the psychosomatic significance of the 'thorn in the flesh'.* This means that, in the case of this dead man, lived experience itself is contested. Later conceptual judgement renders the life itself inauthentic. Kierkegaard lived out badly – in the sense of obscurely, disguisedly – determinations that we can perceive better than he. In short, in the eyes of historical knowledge, one lives to die. Existence is a mild surface ripple that is soon stilled in order to allow the dialectical development of concepts to appear; chronology dissolves into homogeneity and in the end, into timelessness. Every lived venture ends in failure for the simple reason that History continues.

But if life is a scandal, failure is even more scandalous. First we describe and denounce it by collections of words that aim at a certain object named Kierkegaard. In this sense the 'poet of faith' is a signified – like this table, like a socio-economic process. And it is true that death first presents itself as the fall of the subject into the realm of absolute objectivity. But Kierkegaard in his writings – today inert or living with our life – proposes a usage of words that is the converse of this: what he seeks is a dialectical regression from signified and significations to signifier. He presents himself as a signifier, and at a stroke refers us back to our transhistoricity as signifiers. Should we reject this regression *a priori*? To do so is to constitute ourselves as relative – relative to History if we are unbelievers, relative to Dogmas and mediated by the Church if we believe. Now if such is the case, then everything should be relative, in us and in Kierkegaard himself, *except his failure*. For failure can be *explained* but not *resolved*: as non-being it possesses the absolute character of negation. In fact historical negation, even at the heart of a relativism, is an absolute. It would be a negative absolute to declare that at Waterloo *there were no* fighter planes. But this negative declaration remains a formality: as the two adversaries were equally without air power and were both incapable of missing it, this ineffectual absence is no more than a formal proposition devoid of interest, that merely registers the *temporal distance* from Waterloo to the present. There are, however, other

* Translator's note: Referred to by Kierkegaard in the *Papirer*, the *Edifying Discourses*, and *Concluding Unscientific Postscript*.

negative absolutes and these are concrete: it is correct to state that Grouchy's army *did not* link up with the Emperor;* and this negation is historical in the sense that it reflects the frustrated expectation of the head of an army, and the fear turned to satisfaction of the enemy. It is effective in the sense that Grouchy's delay in all probability *settled* the outcome of the battle. It is thus an absolute, an irreducible but a concrete absolute. Similarly in the case of the failure: the fact that an ambition is not realised in objectivity means that it returns to subjectivity. Or, more precisely, the interpretations of such a failure aim via moderate negations (he didn't consider . . ., he couldn't be aware at the time, etc.) to reduce it *to the positive*, to erase it before the affirmative reality of the Other's victory, whatever it may be.

But at once this relative positivity slips back and reveals what no knowledge could ever transmit directly (because no historical advance could recuperate it): failure lived in despair. Those who died of anguish, of hunger, of exhaustion, those defeated in the past by force of arms, are so many gaps in our knowledge in so far as they existed: subjectivity constitutes *nothing* for objective knowledge since it is a non-knowledge, and yet failure demonstrates that it has an absolute existence. In this way Soeren Kierkegaard, conquered by death and recuperated by historical knowledge, triumphs at the very moment he fails, by demonstrating that History cannot recover him. As a dead man, he remains the insurpassable scandal of sujectivity; though he may be known through and through, he eludes History by the very fact that it is History that constitutes his defeat and that he lived it in anticipation. In short, he eludes History because he is historical.

Can we go further? Or must we simply conclude that death irrevocably filches the agents of past History from the historian? Here it is necessary to question *what remains* of Kierkegaard, his verbal remnants. For he constituted himself in his historicity as an absolute contesting the historical knowledge that would penetrate him after his death. But the kind of interrogation with which we are concerned is of a particular type: it is a paradox itself. Kant situated himself in the realm of cognition in order to test the validity of our knowledges. We, the living, can approach

---

*Translator's note: Emmanuel de Grouchy was a general under Napoleon at Waterloo.

him through the realm of cognition, question his words with words, and cross-examine him on concepts. But Kierkegaard stole language from knowledge in order to use it against knowledge. If we approach him, as we are compelled to do, through the realm of cognition, our words encounter his and are disqualified by disqualifying them. The fact is that his use of the Word and our own are heterogeneous. Thus the message of this dead man is scandalous through the very fact of its existence, since we are incapable of considering this residue of a life as a determination of knowledge. On the contrary, the paradox reappears since his thought expressed in words constitutes itself within knowledge as irreducible non-knowledge. Our interrogation must then either disappear without trace, or be transformed and itself become non-knowledge questioning non-knowledge. That is to say, the questioner is called into question in his very being by the questioned. Such is the fundamental virtue of the pseudo-object called the works of Kierkegaard. But let us push our examination to the very moment of this metamorphosis.

This philosopher was an anti-philosopher. Why did he reject the Hegelian system and, in a general way, the whole of philosophy? Because, he says, the philosopher seeks a first beginning. But why, one may ask, did he who rejected beginnings take as his point of departure the Christian dogmas? For to accept them *a priori* without even testing their validity is tantamount to making them the uncontested principles of thought. Is there not a contradiction here? Did not Kierkegaard, having failed to establish a solid beginning himself, take the beginning of others as the origin and foundation of his thought? And as he failed to test it through criticism, and as he neglected to doubt it to the point where it could no longer be doubted, did it not retain for him, even in his most intimate thought, its character of otherness?

This is, indeed, the unfair question that knowledge puts to existence. But, in Kierkegaard's pen, existence replies by rejecting knowledge's case. To deny dogma, it says, is to be mad and to proclaim the fact. But to prove dogma is to be an imbecile: while time is wasted proving that the soul is immortal, living belief in immortality withers away. At the absurd limit of this logic, the day would come when immortality was finally proved irrefutably – except that no one would believe in it any more. There is no way we could better understand that immortality, even if proven, could never be an object of knowledge: it is a particular absolute relationship between immanence and transcendence that can only be constituted in and through lived experience. And of course this is sufficient for believers. But for the non-believer that I am, what this means is that the real relation of man to his being can only be lived, in History, as a transhistorical relationship.

Kierkegaard replies to our question by rejecting philosophy or rather by radically changing its end and aims. To seek the beginning of knowledge is to affirm that the foundation of temporality is, precisely, timeless, and that the historical individual can wrench himself free of History, de-situate himself and relocate his fundamental timelessness by a direct vision of being. Temporality becomes the means of intemporality. Naturally Hegel was aware of the problem since he placed philosophy at the end of History, as truth-that-has-come-into-being and retrospective knowledge. But this is the point: History is never finished, so this atemporal reconstitution of temporality, understood as the unity of the logical and the tragic, becomes in turn an object of knowledge. From this point of view, there is no being at all at the beginning of Hegel's system, but only the person of Hegel, such as it had been fashioned, such as it had fashioned itself. This is the sort of ambiguous discovery that can lead, from the point of view of knowledge, only to scepticism.

To avoid this, Kierkegaard took as his point of departure the *person* envisaged as non-knowledge, that is to say in as much as he both produces and discovers, at a given moment in the temporal unfolding of his life, his relation to an absolute which is itself inserted in History. In short, far from denying the beginning, Kierkegaard testified to a beginning that is lived.

How is it possible that, in the context of History, this historical situation does not contest the claim of the thinker to have disclosed the absolute? How can a thought *that has appeared* testify on its own behalf after its *disappearance*? This is the problem Kierkegaard set himself in the *Philosophical Fragments*. Of course, this paradox was first and foremost a religious one. What was at stake was the appearance and disappearance of Jesus. Or equally, the transformation of one sin – Adam's – into original and hereditary sin. But it was just as much the personal problem of Kierkegaard the thinker: how could he establish the trans-historical validity of a thought that had been produced within History and would disappear into it? The answer lay in 'reduplication': the insurpassable cannot be knowledge, but must be the establishment in History of an absolute and non-contemplative relation with the absolute that has been realized in History. Rather than knowledge dissolving the thinker, it is the thinker who testifies on behalf of his own thought. But these ideas are obscure and can appear to be merely a verbal solution so long as one has not understood that they proceed from a novel conception of thought.

The beginning of the thinker's existence is analogous to a birth. This is not a rejection but a displacement of the beginning. Before birth there was non-being; then comes the leap, and the moment they are born to themselves, the child and the thinker find themselves immediately situated within a certain historical world that has produced them. They discover themselves as a particular adventure, whose point of departure is a set of socio-economic, cultural, moral, religious and other relations, which proceeds with whatever means are to hand, that is to say within the limits of these relations, and which gradually becomes inscribed in the same set. The beginning is reflective – I saw and touched the world, and so see and touch myself, this self who touches and sees the surrounding things; in this way I discover myself as a finite being, one that these same objects I touched and saw condition invisibly in my very sense of touch and sight. As against the constant and non-human beginning that Hegel postulated, Kierkegaard proposed a start that is in flux, that is conditioned and is conditioning, whose foundation approximates to what Merleau-Ponty called *envelopment*. We are enveloped: being is behind us and in front of us. He-who-sees is visible, and sees only by virtue of his visibility. 'My body', said Merleau-Ponty, 'is caught in the fabric of the world, but the world is made from the stuff of my body.' Kierkegaard knew he was enveloped: he saw Christianity and in partic-ular the Christian community in Denmark with the eyes that this com-munity had given him. This is a new paradox: I see the being that fashioned me. I see it as it *is* or as it made me. 'Overview thought' has an easy solution to this: having no qualities, the understanding grasps the objective essence without its own nature imposing particular deviations on it. Idealist relativism has an equally simple solution: the object fades away; what I see, being the effect of causes modifying my vision, contains no more than what these latter determine me to be. In each case, being is reduced to knowledge.

Kierkegaard rejects both solutions. The paradox, for him, is the fact that we discover the absolute in the relative. Kierkegaard was a Dane, born at the beginning of the last century into a Danish family, and conditioned by Danish history and culture. He came across other Danes as his contemporaries, people who were formed by the same History and cultural traditions. And at the same time, moreover, he could *think* the historical traditions and circumstances that had produced them all and produced himself. Was there either deviation or appropriation? Both. If objectivity has to be unconditioned knowledge, then there can be no true objectivity: to see one's surroundings, in this instance, would be to see without seeing, to touch without touching, to possess in oneself an *a priori* intuition of the other and, at the same time, to grasp him on the basis of common presuppositions that can never wholly be uncovered. Even in broad daylight my neighbour is dark and impenetrable, separated from me by his apparent resemblances; and yet I sense him in his underlying reality when I penetrate deeper into my own inner reality and attain its transcendental conditions. Later, much later, the presuppositions inscribed in things will be correctly deciphered by the historian. But at this level, the mutual comprehension that takes the existence of a communal envelopment for granted will have disappeared. In short, contemporaries understand each other without knowing each other, whereas the future historian will know them but his greatest difficulty – a difficulty bordering on the impossible – will be to understand them as they understood each other.

In fact – and Kierkegaard was aware of this – the experience which turns back upon itself, after the leap, comprehends itself more than it knows itself. In other words, it sustains itself in the milieu of the presuppositions that are its foundation, without succeeding in elucidating them. Hence a beginning that is a dogma. A particular religion produced Kierkegaard: he could not pretend to emancipate himself from it so that he could rise above it and see it as historically constituted. Note however that other Danes, from the same society, from the same class, became non-believers: but even they could do nothing to prevent their irreligion questioning or challenging *these* dogmas, this particular Christianity which had produced them – and hence their past, their religious childhood and finally themselves. Thus whatever they did, they remained wedded to their faith and their dogmas while vainly attempting to negate them by using other words to express their demand for an absolute. Their atheism was in fact a Christian *pseudo-atheism*. As it happens, one's envelopment determines the limits within which real modifications are possible. There are times when disbelief can only be verbal. Kierkegaard doubted as a youth, and hence was more consequential than these 'free-thinkers': he recognized that his thought was not free and that whatever he might do or wherever he might go his religious determinations would follow him. If in spite of himself he saw Christian dogmas as irreducible, then it was perfectly legitimate for him to locate the beginning of his thought at the moment when it retraced its steps to them to get at its roots. Such a thought was doubly embedded in history: it grasped its envelopment as a conjuncture, and it defined itself as an identity between the beginning of thought and thought of the beginning.

If such was the case, what then was to become of the universality of historical determinations? Must we deny in absolute terms that there is any social sphere, with structures, pressures and developments of its own? Not at all. We shall see that Kierkegaard testified to a double universality. The revolution consisted in the fact that historical man, by his anchorage, turned this universality into a particular situation and this common necessity into an irreducible contingency. In other words, far from this particular attitude being, as in Hegel, a dialectical incarnation of the universal moment, the anchorage of the individual made this universal into an irreducible singularity. Did not Soeren say to Levin one day: 'How lucky you are to be a Jew: you escape Christianity. If I had been protected by your faith, I would have enjoyed a quite different life.'?* This was an ambiguous remark, for he often reproached Jews with being inaccessible to religious experience. There could be no doubt that dogma was truth, and the Christian who was not religious remained

* Translator's note: Quoted from a letter concerning Kierkegaard from Pastor A. F. Schioedte to H. P. Barford, dated 12 September 1869.

inauthentic, outside himself, lost. But there was a sort of humble birth-right which meant, in the case of a Jew, a Moslem or a Buddhist, that the chance occurrence of their birth in one place rather than another was transformed into a statute. Conversely, Kierkegaard's deepest reality, the fabric of his being, his torment and his law appeared to him in the very heart of their necessity as the accidental outcome of his facticity. Again this contingency was common to all members of his society. He came across others which belonged only to him. In 1846 he wrote: 'To believe is to lighten oneself by assuming a considerable weight; to be objective is to lighten oneself by casting off burdens . . . Lightness is an infinite weight, and its altitude the effect of an infinite weight.' He was clearly alluding to what he called elsewhere the 'thorn in the flesh'. Here we are confronted with pure contingency, the singularity of his conditionings. Soeren's unhappy consciousness was the product of random determinations which Hegelian rationalism did not take into account: a gloomy father who was convinced that he would be struck by a divine curse on his children; the mournings that seemed to bear out these expectations and ended by persuading Soeren that he would die by the age of thirty-four; the mother, mistress and servant, whom he loved in so far as she was *his* mother and whom he reproved in so far as she was an intruder in the household of a widower and testified to the carnal lapses of his father, and so on. The origin of singularity is the random at its most radical: if I had had a different father . . . if my father had not blasphemed, etc. And this pre-natal accident reappears in the individual himself and in his determinations: the thorn in the flesh was a complex disposition whose inner secret has not yet been unearthed. But all authors are agreed in seeing a sexual anomaly as its kernel. A singularizing accident, this anomaly *was* Kierkegaard, it *made* him; it could not be cured, and hence could not be surpassed; it produced his most intimate self as a pure historical contingency, which might not have been and in itself meant nothing. Hegelian necessity was not negated, but it could not be embodied without becoming a singular and opaque contingency; in an individual the rationality of History is experienced irreducibly as madness, as an inner accident, expressive of random encounters. To our questioning, Kierkegaard replies by revealing another aspect of the para-dox: there can be no historical absolute that is not rooted in chance;

because of the necessity of anchorage, there can be no incarnation of the universal other than in the irreducible opacity of the singular. Is it Soeren who *says* this? Yes and no: to tell the truth he *says nothing* if 'to say' means the same as 'to signify', but his work refers us back, without speaking, to his life.

But here the paradox has a twist to it, for to experience original contingency means to surpass it. Man, irremediable singularity, is the being through whom the universal comes into the world; once fundamental chance starts to be lived, it assumes the form of necessity. Lived experience, we discover in Kierkegaard, is made up of non-significant accidents of being in so far as they are surpassed towards a significance they did not possess at the beginning, and which I will call the singular universal.

To gain more insight into this message, let us come back to the notion of sin which lies at the centre of Kierkegaard's thought. As Jean Wahl has noted correctly, Adam exists in a pre-Adamite state of innocence, i.e. of ignorance. Nevertheless, although the Self does not yet exist, this being already envelops a contradiction. At this level, the spirit is a synthesis which unites and divides: it brings body and soul together and, in doing so, engenders the conflicts which oppose them. Dread makes its appearance as the interiorization of being, that is to say its contradiction. In other words, being has no interiority prior to the appearance of dread. But since the spirit can neither flee nor fulfil itself, since it is a dissonant unity of the finite and the infinite, the possibility of choosing *one* of the terms – the finite, the flesh, in other words the Self which does not yet exist – makes its appearance in the form of dread, at the moment when God's Thou Shalt Not resounds. But what is this prohibition? In actual fact, communication is not possible – no more than it was possible between Kafka's Emperor and the subject he wanted to touch but whom his message does not reach.* But Kierkegaard gave this Shalt Not its full value when he deprived the Serpent of the power to tempt Adam. If the Devil is eliminated and Adam is not yet Adam, who can pronounce the prohibition and at the same time suggest to the pre-Adamite that he *turn himself* into Adam? God alone. A curious passage from the *Journal* explains why:

* Translator's note: Franz Kafka: *An Imperial Message.*

Omnipotence . . . should make things dependent. But if we rightly consider omnipotence, then clearly it must have the quality of so taking itself back in the very manifestation of its all-powerfulness that the results of this act of the omnipotent can be independent. . . . For goodness means to give absolutely, yet in such a way that by taking oneself back one makes the recipient independent. . . . Omnipotence alone . . . can create something out of nothing which endures of itself, because omnipotence is always taking itself back. . . . If . . . man had even the least independent existence (in regard to *materia*) then God could not make him free.*

The pre-Adamite state of innocence is the final moment of dependence. At any moment God will withdraw from his creature as the ebbing tide uncovers a piece of flotsam; and by this movement alone he creates dread – as the possibility of independence. In other words, God becomes at once the Prohibiter and the Tempter. Thus dread is the abandonment of being to the forbidden possibility of choosing finitude by a sudden retreat of the infinite. Dread is the internalization of this forsaken condition and it is completed by the free realization of the sole possible future of Adam abandoned – the choice of the finite. The moment of sin is defined by the restitution of original being as *meaning*. Being was the contradictory unity between the finite and the impalpable infinite, but this unity remained in the indistinction of ignorance. Sin as *re-exteriorization* makes the constituent contradiction reappear. It is the determination of it: the Self and God appear. God is infinite withdrawal but yet immediate presence, in so far as sin bars the way to any hope of return to Eden. The Self is chosen finitude, nothingness affirmed and delimited by an act; it is determination conquered by defiance; it is the singularity of extreme estrangement. Thus the terms of the contradiction are the same and yet the *state* of ignorance and sin are not homogeneous: the finite is now constituted as loss of the infinite, freedom as the *necessary* and irremediable foundation of the formation of the *Ego*. Good and Evil make their appearance as the meaning of this exteriorization of the interiority that is sinful freedom. Everything happens as though God *needed sin* in order that man might produce himself in front of him, as if he had solicited it in order to bring Adam out of his state of ignorance and *give* meaning to man.

* Translator's note: Kierkegaard's *Papirer*, VII A 181.

But we are all Adam. Thus the pre-Adamite state is one with the contingency of our being. For Kierkegaard, what produces it is a disunited unity of accidents. In this sense, sin becomes the *establishment* of Kierkegaard as a surpassal of these scattered data *towards a meaning*. The contingency of our being is the beginning; our necessity only appears through the act which assumes this contingency in order to give it a *human meaning*, in other words to make of it a singular relationship to the Whole, a singular embodiment of the ongoing totalization which envelops and produces it. Kierkegaard was well aware of this: what he called sin is, as a whole, the supersession of the (pre-Adamite) *state* by the advent of freedom and the impossibility of retreat. Thus the web of subjective life – what he called passion, and Hegel called *pathos* – is nothing other than the freedom that institutes the finite and is lived in finitude as inflexible necessity.

If I wished to summarize what Kierkegaard's non-signifying testimony has to offer to me, a twentieth-century atheist who does not believe in sin, I would say that the state of ignorance represents, for the individual, being-in-exteriority. These exterior determinations are interiorized in order to be re-exteriorized by a *praxis* which *institutes* them by objectifying them in the world.

This is what Merleau-Ponty was saying when he wrote that History is the milieu in which 'a form burdened with contingency suddenly opens up a cycle of the future and commands it with the authority of the instituted'. The cycle of the future is a *meaning*: in the case of Kierkegaard, it is the Self. Meaning can be defined as the future relation of the instituted to the totality of the world or, if you like, as the synthetic totalization of scattered chance occurrences by an objectifying negation, which inscribes them as necessity freely created in the very universe in which they were scattered, and as the presence of the totality – a totality of time and of the universe – in the determination which negates them by posing itself for itself. In other words, man is that being who transforms his being into *meaning*, and through whom *meaning* comes into the world.

The singular universal is this meaning: through his *Self* – the practical assumption and supersession of being as it is – man restores to the universe its enveloping unity, by engraving it as a finite determination and a mortgage on future History in the being which envelops him. Adam temporalizes himself by sin, the necessary free choice and radical transformation of what he is – he brings human temporality into the universe. This clearly means that the foundation of History is freedom in *each man*. For we are all Adam in so far as each of us commits on his own behalf and on behalf of all a singular sin: in other words finitude, for each person, is necessary and incomparable. By his finite action, the agent alters the course of things – but in conformity with what this course itself ought to be. Man, in fact, is a mediation between a transcendence behind and a transcendence in front, and this twofold transcendence is but one. Thus we can say that through man, the course of things is deviated in the direction of its own deviation. Kierkegaard here reveals to us the basis of his own paradox and of ours – and the two are the same. Each of us, in our very historicity, escapes History to the extent that we make it. I myself am historical to the extent that others also make history and make me, but I am a transhistorical absolute by virtue of what I make of what they make of me, have made of me and will make of me in the future – that is, by virtue of my historiality (*historialité*).

We still need to understand properly what the myth of sin holds for us: the *institution* of a man is his singularity become law for others and for himself. What is Kierkegaard's body of work but himself in so far as he is a universal? But on the other hand the content of this universality remains his contingency – even if elected and surpassed by his choice of it. In short, this universality has two sides to it: by virtue of its meaning it raises contingency to the level of concrete universality. This is its luminous and yet unknowable *recto* side – to the extent that knowledge refers to the 'world-historical' by the mediation of an *anchorage*. Its *verso* side is in darkness, and refers back to the contingent set of analytical and social data which define Kierkegaard's being before his *institution*. Two errors in method are thereby denounced. The first of them, the world-historical, would define Kierkegaard's message in its abstract universality and as the pure expression of general structures; thus Hegelians would categorize it as the unhappy consciousness, incarnation of a necessary moment in universal History, or interpreters like Tisseau*

* Translator's note: Paul-Henri Tisseau, one of Kierkegaard's French translators.

would view it as a radical definition of faith, an appeal by a true Christian addressed to all Christians.

The other error would be to deem his work a simple effect or translation of original chance occurrences: this is what I would call psychoanalytical scepticism. Such a scepticism is founded on the fact that the *whole* of Kierkegaard's *childhood* is present in his work and forms the basis of its singularity, and that in a sense, there is nothing more in the books he wrote than the life he instituted. Soeren's works are rich in Freudian symbols, it is true, and a psycho-analytical *reading* of his texts is quite possible. The same holds good for what I would call sceptical Marxism, that is to say bad Marxism. Although its truth here is mediate, there is no doubt that Kierkegaard was radically conditioned by his historical environment: his disdain for the masses, and aristocratic demeanour, his attitude to money, leave no trace of doubt as to his social origins or his political position (for example his liking for absolute monarchy), which, though well concealed, surface time after time and obviously form the basis of his ethical and religious opinions.

But this is the point: Kierkegaard teaches us that the Self, action and creation, with their dark side and light side, are absolutely irreducible to the one or to the other. The shadow is wholly in the light because it is *instituted*: it is true that every act and every text expresses the whole of the Self, but this is because the Self-as-institution is homogeneous with action-as-legislator. It is impossible to make the general conditions the *basis of it*: this would be to forget that they are general in a 'world-historical' sense – for example the relations of production in Denmark in 1830 – but that they are lived as non-significant chance by each individual, who is inserted in them fortuitously. By virtue of the fact that the individual expresses the universal in singular terms, he singularizes the whole of History which becomes at once *necessity*, through the very way in which objective situations take charge of themselves, and *adventure*, because History is forever the general experienced and instituted as a particularity which at first is non-signifying.

In this way the individual becomes a singular universal by virtue of the presence within himself of agents defined as universalizing singularities. But conversely, the side in shadow is already in light because the same individual is the moment of interiorization of exterior contingency.

Without this pre-instituting unity, the person could lapse into scattered disorder; too frequently psychoanalysis reduces meaning to non-meaning because it refuses to acknowledge that dialectical stages are irreducible. But Kierkegaard was perhaps the first to show that the universal enters History as a singular, in so far as the singular institutes itself in it as a universal. In this novel form of historiality we encounter paradox once again: here it acquires the insurpassable appearance of ambiguity.

But as we have seen, the *theoretical* aspect of his work, in the case of Kierkegaard, is pure illusion. When we *encounter* his words, they immediately invite us to another use of language, that is to say of our own words, since they are the same as his. Kierkegaard's terms refer to what are now called, in accordance with his precepts, the 'categories' of existence. But these categories are neither principles nor concepts nor the elements of concepts: they appear as lived relationships to a totality, attainable by starting with the words and following their trajectory back from speech to speaker. This means that not a single one of these verbal alliances is *intelligible*, but that they constitute, by their very negation of any effort to know them, a reference back to the foundations of such an effort. Kierkegaard made use of irony, humour, myth and non-signifying sentences in order to communicate indirectly with us. This means that if one adopts the traditional attitude of a reader to his books, their words engender a series of pseudo-concepts which are organized under our eyes into false knowledge. But this false knowledge denounces itself as false at the very moment of its formation. Or rather it is constituted as knowledge of something which pretends to be an object but in fact cannot be other than a subject. Kierkegaard made *regressive* use of objective and objectifying ensembles in such a way that the self-destruction of the language necessarily unmasked he who employed it. In this way the surrealists were later to think that they could unmask being by lighting fires in language. But being was still, they believed, *in front of their eyes*; if the words – whatever they were – were burned, being would be unveiled to infinite desire as a surreality, something which was also ultimately a non-conceptual sur-objectivity. Kierkegaard by contrast constructed his language in such a way as to reveal within his false knowledge certain lines of force which allowed the possibility of a return from the pseudo-object to the subject. He invented regressive enigmas. His verbal edifices were rigorously logical. But the very abuse of this logic always gave rise to contradictions or indeterminacies which implied a complete reversal of our own perspective. For example, as Jean Wahl has pointed out, even the title *The Concept of Dread* is a provocation. For in Kierkegaard's terms dread could never be the object of a concept. To a certain extent, in so far as dread is the source of a free and temporalizing choice of finitude, it is the non-conceptual foundation of all concepts. And each of us ought to be able to understand that the word 'dread' is a universalization of the singular, and hence a false concept, since it awakens universality in us to the very extent that it refers to the Unique, its foundation.

It is by turning his words upside down that one can understand Kierkegaard in his lived and now vanished singularity, that is to say in his instituted contingency. His finitude, excluded, corrupted and ineffective, victim of the curse that he believed his father had brought on the whole family, could be described as impotence and as alterity. He is *other* than *all* others, other than himself, other than what he writes. He institutes his particularity by his free choice to be singular, that is to say he establishes himself at that ambiguous moment when interiorization, pregnant with future exteriorization, suppresses itself so that the latter may be born. Kierkegaard, who was afraid of being alienated by inscribing himself in the transcendence of the world, opted for identification with this dialectical stage, the perfect *locus of the secret*. Of course, he could not refrain from exteriorizing himself, as interiorization can only be objectification. Yet he did his best to prevent his objectification from defining him as an object of knowledge, in other words to ensure that the inscription of his person in the realm of reality, far from condensing him into the unity of ongoing History, should remain *as such* indecipherable, and refer back to the inaccessible secret of interiority. He performs brilliantly at a social function, laughing and making others laugh, and then notes in his journal that he wishes he could die. He could make people laugh because he wanted to die, and he wanted to die because he made people laugh. In this way his exteriority – a sparkling wit – was deprived of meaning, *unless* it is to be seen as the intentional contestation of every action reduced to its objective result, *unless* the *meaning* of any manifestation is not precisely incompletion, non-being, non-signification, forcing he who wishes to decipher it to return to its inaccessible source, interiority. Kierkegaard instituted his accidents by choosing to become the knight of subjectivity.

Now that he is dead, Soeren takes his place in knowledge as a bourgeois who came to Denmark in the first half of the last century, and was conditioned by a specific family situation, itself an expression of the movement of history in its generality. But he takes his place in knowledge as unintelligible, as a disqualification of knowledge as a virulent lacuna, that eludes conceptualization and consequently death. We have now gone full circle and can reconsider our initial question. We asked what it was that prevented the late Kierkegaard from becoming the object of knowledge? The answer is that he was not such while he was alive. Kierkegaard reveals to us that death, which we took to be the metamorphosis of existence into knowledge, radically *abolishes* the subjective, but does not change it. If Kierkegaard, in the first instance, can appear to be an assemblage of items of knowledge, the reason is that the *known* is not contested in any immediate fashion by *lived experience*. But at the next moment it is knowledge which radically contests itself in the pseudo-object that this dead man is to us. It discovers its own limits as the object of study, impotent to become an autonomous determination of the exterior, escapes it.

The paradox, at this level, can be seen in a new light: can the contestation of knowledge by itself be surpassed? Can it be surpassed in the face of the living being who bears witness to his secret? Can it be surpassed when this living being has utterly disappeared? To these questions, Kierkegaard has but one reply, and it is always the same: the regression from signified to signifier cannot be the object of any act of intellection. Nevertheless, we can grasp the signifier in its real presence through what Kierkegaard calls *comprehension*. But the knight of subjectivity does not define comprehension, and does not conceive it as a new action. However, through his work, he offers his life to us *to be comprehended*. We encounter it in 1964, in History, fashioned as an *appeal to our comprehension*.

But is there anything left to be understood if death is utter abolition? Kierkegaard replied to this with his theory of 'contemporaneity'. In relation to the dead man Soeren, there remains one thing to be understood, and that is ourselves. Soeren, alive in his death, is a paradox for us: but Soeren had already himself encountered the same paradox in relating to Jesus, in starting from Adam. And his first solution was to say that one comprehends what one becomes. To comprehend Adam is to become Adam. And certainly if an individual cannot become Christ, at least he can comprehend his unintelligible message without any temporal mediation by becoming the man to whom this message was destined – by becoming a Christian. Thus Kierkegaard lives on if it is possible for us to become Kierkegaard or if, conversely, this dead man is ceaselessly instituted by the living – borrowing their life, flowing into their life, and nourishing his singularity with our own. Or if, in other words, he appears at the heart of knowledge as the perpetual denouncer, in each of us, of non-knowledge, of the dialectical stage in which interiorization turns into exteriorization; in short, of existence.

Yes, says Kierkegaard; you may become myself because I may become Adam. Subjective thought is the reflective grasp of my being-an-event, of the adventure that I am and which necessarily ends in my becoming Adam – that is, in recommencing original sin in the very movement of my temporalization. Sin in this case is choice. Every man is at once himself and Adam renewed, precisely to the extent that Kierkegaard was at once himself and his father, the blasphemer whose blasphemy he took upon himself through his own sin. Every sin is singular in so far as it institutes, in particular conditions, a unique individual and, at the same time, it is sin in general in so far as it is the choice of finitude and blasphemous defiance of God. In this way the universality of sin is contained in the singularity of choice. By virtue of it, every man always becomes all man. Each individual moves History forward by recommencing it, as well as by prefiguring within himself new beginnings yet to come. From this point of view, if Kierkegaard could become Adam, it was because Adam was already at the heart of his sinful existence the premonition of a future Kierkegaard. If I can become Kierkegaard it is because Kierkegaard was in his being already a premonition of us all.

If we take up the question again in the initial terms in which we posed it, it comes to this: Kierkegaard's words are our words. To the extent that, within the framework of knowledge, they are changed into non-knowledge and are referred back via the paradox from the signified to the signifier, we are the signifier they regressively disclose. Reading

Kierkegaard I reascend back to myself; I seek to grasp Kierkegaard and it is myself I hold; his non-conceptual work is an invitation to understand myself as the source of all concepts. Thus the knowledge of death, by discovering its own limits, does not issue into sheer absence, but comes back to Kierkegaard. I discover myself as an irreducible existent, that is to say as freedom that has become my necessity. I understand that the object of knowledge *is* his being in the peaceful mode of perennity and by the same token that I am a non-object because I have to be my being. In fact my being is a temporalizing and hence suffered choice – but the nature of this sufferance is to be *freely* suffered, and thus to be sustained as a choice.

Kierkegaard is restored as my adventure not in his unique meaning but at the level of my being-as-adventurer, in so far as I have to be the event that happens to me from outside. In so far as History, universalized by things – the bearers of the seal of our action – becomes, through each new birth of man, a singular adventure within which it enfolds its universality, Soeren could continue to live after his death as my forerunner before birth, when I begin anew in different historical conditions. Curiously, this relationship of reciprocal interiority and immanence between Kierkegaard and each of us is established, not in the relativity of circumstances, but rather at the very level where each of us is an incomparable absolute. And what can demonstrate to us the reality that is common to all and yet in each case is singular, but words? Words are signs turned back on themselves, tools of indirect communication referring me to myself because they refer uniquely to him.

Kierkegaard lives on because, by rejecting knowledge, he reveals the transhistorical contemporaneity of the dead and the living. In other words, he unmasks the fact that every man is all man as a singular universal or, if you like, because he shows temporalization, in opposition to Hegel, to be a transhistorical dimension of History. Humanity loses its dead and begins them absolutely anew once more in its living. Kierkegaard is not myself, however – I am an atheist. Nor is he the Christian who will reproach him tomorrow for his negative theology. Let us say that he was, in his own time, a unique *subject*. Once dead he can be revived only by becoming a *multiple subject*, that is to say an inner bond linking our singularities. Each of us *is* Soeren in our capacity as adventure.

And each of our interpretations, contesting the others, nevertheless subsumes them as its negative depth. Just as each of them, conversely, is contested but subsumed by the others to the extent that, refusing to see in it a complete reality or knowledge concerning reality, they conceive of its possibility by referring to the susceptibility of Kierkegaard to several different interpretations: in fact, divergence, contradiction and ambiguity are precisely the determinate qualifications of existence. Thus it is today's Other, my real contemporary, who is the foundation of Kierkegaard's profundity, his way of remaining *other* within myself, without ceasing to be mine. Conversely he is, in each of us, the denunciation of ambiguity in himself and in others. Kierkegaard, comprehensible in the name of each ambiguity, is our link, a multiple and ambiguous existential relation between existent contemporaries, themselves lived ambivalences. He remains within History as a transhistorical relation between contemporaries grasped in their singular historiality. Within each of us he offers and refuses himself, as he did in his own lifetime; he is my adventure and remains, for others, Kierkegaard, the other – a figure on the horizon testifying to the Christian that faith is a future development forever imperilled, testifying to myself that the process of *becoming-an-atheist* is a long and difficult enterprise, an absolute relationship to these two infinites, man and the universe.

Every enterprise, even one brought to a triumphant conclusion, remains a *failure*, that is to say an incompletion to be completed. It lives on because it is open. The particular failure, in Kierkegaard's case, is clear. Kierkegaard demonstrated his historicity but failed to find History. Pitting himself against Hegel, he occupied himself over-exclusively with transmitting his instituted contingency to the human adventure and, because of this, he neglected *praxis*, which is rationality. At a stroke, he denatured *knowledge*, forgetting that the world we know is the world we make. Anchorage is a fortuitous event, but the possibility and rational meaning of this chance is given by general structures of envelopment which found it and which are themselves the universalization of singular adventures by the materiality in which they are inscribed.

Kierkegaard is alive in his death in as much as he affirms the irreducible singularity of every man to the History which nevertheless conditions him rigorously. He is dead, within the very life that he continues to lead within ourselves, in as much as he remains an inert interrogation, an open circle that demands to be closed by us. Others, in his own time or shortly thereafter, went further than him and completed the circle by writing: 'Men make history on the basis of prior circumstances.' In these words there is and is not progress beyond Kierkegaard: for this circularity remains abstract and risks excluding the human singularity of the concrete universal, so long as it does not integrate Kierkegaardian immanence within the historical dialectic. Kierkegaard and Marx: these living-dead men condition our anchorage and institute themselves, now vanished, as our future, as the tasks that await us. How can we conceive of History and the transhistorical in such a way as to restore to the transcendent necessity of the historical process and to the free immanence of a historicization ceaselessly renewed, their full reality and reciprocal interiority, in theory and practice? In short, how can we discover the singularity of the universal and the universalization of the singular, in each conjuncture, as indissolubly linked to each other?

Mallarmé: The Poetry of Suicide

Mallarmé, born into a family of civil servants, and brought up by a grandmother who left much to be desired, felt revolt welling up inside him at an early age, but was unable to give it expression. Society, nature, the family – he rejected everything, even the pale and wretched child he saw in the mirror. But the efficacy of revolt varies inversely with its diffusion. The whole world needs to be blown up, of course: but the problem is to do it without getting our hands dirty. A bomb is an object just as much as an Empire armchair: it is a little more dangerous, that's all. What intrigues and compromises are necessary in order to place it just right! Mallarmé was not, nor would ever be, an anarchist: he rejected all individualist activity. His violence – and I use the word without irony – was so desperate and total that it became transformed into a peaceful *idea* of violence. No, he would not turn the world upside down: he would place it in parentheses. He opted for the terrorism of politeness: between himself and other things, other men, even his own being, he always managed to preserve an imperceptible distance. It was this distance that he wanted to express at first in his poetry.

Mallarmé wrote his early poems as a form of recreation. He had to reassure himself that he was really on the right path. He detested his birthright, and wrote to obliterate its memory. As Blanchot has put it, the universe of prose is sufficient unto itself, and we cannot count on it furnishing us of its own accord with reasons for surpassing it. If the poet can locate a poetic object in the real world, we can assume he is already acting at the behest of Poetry; in a word, he has found his true progenitor. Mallarmé always conceived of this 'vocation' as a categorical imperative. What drove him on was not the urgency, the wealth of his impressions, nor the violence of his feelings, but an *order*: 'You will proclaim through your work that you hold the universe at a distance.'

And in fact his first poems were concerned with nothing other than Poetry itself. It has been pointed out that the Ideal which was always central to his verse remained an abstraction, the poetic disguise of a simple negation: it was the indeterminate region one is forced towards when one moves away from reality. It would subsequently serve him as alibi: he was able to pretend that he abandoned being, not because his hatred and resentment drove him to it, but in order to reach the ideal.

Yet he would have had to believe in God, for it was God who guaranteed Poetry. The poets of the previous generation saw themselves as minor prophets: through their mouths, God spoke. But Mallarmé no longer believed in God. Yet discredited ideologies do not disappear at one blow, but leave crumbling remnants in men's minds. After having killed God with his own hands, Mallarmé still hankered after a divine sanction: Poetry, in his eyes, needed to retain its transcendental quality – even though he had done away with the source of all transcendence. Now that God was dead, his inspiration could come from tainted sources only. These had to establish his poetic calling. Mallarmé could still hear God's voice, but in it he discerned the vague chorus of sounds that belong to nature. In the evening, for example, someone might whisper into his room – and it would turn out to be the wind. The wind, or the voice of his ancestors: it was still a fact that the prose of the world does not inspire poems; it was still a fact that verse has to pre-exist within the poet; it was still a fact that the poet listens to words ringing inside his head before he writes them down. Facts, yes, but resting on a fallacy: what Mallarmé grasped was that every fresh line of a poem struggling to surface was in fact an older line struggling to revive. Thus the words which seem to reach the poet's lips fresh from his heart, are in fact emerging from cold storage in his memory. What can inspiration be then? Reminiscences – and nothing else. Mallarmé caught a glimpse in the future of a youthful image of himself, beckoning; he drew closer and it turned out to be his father. Time seemed an illusion to him: the future was nothing but the aberrant appearance which the past may assume in a man's eyes. This despair, which at that time Mallarmé chose to call his impotence, as it left him in a state in which he felt he had to reject all sources of inspiration and all poetic themes which were not the abstract

and formal idea of Poetry itself – drove him to postulate a whole system
of metaphysics, an analytical and vaguely Spinozist variety of materialism.
In this system, nothing was supposed to exist other than matter, eternal
murmur of being, space 'indifferent as to whether it expanded or con-
tracted'.* The appearance of man was supposed to lead to the transformation *for him* of eternity into temporality, and of infinity into chance.
In itself in fact the never-ending causal chain was all that it could be.
An all-knowing understanding would perhaps grasp the absolute necessity underlying such a system: but to finite eyes the world appeared
to be in a state of perpetual encounter, an absurd succession of random
events. If this was the case, then the reasoning of our intellect was as
deranged as the reasoning of our heart, and the principles of our thought
and the categories of our action were shams: man was an impossible
dream. Thus the poet's impotence symbolized the impossibility of
being man. In this schema there is only one tragedy, that is always the
same, 'and which is resolved at once, in no more than the time it takes to
demonstrate lightning defeat'. This is how it comes about: 'He throws the
dice. . . . And he who created them assumes material form again, in the
shape of the dice themselves.' There *were* dice; there *are* dice. There *were*
words; there *are* words. Man was a volatile illusion floating above the
movements of matter. Mallarmé, a purely material creature, sought to
conjure up an order of existence superior to matter. His was a *theological*
impotence: the death of God left a void which the poet tried to fill, and
failed. The man Mallarmé envisaged, like that of Pascal before him, had
to express himself in terms of drama and not in terms of essence: 'latent
god who cannot become', he was defined by his impossibility. 'This
insensate game of writing consists in arrogating to oneself on the strength
of a doubt an obligation to recreate everything by means of reminiscences.' But 'Nature is always there – nothing can be added to it.' In
epochs that have no future, when for instance historical advance is
blocked by the weighty prestige of a king or by the incontestable triumph
of a certain class, invention appears pure reminiscence: it has all been
said before – the writer has turned up too late. Ribot† would soon pro-

---

*Translator's note: 'pareil à soi qu'il s'accroisse ou se nie' – see *Quand l'ombre
menace*, Penguin *Mallarmé*, p. 85.

†Translator's note: Theodule Ribot (1839–1916), early French protagonist of an

pound the theoretical basis of this feeling of impotence by compounding our mental images with our memories.

In Mallarmé, then, we find the outline of a metaphysics of pessimism: one which postulates that matter, i.e. formless infinity, possesses a vague sort of proclivity for retracing its steps so as to gain knowledge of itself. In order to illumine its obscure infinity, it produces these ribbons of thoughts, these tattered pennants, we call men. But in the infinite dispersion of matter, the Idea is lost. Man and chance come to be born at the same time – each begotten of the other. Man is a failure, a 'wolf' among 'wolves'. His nobility is to live out this flaw in his making right up until the time of the final explosion.

And wasn't an explosion called for? Mallarmé, at Tournon, Besançon and Avignon, very seriously envisaged suicide. What weighed on his mind at first was the argument that if man is impossible, then this impossibility must be made manifest by stretching it to the point where it destroys itself. For once the *cause* governing our action could not be considered *material*. Being, runs the argument, can only produce being; and if the poet opts for non-being as the logical consequence of his non-possibility, then his No becomes the cause of Nothingness. A human order arises against being – through Man's very disappearance. Before Mallarmé, Flaubert had already written a passage in which he caused St Anthony to be tempted in these words: '(Kill yourself). Do something which will make you the equal of God. Just think of it . . . He created you – and by virtue of your courage, you are free to destroy his handiwork.' Wasn't this what Mallarmé always wanted? In his contemplated suicide there was an element of terrorist crime. And didn't he say once that suicide and crime were the only *supernatural* acts of which man was capable? Some few men have the capacity to confuse their own drama with that of humanity – and this is their salvation. Mallarmé never doubted for a minute that had he killed himself, the human species in its entirety would have died with him. His suicide would have been genocide. Being would regain its purity through his disappearance. Since chance was supposed to have arisen along with man, along with him it would expire: 'So infinity is to elude my family, after their sufferings

experimental psychology. In 1876 he founded the *Revue philosophique de la France et de l'Etranger*.

from it . . . Ancient region . . . devoid of chance . . . Which was to have arisen out of the combinations of the Infinite. On the one hand, the necessary Absolute; and on the other – the Idea.'

Slowly, through generations of poets, the poetic idea had been ruminating the contradiction which rendered it impossible: the death of God was the final blow. And Mallarmé, the last representative of the poetic race, enjoyed the privilege of living this contradiction in its pure form – and of dying from it. Thus he brought to a close the poetic phase of human history. His suicide – at once sacrifice and genocide, affirmation and negation of man – would reproduce the throw of the dice: matter would be matter once again.

If however this crisis did not result in his death, it was because supreme inspiration came knocking at his window. During this dummy run of his voluntary death, Mallarmé suddenly discovered his doctrine: the reason why suicide was efficacious was that it replaced the abstract, fruitless negation of the whole of being, with a negative *mode of action*. In Hegelian terms we could say that Mallarme's contemplation of the absolute act – suicide – enabled him to surpass 'stoicism', as a purely formal affirmation of the mind in opposition to free-being, towards scepticism 'which realizes that of which stoicism was merely the concept . . . (In scepticism) the mind becomes perfect thought, annihilating the being of the world in the multiple variety of its determinations, and the negativity of self-consciousness becomes real negativity.' Mallarmé's first impulse had been to recoil in disgust and condemn the world in its entirety. Driven to the summit of his spiral flight, the dizzy heir 'did not dare move', for fear of falling. But he now become aware that universal negation is equivalent to the absence of negation. To negate is an *act:* every act must be inserted in time, and exercised on a particular content. Suicide is an act because in effect it destroys a being and because it causes the world to be haunted by an absence. If being is dispersion, man by losing his being acquires an incorruptible unity. More, his absence has an astringent effect on the being of the universe; like Aristotelian forms, absence binds things together, seeping into them with its secret unity. What the poet felt he had to capture in his verses was this essential movement of suicide. Since man was incapable of the act of creation yet still possessed the power to destroy, and since he affirmed his identity by the very act of annihilating himself, the poet's work would be a labour of destruction. Considered from the point of view of death, poetry would become, in Blanchot's apt phrase, 'a language whose whole strength is not to be, and whose whole glory is to evoke, in the absence of itself, the absence of all'. Mallarmé could write proudly to Lefébvre that Poetry had become *critical*. In staking his all, Mallarmé discovered himself, under the glaring light of death, in his essence as man and poet. He had not abandoned his rejection of everything, he had simply rendered it effective. He would soon be able to write that 'a poem is the only bomb worth making'. At times, he actually came to believe that he had really killed himself.

It was not by chance that Mallarmé wrote the word – 'Nothing' – on the first page of his *Poesies complètes*.* Since a poem is the suicide both of man and poetry, being must finally close over this death; the moment of poetic plenitude must correspond to that of annulment. Thus the truth that these poems have *become*, is nothingness: 'Nothing will have taken place but the place.'† We are familiar with the extraordinary negative logic Mallarmé invented – how, under his pen, a lace curtain vanishes to reveal nothing but the absence of a bed,‡ while a 'vase devoid of any liquid' agonizes without consenting to hope for anything that might announce an invisible rose,§ or how a tomb is burdened only 'with the absence of heavy wreaths'.‖ 'The virginal, living and beautiful day . . .'¶ offers a perfect example of this internal annulment at work in a poem. 'Today' and its future are only an illusion; the present is reduced to the past; a swan which believed that it was acting is nothing but a memory of itself, fixed without hope 'in the cold dream of scorn'. An appearance of movement vanishes, and all that remains is the infinite and undifferentiated surface of ice. The explosion of colours and forms discloses to our senses a symbol that refers us back to the tragedy of man – which dissolves into nothingness. Such is the internal movement

---

* 'Rien, cette écume, vierge vers . . .' ('Nothing, this foam, a virgin line of poetry . . .') See Penguin *Mallarmé*, p. 7.
† See *Un coup de dés*, Penguin *Mallarmé*, p. 231.
‡ See *Une dentelle s'abolit*, Penguin *Mallarmé*, p. 99.
§ See *Surgi de la croupe*, Penguin *Mallarmé*, p. 98.
‖ See *Sur les bois oubliés*, Penguin *Mallarmé*, p. 89.
¶ See Penguin *Mallarmé*, p. 85.

of these astonishing poems, at once silent words and faked objects. In their very disappearance, they were ultimately to evoke the outlines of some object 'absenting itself in flight', and their very beauty was to be virtually an *a priori* proof that *lack of being* is a *manner of being*.

Virtually an *a priori* proof – but an unsound one. Mallarmé was too lucid not to understand that no single experiment will ever contradict the principles that guided its construction. If Chance were present at the beginning, then 'a dice throw will never abolish it'.* In any act in which there is an element of chance, it is chance alone which accomplishes its own Idea by affirming or negating itself. In a poem, it is chance which negates itself. Poetry, the child of chance and its foe, abolishes chance in the act of abolishing itself, because its symbolic abolition is that of man himself. Yet all this, at bottom, was only a hoax. The origin of Mallarmé's irony was his knowledge of the absolute vanity, yet entire necessity of his work; he could discern in it two unsynthesized opposites perpetually engendering and repulsing each other – chance and necessity. Chance creates necessity, an illusion of man – this fragment of nature gone mad. Necessity creates chance as that which limits and defines it *a contrario*. Necessity negates chance 'word by word' in the body of the poem; chance in its turn negates necessity since the 'full employment' of words is impossible. Necessity abolishes chance in turn by the suicide of the poem and of Poetry. There was in Mallarmé an element of dour humbug: he created and nurtured amongst his friends and disciples the myth of a masterpiece which would suddenly reabsorb the world; he feigned to be preparing for it. But he knew perfectly well that such a project was impossible. All he had to do was simply make it appear that his whole life was dedicated to this absent object: an Orphic explanation of the Earth (which was nothing other than poetry itself). I cannot doubt that he firmly believed his death would eternalize this relationship to Orphism as the poet's loftiest ambition, and its failure as the tragic impossibility of man. If a poet dies at twenty-five, overcome by his own sense of impotence, the event ranks as no more than a curiosity; but when a fifty-six-year-old-poet perishes at the very moment when he has mastered all the preliminaries and is about to commence his life-work – this is the *very tragedy* of man. Mallarmé's death was a memorable mystification.

*See *Un coup de dés*, Penguin *Mallarmé*, p. 207.

But it was a mystification by means of *the truth*: a 'veridical mummer of himself', Mallarmé performed to the world at large for thirty years the tragedy for one player which he had often dreamed of writing. He was himself the 'latent god who cannot become, youthful shadow of all, hence bearer of myth . . . forcing a subtle effacement on the living through the subtle invasion of his presence'. In the complex system of this comedy, his poems had first to be failures in order to be perfect. It was not enough that they should abolish both language and world, nor even that they should annul themselves; what the system demanded was that they should represent the fruitless draft sketches of an unprecedented and impossible masterpiece which only the chance occurrence of death prevented him from beginning. Everything falls into place if we view these symbolic suicides in the light of an accidental death – being in the light of nothingness. Through an unexpected twist, the atrocious ship-wreck ahead conferred on the poems he *actually wrote* an absolute necessity. What is most poignant about them is that whereas they en-rapture us, their author held them worthless. He gave them the final touch when, on the eve of his death, he pretended to be interested in nothing but his future masterpiece, and wrote to his wife and daughter: 'Have no doubt that this work was to be most beautiful.' The truth? A lie? But this was the very man Mallarmé wanted to be – man dying throughout the world from the disintegration of the atom or the cooling of the sun, and murmuring of the Society he had wanted to construct: 'Have no doubt that this work was to be most beautiful.'

A hero, prophet, magician and tragedian all at once, this slight, feminine man, discreet in his ways and little attracted to women, deserved to die at the threshold of our century: in fact he heralded its coming. To a greater degree than Nietzsche, he experienced the death of God; well before Camus, he felt that suicide was the original question confronting man; his struggle day after day against chance would be taken up later by others, yet with no greater lucidity. In a word, what he asked himself was this: Is there a way to be found within determinism that leads outside it? It is possible to turn *praxis* upside-down and rediscover subjectivity by reducing the universe and oneself to objectivity? He systematically applied to art what was still only a philosophical principle and was to become a political maxim: 'Make and in making make yourself.' Shortly before the gigantic onrush of technology, he invented a technique of poetry; at the same time as Taylor was devising methods to mobilize men in order to give their work its maximum efficiency, he was mobilizing language in order to secure the maximum profit from words. But the most striking feature of the man, it seems to me, was the metaphysical anguish which he endured so openly and modestly. Not a single day passed without his being tempted to kill himself, and if he lived on, it was for the sake of his daughter. But this suspended death gave him a kind of charming and destructive irony – his 'native intelligence', which was above all the art of finding and establishing in his daily life, and even in his perception, a 'lethal duet' to which he submitted all the objects of this world. He was wholly a poet, wholly dedicated to the critical destruction of poetry by itself. Yet at the same time, he remained aloof: a 'sylph belonging to cold ceilings',* he studied himself. If it was matter that produced poetry, perhaps the lucid thought of matter escaped from its determinism? So his poetry itself came to be placed in parentheses. One day someone sent him a few drawings; he liked them, but what particularly attracted him was the sketch of an old magician with a mournful smile: 'It comes from knowing', he commented, 'that his art is a fraud. But at the same time he seems to be saying: "*Yet it might have been the truth.*" '

*Translator's note: See *Surgi de la croupe*, Penguin *Mallarmé*, p. 98.

Tintoretto: *St George and the Dragon*

Tintoretto knew or anticipated everything that his predecessor was lucky enough to ignore. What account of himself did this painter of passions give when asked by his clients to commemorate an act? For an answer let us question the painting in the National Gallery.

Jacopo begins by relegating the soldier and the animal to the half-light of the middle-ground. This is a favourite procedure of his: as a rule he makes use of it to rob us of our time. Not so in this case: after all, what believer would not ardently seek out a Christ or Virgin Mary in the depths of a crowd? Yet however great may have been St George's contribution to the welfare of Venice, the most serene City has loftier protectors – among others, St Mark. No one will take the trouble to peer into the half-light to discern the shabby and indistinct scuffle there: St George isn't popular enough. If a painter wants to impose him, let him bring into close-up, out in the light! This is what Carpaccio did, and this is what Robusti refuses to do. Out of sullenness, I believe. This George is the painter's personal enemy, the protagonist of every drama, the adventurer who is called in treatises on morality the *agent*. Tintoretto's brush will exile this captain, who disturbs the universe of *pathos* by the incongruity of an act.

A double and contradictory distension expels him and propels towards us the sumptuous sign of that blindest of passions, fear. On the right, in bright light, a woman throws herself against the glass frontier of the painting. A tilt-shot from below accentuates her. This is where the canvas begins: it is impossible to ignore or pass beyond her. We first contemplate this range of every visible quality – light and form, colour, modelling; we imagine the object endowed with the density and weight of this beautiful, fair flesh. And then diagonally we cross a rarefied wasteland to reach the site of the curious combat. Our itinerary for the moment goes from right to left, from foreground to background. The painter will not let go of us until he has first impressed this luxurious flight on us. A flight, a fall, a collapse, a swoon – it is all these at once. The girl is running straight like a mad thing ahead; but matter resists, sticks to her shoes, slips or crumbles; under her skirt, her shapely legs stumble – one knee is about to hit the ground. Tintoretto keeps us here a moment longer: floating behind this dread he has painted the proudly billowing waves of a cloak. In this remarkable but sombre painting, the only bright plumage is that of fright – fright alone is allowed to be pink. Why? Is an attempt being made to demoralize us? Yes – in a way. For just at this point the canvas opens up: it is time for us to go right into it.

On the left of the painting, by the shore of a putrescent lagoon, we discover a sizeable reptile with gnarled, mangled wings. Our look immediately connects this vermin with the fugitive girl; a slither, a flight or a leap would be enough – and Beauty would be devoured by the Beast. This fulgurating relationship flashes from right to left and from front to back; but it is not reciprocal. The animal has excellent reasons for temporary distraction; it is the girl whose long ostensible rout denounces the evil intentions of the monster. We no sooner glimpse the monster, however, than the time-sequence of the painting is overthrown. So long as we did not know the reasons for it, the girl's attempt to escape was not simply a wild passion – she might have decided, albeit trembling, on the wisest course. She seemed to be losing her balance. Was she about to stumble or would she regain her footing? That such a question can be put implies that an enterprise unfolding in time has suddenly been broken by a false step – the breakage is an instant. Sheerer fissures exist – vertical or scythe-like; and Robusti knows how to summon the necessary angles of our bodies from them. But this time he has other intentions: he deftly compensates for the threat of a fall with the hint of a recovery. Our uncertainty tempers our expectancy – we are not disturbed either by the postponement *sine die* of a too-awaited disaster, or by the perpetual promise of a reprieve forever deferred. In short, our eye demands nothing; the moment of rupture fades into a flabby suspense; it even becomes the guarantee of the temporal dimension of the painting. For since the immediate future is indeterminate, we can guess that a durable enterprise is afoot. Freed from all physical impatience, we have been forewarned that an act will be accomplished or aborted, according to whether events take this course or that.

This initial illusion lasts for less time than it takes to describe it. This is where our itinerary starts, that is all; although it is also where it always begins again. In short, this is a moment – a moment made to disappear. In effect, no sooner is the dragon noticed than the instant triumphs. Not that girl definitely falls – Jacopo is too crafty for that. He merely puts her enterprise in parentheses: Beauty will not escape from the Beast without the intervention of Providence. What then does it matter to us whether she finally tumbles or recovers? We are shown the passive abandonment of a body disordered by fear; as for the fate of the young person it is being decided a hundred metres behind her. In short, the instant retains its delicate balance, but duration decamps from the scene. For the rest, on the left of the painting, in the middle-ground, a corpse suggests a prophecy: the die is cast – if the finger of God does not crush the reptile, the maiden will die. In fact she is *already dead.* The instantaneous violence of her flight and the eternal repose of death balance each other. It was not for nothing that Tintoretto placed this cadaver in our path, between the fugitive and the animal – his canvases are covered with signs whose function is to foretell the future of the principal characters and to figure its imminence. Other men perform what they are about to do, suffering the fate that will overtake them, or which they will only just escape. Robusti had to depict the inevitable downfall of the girl for us – a Natural inevitability, before the intervention of the Supernatural. But he profits from it to suggest that the swift transience of the instant is identical to eternal rest.

The dragon would only have to be on the look-out, would only have to deign to give his attention to the frightened scramblings of his future repast, to pull the whole of the canvas over towards him. It would disappear down his gullet and we would follow it. It would suffice for him to be steady, but ready to spring, and the dramatic action would revolve about him; we would feel the depth of the painting as a threat. But he is not on the look-out – God has rendered him so deaf that he cannot hear the charge of the holy lancer. Now it is too late – the pike has pierced him; he has been killed. No, it is still too soon – he has not yet had time to die, only to suffer. We are enclosed by the instant – his start of wild terror, his jaws wrenched apart with pain, between the visible shock and legible death (foretold, moreover, by the sacred legend itself). Yet another suspended death. Although baleful still, he no longer threatens anyone – his only concern is his own predicament. In short, this dragon disappoints us, as the maiden did before him: she was not really seeking safety from him, just as he is not a real threat to her. At a stroke, the armed intervention of the saint disqualifies the flight of the girl – she runs on, though now out of danger. Terror has driven her mad; she will career forward aimlessly, without stopping, until she faints. Her flight, provoked by an external cause whose disappearance forms the very subject of the painting, survives her; it will continue indefinitely, for want of any inner ability to halt itself. Is this not the definition of inertia ? Scientists would soon establish the principles of it. Robusti knows nothing of science. Yet on his canvas he depicts death, fear, life as inert appearances – borrowed, maintained, removed: always from the outside.

Robusti's itinerary conducts us through a complex play of deceptions: each presence points to the next, and is disqualified by it. The beast and the corpse condemn the princess to death – and the death of the beast transforms the deceased maiden into a mechanical system gone wrong. At the outset one presence – a splendid and massive terror – dominates from the foreground on our right. But we do not have to go very deeply into the picture to see this as the mere residue of an effect that has survived its cause. In fact, once we have discerned the agony of the beast, the true present is revealed while the other slips into the past. The painter's message is clear: everything on his canvas is taking place at once. He encloses everything in the unity of a single instant. But to conceal its too brutal cleavage, a phantom succession is pressed upon us. Not only is the course of events traced in advance, but each successive stage devalues its predecessor and denounces it as the inert memory of things. The repose of the corpse is memory – prolonged, repeated from one moment to the next, forever identical, useless. As for the dragon, his ugliness demonstrated his wickedness. He suffers; his agony distracts or suspends his faculties – and his wickedness passes. His ugliness loses its function, but lingers on – etched in his leather. The time-trap works, and we are caught in it. A false present greets us at every step and unmasks its predecessor, which returns, behind our backs, to its original condition as petrified memory. We believe that we are encountering the true present each time, and that it flows in living form behind us into the past.

Just one thrust of a lance has to produce all these cracks in inertia at once. The painter's itinerary forces us then to go from the flight of the girl all the way back to the death blow of the Saint. What do we find? Is the saint performing an act, or is he merely the passive vehicle of an event? Let us look closer: for this soldier of God can scarcely be seen. I notice that he is charging from right to left, as in Carpaccio's painting. But this time he is more knowing, less bold. Rather than confront the monster candidly, he stabs it by stealth from behind – to make victory more certain. The position of his lance-head testifies to this: It has just struck the beast above the eye. The years have transformed the knight-errant into a condottiere. I see nothing wrong in this – the girl had to be saved, audacity would have been criminal in such circumstances. But something has been lost. Carpaccio's dragon was a sort of prodigy, the child of the devil and of paganism. The two supernatural beings, one the emissary of Providence and the other the instrument of the devil, had to fight it out face to face. In this manichean confrontation, the painter pitted Heaven against Hell – the beautiful prey in her robes was merely a pretext. Here, in this place, as everywhere, God had to triumph over idolatry. Such, moreover, was the meaning of the legend – once the Beast was dead, the whole city was converted to the Christian religion.

Tintoretto believed in the All-Powerful, in original sin, in God's abandonment of man. About the Devil, we cannot be so sure. In any case, he conceived his dragon as a product of nature, a Loch Ness monster. While George, despite the phosphorescent wave that encircles his head, became the victim of a brush determined to naturalize the supernatural. Human, all too human, George grips his lance. It is not he that is the driving force behind the blow, but his horse: the soldier merely uses its momentum to the full. All he does is grip tight with his thighs and bend low over the neck of his mount to cushion the recoil. I am well aware that this was standard procedure in tournaments; but at least those jousts pitted combatants of the same species and the same arms against each other, while the same signal alerted both of them together. A trace of this age can be seen in Carpaccio's painting – he was known for his aristocratic tastes, and took pleasure in depicting a champion striking cleanly, in style. To show the champion's style, he had to show his act, and to show that he had to depict his hands: the saint's left profile is turned towards us, but he is holding up his right hand and all can see his iron fist, the symbol of every human endeavour, gripping his lance and thrusting it at the beast. Carpaccio was so intent on showing us that the saint's weapon was wholly articulated with his hand, that he forced the hand to point the lance obliquely, across the courser's neck. On reflection, it is evident that other modes of attack would have been faster or more certain in their outcome – but from Carpaccio's point of view they all suffered from the same drawback: the saint would have to drive his lance to the right of his horse, so that a few inches of its length would be blocked from view by the horse's head – enough, anyway, to break the durable unity of this lightning stroke. Carpaccio the aristocrat preferred to cheat a little – hardly at all, for the public to see Force in the service of Order.

Tintoretto's tastes were plebeian. What he liked best, I think, was the sweat of artisans struggling with intractable matter: I have said that it was their troubles and the drama of their lot that he depicted. Thus he made his soldier, without even thinking about it, into a good workman, labouring hard and perspiring profusely. In fact, the saint's enterprise changed radically from one canvas to the other: for Tintoretto, George is wholly occupied with charging, lance downwards, a piece of vermin off-guard and stupefied by Providence, that offers no resistance apart from the thickness of its hide and the hardness of its bones. In a word, for Tintoretto, George is a workman driving in a nail.

If only we were shown his hammer and his five fingers gripping it! But this is carefully avoided. Observe the position of the lance. Tintoretto could not prevent it being a foreshortened, rectilinear vector, but he promised himself that he would not let it dominate the painting. In the church of San Giorgio degli Schiavoni, he must, I imagine, have become much more aware of the problem, and may even have glimpsed its solution: two opposed ends could be achieved by the use of opposing means. In his painting, therefore, everything had to be the contrary of what Carpaccio had done. Robusti would conceal the lance, and he would hide George's right hand, because he guessed that his predecessor had

gone out of his way to show both of them. Tintoretto deliberately constructed his painting around a leftward-pointing axis – so that our gaze
penetrates it at an angle – in order to project the left-hand side of the saint
to us and deprive us of this image of practical efficacy – the closed fist
gripping and aiming the instrument. As a consequence the lance is three-
quarters hidden behind the opaque mass of horse and rider; the dim
light does the rest – you need good eyes to see the lance's fourth quarter.
All we pick out is a vague glimmer of steel beneath the soldier's bent
elbow – the end of the lance; and between the horse's head and the
dragon, a black streak – its shaft – whose head has already disappeared
into the monster's skull. Everything takes place as if Jacopo had taken
the precaution of removing all straight lines from his painting.

What he actually did was worse: while scrubbing out these foreshortened lines, these pins that fix people and things to the canvas like
multicoloured butterflies onto cork, he contrived by a stroke of ingenious
malice to leave an insubstantial trace of them – optical phantoms of what
they had once been. The axis of the action thus disappeared, but in its
place he painted, in the far distance, two privileged spectres – horizontal
and perpendicular – in order to figure, in the form of mirages, our
absolute impotence. Before coming back to St George, we must concentrate for a moment on the background of the painting. Let us consider
this distant town, pale with fear, less substantial than a puff of smoke.
The verticality of its tall ramparts proclaims the abandonment of the
princess. Here we may recall the story of this unfortunate maid. The
cowardly citizens of the town have been paying the Beast a tax in the form
of virgins – a diet, it appears, particularly delectable to dragons. One day
Fate picked on the king's daughter, and this interesting sovereign, instead
of beating drums and issuing calls to arms, decided that it would be more
honourable to bow to the common destiny. A democrat from funk,
the enlightened despot had his own child led to the water's edge and
there abandoned. Abandoned? That's putting it mildly – her fellow
citizens delivered her to the dragon. With tears in their eyes, according
to the legend. Indeed, they were still crying, I don't doubt, when an
hour later they had raised all the drawbridges and gone home to sleep
behind bolted doors. Then St George happened to pass by. Outraged by
these events, he decided to stay. On Tintoretto's canvas, everything is

finished: it is for God to make the next move. The community has shut itself up – it is distant, inaccessible. The terrorized maid flees from the dragon, but each step also takes her further away from the capital that rejected her. For the soldier and the princess, the business has to be settled out here in the wasteland, without the assistance of men – where the alternatives are to kill or to die. Such is the meaning of the insubstantial rigidity of those sharp-edged ramparts. 'Don't count on us!' At beginning of our century, another craftsman called K . . . , a surveyor by trade, happened upon a castle built on a hill; it too had elusive ramparts, hewn out of the same matter. Grace alone, the divine concourse, allows those on earth to know and accomplish what must be accomplished. What would the sixteenth century see in a distant figuration of absolute verticality? It would see grace, revealed and erased in a single movement. Why not? Tintoretto is the epic painter of solitude. Like all great solitaries, he was a man who inhabited crowds. He who had been so often humiliated and betrayed, and so often a betrayer, believed that the human community without grace became a den of thieves. In order that man might cease to be a wolf for men, a transmutation of his being was necessary, that verticality could figure and abundant grace alone could accomplish. But God tarries and life rushes by; it passes without his ever appearing, and without our ceasing to await him. Look closely at the mirage of those vertiginous walls – the mirage is that of Godot. But a Godot rooted to the spot – who will not come.

As for the horizontal, here things are worse. If man is nothing but a savage beast, then absolute verticality, even reduced to a spectre of itself, does not prevent him from communicating his hopes to God. But that straight line across the horizon represents precisely such a prohibition. Its office is to separate earth from heaven. Let us look at it more closely: the dead water and the clouds above it fade away in a single movement. But the artist has no liking for sea-voyages; the sombre indistinction of the lagoons and their banks hold no interest for him. The proof: he makes no effort to interest us in them. The sky is his destination: it is there he would like to travel. What emptiness! The tender tormented pink is a summons: 'Flee on high, flee! I sense that the angels are drunk . . .' Fine. But why does he have to go so far? One need only live a few weeks in Venice to find this nostalgia suspicious. If the artist was fond of the rarifaction of being, all he had to do was to take a walk around the Fondamenta Nuove, at dusk or dawn, to encounter it everywhere, virtually tangible – it is a Venetian speciality. In Venice the sky shimmers around the pale fingers of the city, crackles dryly at eye-level – while up there above the stratosphere it appears as a series of loose, grey silken folds receding out of sight. Between this delicate silken scarf and the rooftops there is a void, a wasteland criss-crossed with scintilla of light. Even when the heat is intense, the sun remains 'cool'; yet nowhere in the world does it erode so much. It can make an island vanish, disintegrate a district, fall into a canal and evaporate its water, turn the gentle lapping of the waves into a sparkling stammer.

This was Tintoretto's one great love: all his work testifies to it. The lagoons of air above the lagoon he was born in, these precipitates of inert azure, tumbling into the dead water out of pure space – he loved them so much he wanted to paint them everywhere. Critics have grumbled that Tintoretto never breathed a word of his native city in his paintings. Not a word? But he spoke of nothing else. Not of the gondolas certainly – you will find none in his canvases. Nor of the old wooden bridge of the Rialto. But no matter how you approach it, Venice must give itself to you wholly or not at all. That is its character, and what differentiates it from, say, Rome or Palermo. Jacopo collected up his city and diluted it into a cone of translucidity. He preserved the mottled impenetrability of its palaces in such a dazzling transparency that they hurt your eyes. It was Venice once more that he depicted in his *St George* – a lagoon of air wafting its pink folds above a lagoon of water. Later paintings – the majority – would depict the Pearl of the Adriatic for us as an attack of the sky against the earth. In these, a deadened blueness, tinged with grey and salmon-pink, is blasted through the interminable purity of space, against a stagnant expanse of water. Why? Doubtless to destroy all germs of life in it, utterly to mineralize the gelatinous morass quivering between the walls of the canals. There is no suggestion of this yet in the *St George*: the next phase of Venetian painting would witness a sumptuous return to the vows of poverty. The full-blown colours would be faded or, still more frequently, eroded by exploding lights. Such was the evolution dictated by local history and the inner logic of the art, and in this period they designated their reformer: Tintoretto. This hallucinated weight-lifter was accorded a mandate to give plastic representation to the decompression of matter into luminosity. To confer a mandate is not difficult – all that is necessary is to plant in the depths of the mandated a few insurmountable contradictions; he will always manage to contrive a mandate out of them. Thus it was, we may be sure, in the case of Jacopo. To transmute weight into grace was natural to him; but to show how the latter was no more than an attenuated guise of the former was his mission. One which had, clearly, only very indirect links with man's surroundings – his environment of things and material products of his labour. Critics long ago ceased to look for the secret of Sienese painting in the strange relief of the Appennines. Everything was floating, everything now has weight, everything will flow away: the painter must dive into the Adriatic and flow with it to discover its luminous energy. This is the order of the questions with which we are confronted. Nevertheless the negation of a negation does not of itself – whatever may have been said – change it into an affirmation; a 'no' is never surpassed towards a 'yes' save under the impulse of a premonition. Without a mandate, signs cannot be deciphered; without signs, a mandate remains what it is – an abstract and stuttering mission. Where other than in Venice could Jacopo find the weight of fire and the heat of being, the hopeless proximity of walls, the aimless wandering in a labyrinth and then, suddenly, the cinemascopic vision of a pale glow in the distance? He would merely have seen blue there, of course, had predestined interests not made him invent the ordinary. But he would have had no idea of the 'terrible wonders' he was about to produce, if his disquiet had not previously discovered them about itself, as the brute response of things.

Now let us take a brief look at something that troubles me. The light in Venice – in other words, the metamorphosis of light into the city, and of the city into light – is to be found on all his canvases, even where the subject demands an interior décor. In spite of appearances, it is not flaming torches that illuminate the great halls of his banquets: sham suns flood them with the blonde light of the Venetian dusks, or with the steely tint of its dawns. Yet the sky itself is blocked off. Even today in Venice the devotees of tenuity merely have to lift their heads for inspiration – the air is made of nothing. Didn't Jacopo ever lift his? Yes, he had to. His gaze too would have been lost in this rarefied gas. But this did not deter him: he preferred to bottle up his local firmament, this glittering island above his city, with heavy traffic – inky, gravid, immobile clouds. Better yet when he could bar our look with a ceiling. He allowed himself to paint the distillation of this volatile light – such as it was, floating above his head – but only on condition that he cast it out, beyond our reach. In his paintings of the Last Supper, the apostles gather in a long low room to drink Christ's blood and to eat his body. Robusti does not spare us a single detail of the ceiling. But for the background he puts a door in the wall, opening onto a luminous void. On the horizon, the sky is an airy summons – to be engulfed, to soar into it. *On the horizon*: in other words, this impossible relief (for who can boast of having reached the horizon?) provides the measure of our distance from it. All of us are born in exile. This, again, is what he attempted to depict in his *St George*. The dragon, the soldier and the princess are fighting under a leaden sky: we cannot make the mistake of confusing the supernatural light emanating from beneath it with a natural transparency. This halo comes from a plunging angel piercing through the flattened dome of clouds. Farther on, much farther on, above the horizontal line, we see Venice, a delicate bouquet of radiance, the rose of the winds. It opens up – and all the pleasures of gliding in the air seem to await us. They will continue to wait until the day of the Last Judgement: man must win or lose his trial beneath the bituminous lid of an enclosed sky.

What is the origin of this vision of Tintoretto's? The religious symbolism is plain and I grant that it implied these procedures to some extent; but I do not believe that it was powerful enough to ensure their adoption. Still less so, in as much as the macadam laid down on the celestial avenues seems to me a trifle Huguenot at the edges: those who are called are without number, but who knows if there have ever been any elected? Tintoretto's original obsession, moreover, must be remembered: relief looms overhead; depth, in general, is a tidal ebb and flow which we shall never rejoin. At a distance, weight diminishes, and can be defeated. By the same token, distances can raise man up to God – on condition that he reach them. A condition Tintoretto pitilessly refused his clients. Obsession and prejudice are the driving forces behind his composition. But they cannot explain everything. If an object or a character become heavier close up, and lighter in the distance, well and good: there is a perfect concordance with our experience of Venice. But Robusti must have been oddly made to catch handfuls of ancestral sky and then cast them into the background of his canvas, till they nearly disappear. After having swept his canvas of light, subtle spirit of his homeland, as if it were unclean, it is stranger still that he should have filled the hole it left on high with tar. Did the subject demand this sort of treatment? One could hardly believe so. Horror, after all, can be solar too. The proof is that, in the case of Carpaccio, small clouds – scattered, moreover, along the *horizon* – are merely employed as extras: the saint transfixes the Beast under an avalanche of gold. The sinister aspect of the painting lies elsewhere – in the corpses, for example, and the patient and sadistic care with which Carpaccio painted them. No; one can certainly be eviscerated in the sun. One man alone demanded that the sky should be leaden, so that the clouds form a ceiling above our heads, and that man was Tintoretto. I cannot help seeing this systematic betrayal of his City of Light as the effect of a secret bitterness, of a nameless resentment.

Did he love Venice? Passionately. He lived there, and he hoped to die there, in the midst of those he knew. He found the wide world frightening and sequestration suited him. He would not have complained of his fate, in short, had he been quite sure of not finding, up above in heaven, the city he preferred to all others down here on earth. Unfortunately this would hardly be likely. When one enjoys the conspicuous glory of belonging to the Serenissima, it is for all time – death does not count. This man of the people painted too many official Paradises not to know that each national community maintains a permanent commission by God's side: new recruits, after a brief session at the reception and sorting centre, are ushered in the direction of their reconstituted homeland. The Venetian dead, in particular, were attached officially to the celestial Serenissima, which resembled its terrestrial counterpart in every detail, save that deceased doges formed a college in Paradise, and the number of senators was multiplied by the succession of generations. Against the anarchism of the apostles, celestial Venice saved moral order by preserving its social hierarchy. It provided new arrivals with jobs equivalent to those they had left behind, and conferred the same honours they had received on earth.

For Tintoretto there were no honours – Titian had taken them all.

Tintoretto had to endure snubs, he felt disgust, he fawned on people without pleasing them, and displeasing himself. A dog's life. This was how he dreamed: if he had to keep company forever with the old man who poisoned him, and if Caliari* the forger, the usurper, was coming to join them, what could distinguish heaven from hell? Of course he would enter the wheel of souls, and revolve around the All-Powerful – but his neighbour would be Veronese, predictably managing to steal God's smiles from Tintoretto. And then, in any case, his neck would have to bear the weight of a patrician bearing the weight of a doge. In reality, the still-medieval servility of the artisan masked an uneasy liberalism whose origins lay in economic competition, and a morose egalitarianism born of his social intercourse with the bourgeoisie. He painted Elysian fields for high bureaucrats and this was repugnant to him. To die in Venice, of course, would be a fine dream. But in the end he dreamt of something finer: the angels would receive his soul and, at the end of a long oblique ascension, introduce him clandestinely into heaven via other heavens. He would live through a few centuries as a tourist, without settling down in any one place, comparing institutions and regimes; then, if he came across a homeland he liked, he would have himself naturalized discreetly before even the college of doges was notified of his arrival.

This was not what he thought? Agreed: it is what he painted. With the result that in his *St George* he figured the impossible universe of verticality in the distance, and everywhere else erased all straight lines from space, as if they were so many whalebones corsetting it. Space, without axes or tutors, collapses into a rounded huddle. It buckles. Any being or movement introduced into it – a lump, a puffiness, an inflammation – is bent by irresistible forces. The curved line became the shortest distance between two points.

Let us return to the one-way itinerary the artist prescribes: we discover a series of arcs. In the first place, the princess: it is possible to trace a semi-circle from the tip of one hand, via her hair, to the other hand. On her left, we come across a series of characteristic domes: that formed by the upper edge of the spreading corolla of her cloak; that of the corpse; that of the shadowy lines running along the belly and mane of the horse; and that of the back of the saint. I mention only the essential. Observe,

---

* Translator's note: Paolo Caliari was the original name of the painter Veronese.

moreover, on the extreme left, the beginnings of an arch – simply a tree trunk – and up above, on the screen of the sky, those pink ellipses about an angel. There can be no doubt about it: Tintoretto has taken an old tale whose events occurred within our daily physical compass and, with the tip of his brush, projected it into curved space. At a stroke, the instant dilates and overflows. On both Carpaccio's and Tintoretto's canvases our eyes are forced to follow one-way paths – but the roads have changed. In Carpaccio's painting, our gaze slides promptly and immediately to the rigidity of a lance; in Tintoretto's, it wanders through valleys, pivots round a bulge, swings between rotundities in search of an exit, envelops the hindquarters of a horse and ascends to its neck by the only acceptable route – that of the least deviation. The painting admits no difference between a short cut and the longest way round. This thickening of duration has at least one advantage: since the speed of time on the canvas is much faster then the real time of our ordinary experience, yet it is this real time that rules the behaviour of the princess and the saint, the instant evoked for us on the canvas – soft, stuffed with itself like prunes from Tours – no longer disturbs us. It is a molecule, of course, but a giant molecule, which exceeds and envelops our fitful attention. Here Baroque time was born – that heavy time which the following century would try to slow down even further, and eventually die of the attempt. In short, Robusti painted the instantaneous, but a curved instantaneity which *we* identify as a duration.

To come back to our soldier, I concede that his heroism suffers somewhat from this metamorphosis. It is not very often that curved space is apparent to inhabitants of rectilinear space. But, as we can see from this example, in every case the confrontation is scandalous. The spectator is indignant: his time is confiscated, and to what purpose? To be wasted heedlessly – to be poured away. The duel between Man and the Beast would have finished long ago if the painter had not rounded each movement, replaced all straight lines by twirls and forced his creatures to telegraph their blows, to suspend them, or delay them indefinitely.

Is this action? Is this soldier performing an act? He is killing, I agree. But a fall of rock can kill as well, by chance. What is St George doing? What can he do in this hemispherical world in which he is assigned residence? He *weighs*. But because Tintoretto has suppressed the prac-

tical axis of the lance, the knight merely weighs on the horse rather than
on the monster. This is only appearance, no doubt – but it is extremely
legible: nothing seems to me more difficult for an artist than to banish
false illusions from the illusory. In any case, the secret balance of the
painting's forms evokes a dull heaviness, and reduces the saint to his
weight. When one looks at a painting of this period, one starts, as we said,
by perceiving an Apollonian range of fantasies: we recognize the characters in the painting, the locations, the events portrayed. Knowledge is
our guide, even words – those of the title, for instance. In this way
anecdotal meaning becomes a part of the process of seeing. However, a
duller and darker world exists below: the same forms participate in its
composition, but they lose their sense in it and become part of a sub-
terranean and non-figurative order which filters through the brilliant
ceremonies of the eye and ends by conditioning our perception. From
this point of view, the killer on his mount never ceases for a moment to be
the secret dome which crowns, yet crushes, the superimposed arcades of
the painting. In other words this providential saviour, rather than pillaging
space at a gallop, is himself borne along by all the voussoirs of the canvas.
The world bends about this true soldier, hero and lounger, like a brooding
hen: hatched in a curved wasteland, he adapts himself by striking a pose
and lets a mare carry him off to the scene of the crime.

However, Tintoretto was not so foolish as systematically to deny a
saint the chance of being one of the subjects of History. He left suggestions and clues in the painting, which show virtually nothing, yet let us
decide whether an act is actually occurring or not.

The suggestions first: the saint's lance and hand have not abandoned
the canvas – their presence is masked. You will understand that your
eyes do not demand that they be visible; they can accommodate themselves to not finding any trace of them. But experience tells us that they
exist, that the saint has not had his right hand amputated, and invites us
to a casual quest for the signs of combat. At a lower level, our knowledge
and feelings come together: the former enlightens the latter, the latter
condition the former. Our blind sensibility receives the information that
the saint is not an inanimate mass, that he is a man and is leaning his
weight on the dragon more than on his mount. By the same token, the
centre of gravity shifts, and the delicate balance we thought we have

surprised turns out never to have existed; our muscular sensations demand that a new distribution of weight be established – they seek a prop. But the painter has done his job well. We accord him complete freedom of action; neither our eyes – nor our muscles – demand that the support be visible; we will be satisfied if it is visibly *signified*. Tintoretto provides every possible appeasement: we know the lance is there – we can see a snatch of it. If the honourable onlooker insists on seeing all of it, together with the hand holding it, he is welcome to turn round and back into the painting. When he has got to the other side of the combatants, in the far depths of the painting, he can contemplate the limpid mystery of the captain's right flank. What will he see there? Whatever he wishes. Since this journey through the canvas can only be accomplished in the imagination, it is the latter, in the last analysis, which will be the final arbiter in each case. Conversely, each of us will be reflected wholly in this final option. It will be a projective test, in short. Tintoretto is no more responsible for what we imagine to be on his canvas than Rorschach for what we perceive in his ink-blots. It is true: *from without and from the left side of the rider* we only know the saint by his mass. But only a curmudgeon could claim without proof that the view would be the same from within and from the right side. The paint-brush has not prejudged the issue in any way: who says that weight, approached from the opposite direction, might not appear as the best help-meet of men and saints, as their servant and mistress? Perhaps we might have the good fortune to surprise George in his true miraculous self. Suddenly he would teach us, perhaps, what we really are: unstable miracles, submitting the universe to our domination by intelligent control of the servitudes it imposes on us. Nothing should be excluded, so much is clear: not even the wild supposition that the painting is uninhabited, that all that can be discerned in it is the clash of inhuman forces, that man is a haunted mineral.

But, as the work was commissioned by a devout clientèle, the most pious conclusion will no doubt be the closest to the truth. In short, Robusti was paid to paint a sacred action; he took pains to ensure that it did not appear on the canvas – knowing that frantic bigotry and conformity would suffice to ensure that every spectator saw action where there was none. The tailor who banked on courtiers admiring on trust a fine suit of royal clothes on a naked monarch was hardly more wily: he himself knew, of course, that his Majesty was opening the ball or presiding over his Council in his birthday suit. But was Robusti, the trickster, any less cunning? If we looked at the saint from the other side, the painter's opinion is that we would see the same mass, borne along by the same momentum: neither lance nor hand could change matters in any way. 'So then', you will say, 'why wasn't he franker? He had nothing to fear: from one side or from the other, with or without a lance, the impotence of man is denounced.' Ah! Quite so. If he were to denounce this impotence, he would lose his client. He was irksome to his clientèle, without wanting to be, he knew it and was scared of that. Do you think he would want to make matters worse by a premeditated scandal? Stay out of trouble – that was his motto. If he had to paint an act that savoured of heresy, it was just as well not to paint it at all. And, rather than refuse the commission, the whole scene would be painted leaving out the act – a hierarchy of characters and events would usher us, from right to left and from foreground to background, to the left-hand side of a patently right-handed soldier. At the same time, Robusti showed his guile by choosing a powerful protector – he let his customers know that he would reproduce, point by point, the composition of the great and pious Carpaccio, and that this was the only course open to him since his predecessor's *St George* was and would remain (perhaps) unequalled. His clients congratulated him. The contrivance appeared triply guaranteed to them: it was fifty years old, it was the work of a dead man, another parish had tried it out and declared itself satisfied. Running-in expenses would be saved. As it happened, Jacopo did not lie: the new master was to draw his inspiration from the old, taking over from him the general features of his composition. What he neglected to say, however, was that he would push this composition to the limit, until it would rock and overturn. Robusti saw at a glance the weakness of Carpaccio's composition – the lance that crosses over the horse – and knew that all he had to do was correct it to obtain the result he wanted. His aim, as we now know, was to leave, in the midst of the most rigorous causal chain, a calculated indetermination – he *would not paint* the actual battle, he would depict an eclipse of the action by obscuring it with the very bodies which were supposed to be producing it. He would make a secret of the act – *the* secret of the canvas. He would exile this absence as far away as possible, to the ranks of all the other exiles, on the pallid ramparts, in the fleeing sky. He would decide nothing, but would leave the client with the task of assigning a name, an essence to the invisible event: the bewitching of a mass by a void, wink of God to His soldier, or a drama, a conflict arising from man and engendering him.

'What a fuss', you're going to say. And it's true – Robusti did make a lot of fuss, an enormous amount, like all painters, though less than writers. But I can't help that: it's all there on the canvas. You can easily verify if you like. Of course, I have had to spell out what came to him in a flash. I have taken friends to see the painting, each time I've been in London, and all of them react in the same way: what astonishes them is Tintoretto's transparent desire to paint a dazzling action by starting with a rout and then proceeding to relegate the thrust of the lance off-stage. But if we restore the painting to its time – the last years of the painter's maturity – we will understand that this was a familiar disposition of Tintoretto's. In a way, he used it everywhere, and one could say that in the *St George* he did not invent it so much as comprehend it. It recurred in his work for quite other reasons; but he understood the advantage, in this particular case, he could take from it.

4. Psychoanalysis

The four texts in this section were published as a single feature in *Les Temps Modernes*, April 1969. J-P. Pontalis (a psychoanalyst) and B. Pingaud (a literary critic) were members of the editorial board of *Les Temps Modernes* who disagreed with the journal's decision to publish the tape-recorded document in question. The footnote appended by Sartre on p. 199 refers to the subsequent resignation of Pontalis and Pingaud from *Les Temps Modernes* a year later, over an article calling for the destruction of the present system of higher education in France.

The Man with a Tape-recorder

A . . .'s text divided us deeply. Eventually we made a compromise peace which I hope will last.[1] I will set down here why I felt from the moment I saw the text that we should publish it; Pontalis and Pingaud, who were of the contrary opinion, will state the reasons for their opposition to the decision. Here then is the document, sandwiched between our articles.

A few words at the outset, to avoid a probable misunderstanding. I am not a 'false friend' of psychoanalysis, but a critical fellow-traveller, and I have neither the desire, nor the wherewithal, to ridicule it. Some people will find the dialogue below funny; it's always good to see Punch give the officer a hiding. Personally I don't find anything funny in it, neither from the point of view of the analyst, nor from that of the patient. Obviously A . . . has the upper hand, and I will say presently why I find him exceptional; but the analyst, after all, came out of the affair, if without glory (who, apart from a judoka, could have done better?) also without defeat – he did not speak. In addition, I am more than willing to admit that the interview occurs within the context of the analytic relationship itself: the dispute hinges, it would seem at first sight, on a particular interpretation, that according to A . . . Dr X has given of his patient's symptoms for many years, and then suddenly retracted (it goes without saying that we will not take sides over the issue of the interpretation nor its retraction, since the tape-recorder did not pick up the first part of the conversation). Besides, A . . . is the first to concede this: he gives the document the title 'Psychoanalytical Dialogue'. There is irony in this title – it reminds us of Merlin's remark that 'such a man thinks he is analysing someone else, whereas frequently he is analysing himself'. Dr X is supposed to have projected his own 'childhood problems' onto A . . . This is only A's side of the story, and anyway it is not the most important aspect from our point of view: if I stress it, it is only

1. It did not last (7 October 1970).

because it illustrates the *problematic* aspect of the dialogue. A . . . refers to Freud on two occasions with sincere respect: he cannot make up his mind whether it is psychoanalysis *as such* that has failed, or whether he would have been cured by a better analyst. In any case, *for us* this is not the point. If mistakes had been committed, we can quite understand that A . . ., as the victim of them, should be angry – but in our eyes an isolated case cannot call the whole of psychoanalysis into question, any more than an ecclesiastical crime could imperil the Church in the eyes of believers. Psychoanalysis is a discipline which aims towards rigour and whose goal is to cure. For that matter it is not a single discipline, but several. If objections to it are raised – objections to certain aspects of psychoanalytic practice, rather than to its principles – discussion of them should be conducted with as much rigour as is invested by practitioners in their clinical and therapeutic procedures.

Why then did I find this dialogue so fascinating? Because it spotlights, with dazzling clarity, the irruption of the *subject* into the consulting room, or rather the overthrow of the univocal relationship linking the subject to the object. And by subject here I do not mean the Self or the Ego – a quasi-object that is a product of reflexion – but the agent: in this brief encounter, A . . . is the subject in the sense in which Marx called the proletariat the subject of History. Let us be clear on this point: A . . . acknowledges that he 'needed help', and he reproaches Dr X for 'not having cured him', for having kept him in a state of dependence while 'promising' that he would one day 'authorize' him to recover his health. He speaks of Dr X's clients as 'ill' – in inverted commas – by which he means: those whom analysts *regard* as ill, but not those they have rendered such. 'You have', he says, 'made me worse.' Thus he does not present himself as a perfectly free and healthy subject (who is?) nor as one of those whom Jones calls 'adults' (a terrible word when one considers that Jones thought that Freud's wife was an adult, but not Freud), but as a damaged subject, or, if you like, as the subject of his damage, as the tormented unity of grave yet elusive problems to which he asks others to help him find the solution. Having said this, what does he attack Dr X for? Let him say why in his own words: 'One can't get better lying on that thing (pointing his finger at the psychoanalyst's couch) . . . You're scared of looking people in the face. A moment ago you told me to "face up to my fantasies". I could never have faced up to anything! You made me turn my back on you. You can't cure people like that. It would never work because . . . living with other people means knowing how to look them in the face.' Is he challenging the method, the couch, the studied mutism of the great professional listeners? Yes and no: for several years he has poured himself out, exposed himself, well aware that his apparently random and free-spoken remarks corresponded to a dark and hidden text that he had to construe rather than discover – a text contained in the spoken word in the sense in which, as Eluard said, 'There is another world, and it is inside this one.' But in the arresting juxtaposition: 'face up to . . . turn my back', he reveals his deepest experience. By his presence alone, the invisible and silent witness of the discourse of the patient (by which we should understand: what he says and what is said through the indispensable mediation of a subject) transforms his speech, even as it is uttered, into an object. Why? For the simple reason that there could never be any reciprocity between these two figures, the one lying on the couch, his back to another sitting down, invisible and intangible. I am well aware that the 'patient' has to emancipate himself; his task is one of gradual *self*-discovery. The trouble, A . . . tells us, is that it is understood *at the outset* that he will embark on this voyage of discovery *passively*, through a gaze that he cannot see and that judges him. The man with the tape-recorder is convinced that the road to independence (facing up to one's fantasies, and to other people) cannot pass via a situation of absolute dependence (transference and frustration; an at least tacit promise – I will cure you; waiting for 'authorization'). He is disappointed, it is true; he takes it out on his doctor and some will say that he thus merely demonstrates an incomplete transference, gone awry. But how are we to answer him when he tells us that a 'patient's' cure has to begin with a face-to-face encounter and should subsequently develop into a joint undertaking in which each person takes his chances and assumes his responsibilities? He has been castrated? So be it. He certainly wants to be told this unpleasant fact, but by someone looking him in the face. The interpretation should be proposed to *him* in the course of a long common adventure, in *interiority*, and not 'come' to him anonymously, like stone tablets. This particular subject hopes to gain some comprehension of himself as a damaged, derailed subject. For lack of any inter-subjective collaboration, he 'acts it out' – as the analysts say – which means he turns praxis, and the situation, upside-down. In the 'Psycho-analytical Dialogue', the roles are reversed, and the analyst become the object. For the second time, a rendezvous of man with man is missed. This episode, which some people will find funny, represents a tragedy of impossible reciprocity.

'Violence has occurred' says Dr X – and it certainly had. But was it not more a sort of counter-violence? A . . . poses the question admirably: is not the 'interminable psychoanalytical relationship'; the dependence; the anticipated and induced transference; the feudal bond; the long confinement of a man lying prostrate on a couch, reduced to the bab-blings of childhood, utterly drained – is not all this original violence? I know what Dr X would reply (or what he would have replied had the tape-recorder not been there): 'We never use coercion; everyone comes and goes as he pleases; when a patient wishes to leave us, we may try to dissuade him for his own good, but if he insists, we don't stand in his way; the proof is that three years ago I regretfully let you go.' This is quite true and in my view, the analysts themselves are not in question. But A . . . would refuse to be quelled. He tells us: if the men are set aside, and the situation itself is considered on its own, then the weekly or bi-weekly abdication of responsibility of the analysand to the analyst becomes an increasingly imperious need. For the condition of an object has certain advantages – violence becomes at least latent and insinuating, and then to be a subject is so exhausting. On the couch, everything solicits one to substitute the agonizing responsibility of being an individual, for aban-donment to the incorporated company of basic drives.

This inversion of praxis is a clear demonstration that the psychoanaly-tical relationship is, *by its very nature*, a violent one, whatever may be the particular doctor-patient duo we have in mind. In fact, when violence turns the situation upside down, the analyst becomes at once analysand, or rather analysable: the use of force against his helplessness places him artificially in the situation of a neurotic. A . . . certainly counted on this: he had been pondering his course of action for three years. Listen to him: 'Until this moment you were accustomed to total control over the situa-tion, and then suddenly a new element is introduced, and upsets things . . .', and the analyst's reply shows that he has been abruptly transformed into a patient. His discourse, at this stage, now in turn needs to be deciphered: 'I'm not used to physical violence.' What a strange turn of phrase – why didn't he say '. . . to violence'? Is he used to *moral* violence then? And why does he treat the act of 'pulling out a tape-recorder' as an example of physical violence? Far be it from me to make an issue out of a few words uttered in a moment of quite understandable stress: all I hope to do is show that when violence breaks into a discourse, each word becomes an over-signifier that either means too much or too little. The abrupt transformation of Dr X – the subject of the analysis, the agent of the therapy – into an object precipitates a crisis of identity in him: how is he to *recognize himself*? This is what lies behind the uncanniness (or 'estrangement' as Lacan would say, translating the Freudian term *Unheimlichkeit*) that he suddenly feels, and his desperate resistance to A. . .; he absolutely refuses to speak in front of the tape-recorder. The reason for this must be sought in the first instance in his professional de-ontology. But is this enough? Does it adequately account for his feeling of horror when confronted with the tape-recorder? Was he not in fact making the discovery, like the object of an analysis, that his words, which he guarded so jealously and which floated away so lightly in the silence of his office (a 'patient' is not a witness), were about to be registered and preserved for ever more? They had been nothing but the gay murmur of his sovereign thought, and now they threatened to become the petrification of it. Once inert, they would testify against him. A tape-recorder can enrage even the mildest person because it evokes the warning of English justice to the accused: 'from this moment, everything you say may be taken down and used in evidence against you'.

Dr X makes one last effort to intimidate A. . ., to treat him like an object in order to recall him to his dependence: 'You're dangerous because you don't have a grasp on reality.' But all he gets for his trouble is the inspired response: 'What is this "reality"?' Yes, what is reality when analyst and patient are face to face; when, with the aid of violence, the analyst can no longer decide what is real in solitary sovereignty, in other words can no longer privilege a certain conception of the world? What is reality when henceforth the patient refuses to speak? Or when in the course of a farcical exchange of mutual antagonism, each man psychoanalyses the other, or rather when the two of them apply the same schema to each other: 'You're imitating your father.' 'No I'm not, you're imitating yours.' 'You're acting the child.' 'No, you are.' What is reality then, when the language of psychoanalysis, reduplicated, echoic, seems to have gone mad?

Such a 'limiting situation' (I should add that other analysts have found themselves in similar situations, and that is one of the risks of their profession) allows us to pose the real question: must we choose between the *subject-being* of the 'patient' and psychoanalysis? Consider the man with the tape-recorder. Consider how he has turned the whole problem over in his mind for three years (whether he erred in his conclusions or not is of little importance); consider how his plan matured; how he decided on his attack; how he implemented it. Listen to him speaking; hear the irony and anguish in his voice ('I'd have to have a nerve to let myself in for such a thing . . .') and listen to the confidence in his voice as he juggles with concepts that for so long were applied to him. I ask you: at this moment, *who* is he? Who is this man A . . . speaking? Is he no more than a blind psychological process, or is he the transcendence of this process by an act? I have no doubt that his every word and action could be given a psychoanalytical interpretation – provided he were reduced once more to his status as the object of analysis. What would vanish along with the subject, is the inimitable and singular quality of the scene – its synthetic organization, in other words the action as such. And let no one tell me it's a 'patient' who is organizing it: I agree, I agree that he is organizing it like a *patient*. But he *is organizing* it, all the same. Psychoanalysis can explain the motivation behind someone who 'acts out' his drama, but the acting itself, which interiorises, surpasses and preserves the morbid motivations within the unity of a tactic, the act which gives a meaning to the meaning conferred on us – hitherto psychoanalysts have not bothered to take account of this. Why not? Because it would mean reintroducing the notion of the subject. A. . ., the indisputable subject of this episode, might find valid interlocutors in England or in Italy:* a new generation of psychiatrists are seeking to establish a bond of reciprocity between themselves and those they are treating. Without abandoning anything of the immense gains of psychoanalytic knowledge,

*Translator's note: A reference to the work of Ronald Laing and others in London, and of Franco Basaglia and his colleages in Gorizia.

they respect above all, in each patient, their mislaid freedom to act – as subjects and as agents.[2] I do not see why conventional psychoanalysis should not join them one day. In the meantime, I offer this 'Dialogue' as a beneficent and benign scandal.

2. I am not unaware of the difficulties they face; 'depth psychology', as Lagache notes, presupposes a general loosening or self-abandon on the part of the patient, and thus makes the couch mandatory. Face-to-face encounters, on the contrary, demand vigilance, sovereignty, and a certain tension. But no progress will be made unless both approaches are grasped together.

Psychoanalytic Dialogue

A: I want something to come to a definite conclusion. Up till now I've followed all your orders; now you should try to . . . Anyway, I don't see why . . .

Dr X: Now if you please . . . we are agreed; there, we'll stop here. You'll regret this.

A: Are you frightened of this tape-recorder then?

Dr X: I don't want it near me. I'm not going along with this.

A: But why not? At least explain to me why not. Are you afraid of the tape-recorder?

Dr X: Cut it out!

A: You're cutting me off? Now this is interesting; you're bringing up the question of 'cutting' again. A moment ago you were talking about my penis being cut off – and now you're the one who's doing the cutting.

Dr X: Listen! I've had enough of this tape-recorder!

A: How do you mean?

Dr X: Either you take it out of the room, or the interview is over. Agreed? I would certainly like to explain to you what I was going to explain – but as things stand, either you take this tape-recorder outside, or I'll refuse to say another word. I'm sorry but that's how it is.

A: I think you're frightened! I think you're frightened and that's silly because what I've just done is in your interests; without making a fuss about it I'm taking a big risk and I'm doing it for you and for lots of other people. But I want to get to the bottom of this whole mystification and I intend to go on.

Dr X: Fine, well then . . .

A: No! Stay where you are, Doctor! You're going to stay there and you're not going to pick up that phone; you're going to stay where you are and above all don't start threatening me with the strait-jacket.

Dr X: I won't threaten you so long as you leave this room.

A: I will not leave this room! I'm calling you to account. I mean it – you'd better be able to account for yourself. And I'm not doing so purely on my own behalf, but on behalf of . . . Come on now – sit down; don't let's get angry. You'll see . . . you won't be hurt. I'm not out to get you. Come on, calm down. Sit down . . . you don't want to? Very well then, let's stay standing. Right then, let's get back to my 'penis being cut off' – wasn't that the expression? My father wanted to cut off my . . . Wasn't that it?

Dr X: Listen! At the moment you're not in a state for a discussion.

A: Of course I am! You're the one who doesn't want to talk. You're the one who's not in a state for discussion.

Dr X: I've asked you to put away your tape-recorder.

A: But my tape-recorder isn't a tail, you know. It's a listening device that keeps a benevolent check on us.

Dr X: I was trying to explain something to you . . .

A: Right. Carry on.

Dr X: And then suddenly, instead of trying to understand . . .

A: Because you were about to drop a capital remark, the sort of thing you've been stuffing my head with for years, and I don't want you now to try and get out of it by dodging the issue – or I should say, by avoiding your responsibility for the hundredth time.

Dr X: *Your* responsibility, you mean.

A: What?

Dr X: At the moment, you want to make me responsible for things that are your own responsibility.

A: Not at all! I'm making a study at the moment, a scientific study.

Dr X: Perhaps you are . . .

A: Good, then let's continue. No doubt you know that things run far more efficiently when you use a tape-recorder for these studies. You're freer; you don't have to take notes. We're getting somewhere.

Dr X: This is not the place to carry out scientific studies!

A: But it is! I thought I was the guest of a man of science. Anyway I've entrusted myself to the care of a man of science, and now I'd like to know just what the science it is he practises, for I have my doubts about this 'science' – it may be nothing but charlatanism.

Dr X: Well, I have the right to refuse to talk in front of a tape-recorder.

A: Of course you have the right, and you're not backward in exercising it; many thanks . . . You feel you're being accused; you're talking like an American who won't make a statement unless he has his lawyer with him . . . Sit down!

Dr X: I'm ready to talk to you and explain things to you.

A: Fine, let's carry on then!

Dr X: But I'm not ready to talk in front of a tape-recorder.

A: But why were you just about to telephone?

Dr X: Because I had told you that if you insisted on using a tape-recorder you had to get out.

A: But why? Why were you going to telephone?

Dr X: Because I had told you that if you insisted on using a tape-recorder you would have to get out; I didn't want to have you put away, but . . .

A: But why did you . . . You can't have me put away, you know! If anyone deserves to be put away, it's you – that's if we're trying to find out who's unbalanced.

Dr X: I . . . I . . . This really is . . .

A: Listen, I've got nothing against you. I don't want to harm you; on the contrary . . .

Dr X: Right then, we're agreed. Turn off your tape-recorder.

A: This is fun, isn't it; except that I wish you'd stop being frightened . . .

Dr X: I don't think it's fun.

A: But you're frightened. And your libido, what are you doing about that? Do you think I want to cut off your little willie? Of course I don't! I'm here to give you a real . . . But it's fantastic! You've had this little occasion coming to you for a long time. Listen, admit that you're getting out of it very nicely. Doctor!!! Doctor, I've got nothing against you, but you obviously have . . . you've got something against yourself.

Dr X: At this moment you're . . .

A: I've got nothing against you, but . . . I feel you abuse your position. Yes, that's it, You have abused me. I would even go so far as to say that you've defrauded me, if we're going to use legal jargon: you haven't met your obligations. You don't know how to cure people – you only know how to make them worse. That's a fact – all we need do is ask your other patients, your 'patients', or people you call your patients, people who come to you for help and get nothing, who get nothing but one long wait . . . Come on, sit down! Let's be reasonable. Let's be reasonable! There. Are you a man or a mouse? Are you a man?

Dr X: For the last time, you've got a tape-recorder there and I won't put up with it.

A: I'm sorry. I have to repeat that I pulled this tape-recorder out – to use your words – because I didn't like the way you suddenly demanded that we drop the question of castration.

Dr X: Well I'd certainly be willing to discuss the question of castration, if that is in fact your real problem, but I won't say anything in front of a tape-recorder.

A: Fine, well we won't talk about it; we'll wait until you change your mind. You're trapped.

Dr X: What do you hope to get out of trapping me?

A: I've got nothing to lose!

Dr X: Maybe.

A: You're frightened! Come on now, Johnny. Buck up, eh? You don't want to?

Dr X: You don't regard this as a serious situation?

A: It's terribly serious. That's why it would be much better if you'd put a different face on it than the one you are . . . I'd have to have a nerve to let myself in for such a thing! Yet even so I need to be absolutely sure . . .

Dr X: No, you don't have to be sure. If you were sure you wouldn't be acting like that! Now let me go; this is a highly dangerous situation.

A: Dangerous?

Dr X: Yes, you're dangerous.

A: I'm not dangerous at all; you're only saying that. You never stop trying to make me believe I'm dangerous, but I'm not in the least bit dangerous.

Dr X: You're dangerous because you don't have a grasp on reality.

A: That's not true.

Dr X: You don't have a grasp on reality!

A: I'm a little lamb. I've always been as gentle as a lamb.

Dr X: You don't have a grasp on reality!

A: You're the one who's dangerous. It's he who says it who is it!

Dr X: You don't have a grasp on reality!

A: What is this 'reality'?

Dr X: At the moment you're dangerous because you don't have a grasp on reality.

A: But what is 'reality'? We have to agree on our definitions first. I know one thing, from the point of view of your reality, and that is that you're very angry, you're having difficulty controlling yourself – you're going to explode any minute. You're going to snap; you're under pressure; you're getting yourself into a state and that helps no one. I've got nothing against you; you've got no reason to be angry. I'm not your father!

Dr X: You've got your tape-recorder there!

A: So?

Dr X: Switch it off!

A: Come on, it's not so bad as all that. Does it frighten you? It's not a gun.

Dr X: Switch it off!

A: Are you frightened?

Dr X: Switch it off!

A: What do you mean – switch it off?

Dr X: I don't like this sort of interview.

A: Now listen, do you want a spanking?

Dr X: There, you see, you're dangerous!

A: Do you want a spanking?

Dr X: You see, you're dangerous.

A: No, I'm not, I'm simply asking you this question: would you mind stop acting like a child?

Dr X: I tell you you're dangerous.

A: And I'm telling you you're acting like a child.

Dr X: And you're going to show me what for, I can see.

A: No, I'm not going not to show you what for.

Dr X: Switch it off!

A: But what do you mean – 'Switch it off!'?

Dr X: I've got nothing more to say to you: you're dangerous.

A: What do you mean, you've got nothing more to say? You've got to square accounts with me.

Dr X: I've asked you to go.

A: I'm sorry! I've no intention of going!

Dr X: See how dangerous you are!

A: You've got to square accounts with me!

Dr X: See how dangerous you are!

A: I'm not dangerous. All I'm doing is raise my voice, and you can't take it. If someone starts shouting, you get frightened, don't you? When you hear shouting you lose your cool. You're terrified – it's your daddy shouting at you (*the two men are now standing within inches of each other*), but all I'm doing here, Johnny, is shouting to show you that it's not serious this time. Now, you see, you've got over your fear already. There! You've overcome your fear. That's better, isn't it? You're all right now. That's better. You see, it's not all that serious: I'm not your father. And I could shout some more, but I won't. There, that's enough.

Dr X: Are you mimicking your father at the moment?

A: No, come on, I'm mimicking yours! The one I can see in your eyes.

Dr X: You're trying to play the part of . . .

A: I don't want to play any part with you; all I want is to be free of the pain you put me through! Now it's you who's shitting in your pants! Of course. Look at you – what are you folding your arms like that for? You're protecting yourself. Do you really think I want to hit you? Where did you get that idea from? I'm far too reasonable for that! I've got myself under control; I don't want to do what you'd like me to do. Things would be much simpler then, wouldn't they? I'd hit you; I'd be in the wrong; I'd have started it; I'd have done something which would give you the power to . . . who knows? . . . to play the doctor, yes, to play the psychiatrist.

If I'm threatening anyone, it's not little Johnny, but the sadistic doctor . . . Not little Johnny. He's suffered enough already. I have no wish to hit him – but the doctor, the psychiatrist, the one who took the place of my father, he deserves a good kick in the pants. Now let me explain. Sit down. No? You don't want to?

Dr X: You can speak. I won't. I've told you that I . . .

A: All right then, I'll speak. So, there you are! I wanted to say this the moment I pulled out the tape-recorder – I only pulled it out to speak, because I had something to say. Obviously you can be recorded too, if you like – I'll send you a transcription. You should find it very interesting.

Well I hope you will, anyway . . . Well, here we go! You can't get better lying on that thing! (*pointing his finger at the psychoanalyst's couch*); it's impossible! You can't get better yourself, because you've spent too many years on it. You're scared of looking people in the face. A moment ago you started to tell me how I had to 'face up to my fantasies'. I could never have faced up to anything! You made me turn my back on you. You can't cure people like that. It would never work, because in fact living with other people means knowing how to look them in the face. What did you think I'd learn on that couch? The way things are, you've robbed me even of my wish to live with others or to face up to anything, and that's your problem! That's why you make people lie down like that! Because you can't look them in the face. You can't cure them; all you can do is palm off on them your own father-figure problems, the ones you've never been able to come to terms with. From one session to another you drag your victims along like this with your father-problem, don't you? Do you see what I'm trying to say? And I've had a terrible time trying to understand this and get out of it. You've certainly made me perform some mental gymnastics. A few at any rate – and you have to agree, it cost me quite a lot, if that's all it was! But there is worse: you've robbed me of my ability to face up to things by promising me . . . I put myself in your hands, but because I couldn't see you I had no idea when you were finally going to give me what I had come to you to get. I was waiting for your authorization. That's what I was doing! You would have been stupid to give it to me, wouldn't you, to get me out of it, since I was keeping you; you lived off me, you sucked me dry – I was the patient, and you were the doctor, and in the end you'd turned your own childhood problem over to me – I was the child and you were the father . . . You had all the rights, didn't you? You had the right to have me put away at some time, well not perhaps me, but other people anyway . . .

Dr X: I was dialling 999 to have you taken out of here – 999, the police, to get rid of you.

A: The police? Daddy? So that's it! Your daddy was a policeman. And you were ringing daddy to come and get me.

Dr X: Because in my opinion . . .

A: But listen, this is interesting. Why did you want to ring for the police? You would have missed all this. You have to admit . . .

Dr X: You're a qualified lawyer . . .

A: . . . that I was right to stop you.

Dr X: When someone refuses to leave your home you call the police.

A: You're right. That's a fact. You brought me here, you drew me into your little sanctum, your little cave . . .

Dr X: I asked you to go.

A: Listen! If you take the floor to say things like that, then you might as well let me go on because if you don't we're going to get fed up, we're going to waste time, agreed?

If you've really got something important to say, you should say it, all right? Of course you should come out with it. It's a fact - you're a mass of inhibitions. But if all you can say is you're calling the police or you wanted to call them, then that's something we really should analyse.

All right then, is that better? (*speaking in a very calm and gentle voice*) All right now?

Dr X: No (*he gets up*), you're going to go and listen to that tape-recorder you've got.

A: No, no, no, no, that's not the important thing now. Just look at how you reacted – what a fuss! You've got yourself all worked up just because I pull out a little machine that allows us to understand what's going on here. It doesn't make sense. Besides you haven't really explained *why* you don't want to be recorded. Wouldn't you like to tell me why you're so angry? I'll tell you why – because suddenly there I was, in control of something! That's why. Up to now you were accustomed to having total control over the situation, and then suddenly a new element is introduced, and upsets things.

Dr X: I'm not used to physical violence.

A: What do you mean – 'physical violence'?

Dr X: Pulling out that tape-recorder was a violent act.

A: An act of physical violence? (*Utter astonishment*)

Dr X: Besides, you're perfectly well aware it was – all you have to do is look where my telephone is to see there has been physical violence. (*The telephone ended up on the floor after the previous episode: 'You're not going to pick up that phone . . .'*)

A: Now listen, are you serious? Did you enjoy saying what you just said? Are you happy now? I want to be sure you're all right. Are you

feeling OK? Everything working? Ooh, ooh . . . (*using baby language*)
Doctor! (*speaking very softly and gently*) Coo-coo . . . Come on, you've
got to say something; don't you want to tell me? Well! Just look at this
situation. It's ridiculous! Let's try to rise to the occasion, will we?

Dr X: Look – all this you've just been saying – what you were just
explaining to me . . .

A: Yes? What?

Dr X: You would do well to listen to it over again.

A: Of course – and you as well – to listen to your silence . . . You're
the one who's repressed, since you can't speak. I pull out a tape-recorder
and all of a sudden you cut off! That was the image you used – you said:
'Cut it out.' Well you've cut out your own game, haven't you, the way a
murderer cuts out when he gives himself up. I'm not cutting out; on the
contrary, I want to carry on, I want us to get closer to the truth . . .

Dr X: Your time is up; you'll have to go.

A: No, time doesn't exist!

Dr X: Yes it does!

A: No it doesn't . . . We'll have a good time from now on, believe me.

Dr X: You have now explained something – well, all you have to do
is draw the right conclusions from it. But you have explained something. . . .

A: Yes?

Dr X: . . . that you should have understood a long time ago.

A: What?

Dr X: Your attitude.

A: What do you mean, my attitude?

Dr X: Your attitude, what you've just explained . . .

A: My attitude? What about yours – (*buzz at the door*) you think you
can just cut me off.

Dr X: What you have just explained is your attitude. Did you hear
that? Someone else is waiting to see me.

A: What do I care? The next victim's in no hurry.

Dr X: Well I do care.

A: (*speaking stiffly and authoritatively*): We will not leave this room
until matters have been cleared up concerning what has taken place and
the problem of your responsibilities and your failure to meet them.

Don't talk to me of physical violence; it was *you* who began the physical violence by forcing me to lie down on that couch; it was you who twisted me, who turned my head upside down. It was you who distorted things, don't you realize that? Don't you realize that all of a sudden you look ridiculous? There's something beyond this moment here now! There's something shameful about your present, infantile behaviour!

Dr X: You see how dangerous you are; I told you that you were dangerous.

A: Doctor X, you're a clown! . . . and an ominous clown at that! You're dodging the issue . . . I've come two or three times a week to you for I don't know how many years, and what have you given me? If I'm mad and dangerous as you say I am at the moment, all you're doing is reaping what you've sown, what you've invested with your erroneous theory. Take note of that. And after all, this little scare should do you a lot of good – all I'm asking you to do is think a bit about what you're doing: it's sort of a little assignment I'm setting you – it's not all that serious! It's not going to hurt you! Come on, what about a smile? Don't look so sullen. It's a very important thing, you know, to be concerned with curing people, to be a doctor; and psychoanalysis is very important – people are always writing books about it; it's worth thinking about, it's worth talking frankly to each other and trying to understand just what has gone on between us, because maybe we can learn something and pass it on to others. I'm not dangerous, so don't keep saying I am – all you're trying to do is get us off the subject. You've profited from a ready-made situation, you're very privileged: you came after Freud, you were put through a course, and you ended up with a little brass nameplate on your door. And now you give yourself the right to muck about with people's lives, and you hope to get out of it like that. You're a failure; you'll never do anything with your life but burden other people with your own problems . . .

Well, it's all over now, you understand! No more! You should be very pleased with what I've just made you put up with, because in fact it was nothing, nothing at all.

Dr X: It was: you're making me put up with your presence.

A: I'm not making you put up with my presence . . . I'd like you to stay sitting down.

Dr X: Physical violence!

A: Don't be silly. (*In a paternal and reassuring voice.*)

Dr X: Physical violence!

A: Don't be silly, it's theatre.

Dr X: You're inflicting physical violence on me!

A: Not at all, I'm not inflicting any physical violence on you.

Dr X: I gave you the opportunity to explain yourself.

A: Well now I'd like to hear you explain yourself.

Dr X: I gave you the opportunity to explain yourself, and I suggested that . . .

A: Rubbish, you cut me off; you interrupted the explanation I wanted to give you to begin with.

Dr X: Only in so far as I did not wish to speak in front of a tape-recorder.

A: But to begin with, I didn't ask you to speak, I just asked you to let me speak.

Dr X: No, you asked me to speak.

A: You interrupted me, that's what happened; you suddenly mentioned the police.

Dr X: The interview is now over.

A: No kidding? Rats! I say it isn't. Well? Who's going to take the first step towards physical violence?

Dr X: You're the one who's moving in that direction.

A: Not at all, I'm fine here; I'm like a southern senator who won't leave his seat.

Dr X: You're very dangerous, yes, you're really extremely . . .

(*The doctor goes across to his window; the office is on a first floor; loud noise of shutters opening.*)

A: Are you going to jump out the window? How amazing! Are you really going to? (*Clatter of shutters again as A . . . closes them, laughing.*) You see, this really is theatre.

Dr X: This is going to get nasty.

A: It's going to get theatrical! A blood-curdling drama. There will be blood!

Dr X: Right, there will be blood.

A: Whose blood?

Dr X: There will be blood.

A: No there won't be, it won't turn out like that. It's going to end very nicely. We're having a great time.

Dr X: This is going to end with violence.

A: No it's not.

Dr X: Let me open the door and go . . .

A: Are you frightened? Are you back at the beginning? Hooh!

Dr X: See, you're dangerous!

A: No, I need to relax.

Dr X: Strange way you have of relaxing; you're frightened.

A: You want to frighten me.

Dr X: You're dangerous because you're frightened.

A: Dangerous? What do you mean, dangerous?

Dr X: You're being a physical nuisance by staying here.

A: Is that how I'm being dangerous?

Dr X: That's right.

A: And what about moral torture! What do you make of that?

Dr X: You're acting in a physical manner.

A: Listen, when slaves revolt, there's obviously a little blood spilt, and yet you can see that no one here is bleeding yet.

Dr X: You're acting in a physical manner.

(*It should be pointed out that A. . . is occupying a strategic position, leaning against the only door in the room.*)

A: You're shitting in your pants.

Dr X: Would you like me to?

A: Not at all, but I can see you are.

Dr X: You think you've got the upper hand . . . you think you're dropping me in it.

A: I'm not dropping you in it; I've got no intention of dropping you in it. All I want is for you to start talking seriously.

Dr X: Well I am talking seriously: your time is up.

A: What?

Dr X: It's time; I have other people to see.

A: It's time? How? It's the time of reckoning! It certainly is – the time has come.

Dr X: I'm very sorry.

A: What do you mean, you're very sorry? Excuse me, but I'm the one who's very sorry, you don't seem to realize that. You've sent me round the bend, you've driven me crazy for years! Years! And you want to leave it there?

Dr X: Help! . . . help!!

(*The doctor goes on to shout another dozen times, more and more loudly, and in a voice that sounds more and more high pitched.*)

Murderer! Help! HELP! HELP! HELP!

A: Shut up and sit down.

Dr X: Help! Help!

A: Shut up, or I'll have to gag you.

Dr X: He-e-e-elp! (*Long wailing sound.*)

A: You silly fool! You poor idiot! Sit down!

Dr X: He-e-elp! (*Very feeble murmuring.*)

A: What are you frightened of?

Dr X: He-e-elp! (*Wailing again.*) You see, you are dangerous.

A: But I'm not dangerous.

Dr X: He-e-elp!

A: Are you frightened I'll cut off your little willie?

Dr X: He-e-e-e-elp! (*This is the finest cry of all.*)

A: This will be a hilarious tape.

Dr X: It will be hilarious? Help! Help! Help!

(*This time he utters a final dismal sound like a dying animal – followed by a long silence.*)

A: Come on, my good man, put on your glasses.

Dr X: They're broken. (*This is not true.*) (*A new pause.*)

A: Well, I certainly didn't expect this; I didn't think you'd behave like that, I really didn't. What a child you are! It was you who started the whole scene. Sit down. And you a man of science! That's really something; Freud would be delighted. He never got himself into a situation like this, like a madman raving on.

Dr X: I think we'd better leave it there. People outside have heard us, and I think perhaps it would be better if you left.

A: For my part, I'd be delighted if you took this to the very end.

Dr X: You're running the risk of being put away, but there's nothing I can do about that.

A: Very nice; delighted I'm sure. I'm willing to stay here, to see if you'll really go that far. We're writing a fine chapter in the history of psychoanalysis right now.

Dr X: What else do you want me to say?

A: Well then, let's sit down and wait for the police; let's wait for your daddy to come. Go on, sit down, relax. You're terribly worked up, Dr Jekyll . . . Eh? Mr Hyde is never far away, eh? . . . and to think that I meant you no harm . . . (*pause*) I'm not dangerous, I'm very kind.

Dr X: Yes, you certainly are.

A: No, no . . . we're going to make the psychoanalysts stand trial now, and we're going to have a look at what goes on, at what they do in their consulting rooms, and we'll see where they're at with their clients, yes we'll see . . . And I think we're going to make a very interesting discovery and find out just who's got his head screwed on back to front. What, do you want to go? You want to run off? Coward!

(*The doctor can be heard in the background, talking to his wife: 'Lulu, please, dial 999!'*)

A: (*mimicking the doctor's voice and expression*): For God's sake, hurry . . . Right, we're off . . .

You have nothing more to say Doctor – before we part?

Dr X: Next time . . .

A: Yes?

Dr X: Today I'll say no more; I would like to speak with you, but only in front of people who are capable of restraining you.

A: Very good!

Dr X: But I'm ready to explain myself to you, without a tape-recorder, and in front of people who can restrain you.

A: Very good! You have nothing more to say? We're finished then? This is where you cut me off? The session's over?

Dr X: Yes!

A: Very good, the session's over then. That's the first one; until the next one then. Good-bye, Doctor.

I hope it will be understood that I do not wish to comment on the 'document' that Sartre has taken the responsibility for publishing: all I wish to do is add a word to the presentation.

What interests me is the fact that Sartre tells us he was 'fascinated' by the record of A. . .'s exploit in challenging his feudal oppressor face to face. Sartre evidently recognizes himself in this mirror, even if the reflection is distorted. He projects into it the antagonistic couples of which he is so fond, rediscovering them all the more easily in that A. . . seems to obey his schemas.

But to conclude from this tragic-comic fragment that the time has come for all those undergoing analysis to follow the command daubed at Censier:* 'Analysed of the earth, arise' (unless they should emigrate to Italy) and for all psychoanalysts to announce the good news 'You have been castrated' to their patients, looking them straight in the eye, subject to subject – would seem to me to jump to rather hasty conclusions. Further, I feel that to reach such conclusions is to reveal a fundamental misunderstanding of the *whole* of psychoanalysis. How, for example, can one salute its 'immense gains in knowledge' and at the same time reject the very *principle* of the psychoanalytic relationship? Is it not praxis, here as elsewhere, that makes the appearance of the theoretical object possible? One day the history of Sartre's thirty-year-long relationship with psychoanalysis, an ambiguous mixture of *equally* deep attraction and repulsion, will have to be written and perhaps his work reinterpreted in the light of it.

As for the virtues of dialogue, I have never seen them celebrated before by Sartre – fortunately! Otherwise he could never have given such powerful witness to the failure of reciprocity, nor been able to confer on what he has called 'limiting situations' (madness, amongst others) their exemplary value. We might recall *Huis Clos* or *La Chambre*, and above all, in this regard, the hero of *Les Séquestrés d'Altona* – that admirable play in which in another theatre, a tape-recorder was already used to register the course of an 'inner dialogue'.

*Translator's note: A reference to one of the slogans inscribed in the University of Paris during the May Revolt of 1968.

REPLY TO SARTRE   [BERNARD PINGAUD]

As I am neither a psychoanalyst nor a psychoanalyst's patient, I do not
feel I need be so restrained in my remarks as Pontalis. I will thus try to
explain why this text 'divided us deeply'. Anyone who just reads Sartre's
prologue might wonder at this. But if he reads A. . .'s text concurrently,
he will soon see the gulf between the two of them. It is obvious – at least
to myself, speaking in my full freedom as a 'subject' – that what Sartre
sees in this dialogue that has been partially transcribed by A. . . is simply
not there, or is there only in the vaguest outline. It is equally obvious
that Sartre is blind, or pretends to be blind, to what *is* there. For this
certainly is an interview that takes place 'in the framework of the psychoanalytic relationship' – and one moreover that we have to judge only
from its ending, since 'the tape-recorder did not pick up the beginning
of the conversation'. There is no need to be very expert in psychoanalysis
to understand that this 'acting out' is part of the very cure it is supposed
to be challenging so radically, and that in publishing it like this we are
making an irresponsible intervention in a 'patient-doctor' relationship
about which we know nothing, or next to nothing. Thus the first question
we had to ask ourselves was: what is the purpose of publishing this
interview – whom will it help ? I cannot say that the answer to this question
is in any way clear.

Now let us look at the background. Sartre has nothing against psychoanalysis. So be it. But what is he doing, after having made a show of his
good intentions, if not denouncing both the practice of psychoanalysis
and the theory on which it is based ? To insist that the psychoanalyst's
refusal to engage in a face to face encounter with his patient amounts to
transforming the latter into an object, is too gross and hoary an argument. Sartre himself gives the answer to it, when he says: 'I am well
aware that the "patient" has to emancipate himself; his task is one of
gradual *self-discovery*.' But let us see what comes afterwards: 'The
trouble, A. . . tells us, is that it is understood *at the outset* that we will
embark on this voyage of discovery *passively*, through a gaze that he
cannot see and that judges him . . .' I like this 'A. . . tells us' and wonder
if it should be understood in the sense: 'Sartre tells us.' For we have two
options here, which exclude each other. Either Sartre adopts this thesis

as his own, and it is a different psychoanalysis he is offering us, one which is based on a different conception of man, and employs different therapeutic methods – those, for example, of the Italian and English psychiatrists who 'are seeking to establish a bond of reciprocity between themselves and those they are treating'. But we would still have to know whether the two situations are comparable, and why psychoanalysts, apparently, reject this 'reciprocity'. Or alternatively Sartre leaves A. . . with the responsibility for his interpretation, and the problem then is to ascertain the meaning of such an interpretation within an analysis, why it arises – whether it was because the therapeutic treatment was wrong, or badly handled – or whether a reversal of the analytic relationship is not *always* a part, at some stage or other, of the cure itself. I am speaking as an outsider here, and will refrain from any summary conclusions. But when I read Sartre's text, and see the way in which he uses phrases like 'weekly or bi-weekly abdication' to suggest an assimilation of psychoanalysis to narcotics – I cannot help thinking that it is the whole of psychoanalysis that he is calling into question, in the name of his personal conception of the subject.

It is quite normal, besides, that debate should focus on this question, since Freud's essential discovery was not, as some have over-hastily claimed, to deny the existence of the subject, but to displace it, to 'decentre' it by demonstrating the *non-subject* on the basis of which it is constituted and from which it always derives. The question is then simply this: is the interview transcribed by A. . . a suitable text with which to launch such a debate?

I should say not. Even if we were to assume that one can elicit the lesson from the dialogue that is drawn by Sartre (i.e. assume we were really dealing with a challenge to psychoanalysis as such, rather than to a particular analyst), it would still be a misleading over-simplification to decree that, in the therapeutic situation, the patient is reduced to total passivity and the analyst 'can decide what is real in solitary sovereignty'. For it would not be difficult to assemble many witnesses to the contrary, who could testify that it was precisely an initial alienation that helped them to become freer subjects. It seems to me that the non-reciprocity criticized by Sartre (and which the analyst has himself experienced in his own time) is the very condition of the discovery or restoration of a 'subject-being', that has been compromised, obscured, 'alienated', by what is known as the 'malady'. The psychoanalytic relationship can never be equal, or reciprocal, except at the point where it is terminated – the ideal point that is called a 'cure'. This in no way gives any privilege to the analyst, as an individual. It rather privileges the Other by the detour of whom reciprocity is re-established – a re-establishment which, in a certain way, always comes too late, or as Freud said, *nachträglich*, 'after the event'. Thus there is no contradiction or incompatibility between the 'subject-being of the patient' and the psychoanalytic method: in one sense, his subject-being is always present, and in another sense, it always remains to be achieved. The most 'afflicted' patient, it is true, 'organizes' his illness. Psychoanalysis does not therefore give him the means to organize himself. But neither does it take it away from him. All it can do, when it is successful, is to help him to modify an organization in which he is alienated. And, of course, it is the subject himself who accomplishes the modification by 'discovering himself' through the psychoanalytic relationship.

Sartre is entitled to criticize Freud's conception of psychoanalysis in the name of another conception, and to oppose a therapy of reciprocity to a therapy of 'violence'. But to do so would be to embark on a debate over fundamentals. The principal merit of the 'compromise' we have reached in this dispute is to have forced us to pose the problem in these terms. But I still hold that A. . .'s text, precisely because it goes no further than an 'acting out', was the worst way of inaugurating such a debate.

5. Intellectuals

A Plea for Intellectuals consists of three lectures delivered by Sartre at Tokyo and Kyoto in September-October 1965, during a visit to Japan.

A Friend of the People was an interview given in October 1970 to the French periodical *L'Idiot International*, which has since ceased publication.

NOTE: I reproduce these lectures and this interview – separated by a gap of five years, and by the events of May 1968 – in order to demonstrate how unstable the notion of the intellectual is today. In my Japanese lectures I described, without naming him as such, the type that since May 1968 has often been called 'the classical intellectual', and even then I showed, though, without exactly being aware of what I was doing, how heteronomous – or *unselbständig*, to use a German phrase – he appeared to be. In fact the moment of 'unhappy consciousness' – that is to say the intellectual proper – in no way represents a stasis but rather a provisional halt in the steady transformation of a technician of practical knowledge into a radicalized companion of the masses, *on condition* – and that is what I failed to say at the time – that he takes a new distance from his profession, in other words from his *social being*, and understands that no *political denunciation* can compensate for the fact that in this social being he remains objectively an enemy of the people.[1]

Today I have finally understood that the intellectual cannot remain at the stage of unhappy consciousness (characterized by idealism and inefficacity): he must resolve his own problem – or, if you like, negate his *intellectual moment* in order to try to achieve a new *popular* statute.

1. Of cours any pro tst against the war in Vietnam by many American college professors is welcome. But this protest counts for little (relative inefficacity) in comparison with the work which others perform, in the laboratories put at their disposal, in providing the US Army with new weapons.

A Plea for Intellectuals

I. WHAT IS AN INTELLECTUAL?

A. *The situation of the intellectual*

Were we to consider only the attacks made on intellectuals, we would have to conclude that they are guilty of many crimes. It is striking, too, that these attacks are everywhere more or less the same. In Japan, for example, reading several newspaper and magazine articles, translated into English for the Western world, I gained the impression that after the Meiji era, the intellectuals were divorced from political power; after the Second World War however, and especially in the years from 1945 to 1950, one would have thought that intellectuals had seized political power and proceeded to do much damage. Over the same period, if you read the French press, it might have looked as if intellectuals had reigned supreme in France too and been responsible for various disasters. In your country as in ours, a military collapse (we called ours a victory, while you called yours a defeat) was followed by a period of remilitarization of society in the service of the Cold War. Intellectuals are commonly believed to have understood nothing of this process. Here in Japan, as in France, they were condemned for the same violent and contradictory reasons. In Japan, their proper function is held to be that of preserving and transmitting culture, and thus by definition to be *conservative*; accordingly they are attacked for having mistaken their office and their role by becoming critical and negative, so that in the end, in their ceaseless sniping at authority, they saw only the evil in their country's history. The result was that they went wrong in *everything*, which would not have been so serious had they not misled the people at every important conjuncture.

Mislead the people! This presumably means: inducing them to turn their backs on their own interests. Do intellectuals then exercise a certain amount of power in the same sense as the government? No – once they depart from the cultural conservatism that defines their activity and vocation, they are attacked, accurately enough, for their impotence. Who listens to them? In any case, they are intrinsically weak – they *produce* nothing and possess nothing but their salary to live on, which prevents them from standing up for themselves in civil society, let alone political society. Intellectuals are thus ineffective and unstable; they compensate for their lack of political or social power by taking themselves for an elite qualified to deliver judgement on everything – which they are not. Hence, their moralism and idealism (they think as if they were already living in the distant future and pass judgement on our times from the abstract point of view of posterity).

Let us add one more characteristic: their *dogmatism*. Intellectuals invoke certain intangible but abstract principles as arbitrary criteria of action. Here the allusion is usually, of course, to Marxism. As such, it is a further contradiction since Marxism is opposed in principle to moralism. The contradiction is solved by projecting it onto intellectuals themselves. In any case, their attitudes are invariably compared unfavourably with the realism of politicians: whereas intellectuals betrayed their function, their *raison d'être*, and identified themselves with 'the spirit that always denies', politicians both in Japan and France modestly set about re-constructing their war-torn country, displaying a wise empiricism imbued with the traditions and, in certain cases, the new techniques (and theories) of the Western world. Europe has gone farther in this direction than Japan. You consider intellectuals to be a *necessary* evil: they are needed to preserve, transmit and enrich culture; some will always be black sheep, but their influence can be neutralized. In Europe, intellectuals have already been pronounced dead: under the influence of American ideas, the imminent disappearance of men who claimed to know everything is widely predicted. The progress of science will replace such universalists with rigorously specialized teams of researchers.

Is it possible, despite their mutual contradictions, to find a common element in all these criticisms? Yes, it is. We may say they are all inspired by one fundamental reproach: *the intellectual is someone who meddles in what is not his business* and claims to question both received truths and the accepted behaviour inspired by them, in the name of a global conception of man and of society – a conception that is today untenable and hence abstract and false, because the industrialized countries can be defined by the extreme diversity of their life styles, social functions, and concrete problems.

Now, *it is true* that the intellectual is someone who intervenes in problems that do not concern him. So much so that in France the word 'intellectual', as a pejorative term, dates from the Dreyfus affair. In the opinion of the *anti-dreyfusards*, the acquittal or condemnation of Captain Dreyfus was a matter for the military tribunals and, in the final analysis, for the General Staff: the *dreyfusards*, by insisting on the innocence of the accused, were interfering in a domain *that was outside their competence*. Originally, then, the category of intellectuals was seen as a heterogeneous collection of individuals who had acquired a certain fame by exercising their intelligence (in the exact sciences, the applied sciences, medicine, literature, etc.) and who subsequently *abused* this fame by straying outside their proper province and criticizing society and established authority in the name of a global and dogmatic conception (vague or precise: moralist or marxist) of man.

If we want an example of this common conception of the intellectual, I would suggest that the scientists working on atomic fission in order to perfect the techniques of atomic warfare should not be called 'intellectuals': they are scientists, and nothing more. But if these same scientists, terrified by the destructive power of the devices they have helped to create, join forces and sign a manifesto alerting public opinion to the dangers of the atomic bomb, they become intellectuals. This is the sequence of events: (1) they stray outside their field of competence – constructing bombs is one thing, but evaluating their use is another; (2) they abuse their celebrity or their authority to do violence to public opinion, by concealing the unbridgeable gulf that separates their scientific knowledge from their *political* appreciation – deriving from *very different principles* – of the devices on which they are working; (3) they do not protest against the use of the bomb on the grounds of any technical defects it may have, but in the name of a highly controversial system of values that sees human life as its supreme standard.

How important are these basic complaints? Do they correspond to anything in the real world? We cannot answer this before we know *what an intellectual is*.

B. *What is an intellectual?*

Since the intellectual is criticized for straying outside the field of *his own* competence, he is seen as a particular case of a wider set of persons who are defined by various socially *recognized* functions. Let us see what this means.

All praxis has several moments to it. Action partially negates that which *is* (the practical field represents a situation *to be changed*) to the profit of that which *is not* (the end in view, a redistribution of the initial elements of the situation in order, ultimately, to reproduce life). But this negation is a disclosure and is accompanied by an affirmation, since *that which is not* is realized by *that which is*; the act of disclosure of that which is, on the basis of that which is not, should be as exact as possible since this act has to find in what is given the means of achieving that which does not yet exist (the resistance to be expected from a material is revealed as a function of the pressure that must be applied to it).

Thus all praxis contains a moment of practical knowledge that reveals, surpasses, preserves and already modifies reality. This is the level of research and practical truth, defined as a grasp of being in as much as it encloses the possibility of its own directed change. Truth comes into being out of non-being, into the present out of the practical future. From this point of view, an enterprise that has successfully been *accomplished* is a *verification* of possibilities discovered in the course of it. (If I manage to cross a river with a make-shift bridge, the material selected and assembled for the purpose will have demonstrated the solidity expected of it.) From this we may conclude that practical knowledge is, in the first instance, *invention*. If various possibilities are to be discovered, utilized and verified, they must first be *invented*. In this sense, every man is a *project*: he is a *creator*, because he invents what *already* exists, starting with what does *not yet exist*; he is a *scientist*, because he will never succeed in anything without first assessing exactly all the possibilities that will help him to realize his project; he is a *researcher* and a *challenger*, for since the end in view will indicate only schematically the means needed to attain it, in so far as it is itself abstract, he must seek concrete means which will in their turn delimit the end and sometimes enrich it by deflecting it. The result is that he puts the end in question by the means, and vice versa, until the point is reached where the end becomes the integral unity of the means used to achieve it. It is at this point that he has to decide whether 'it is all worth it' – in other words, whether this aggregate end, envisaged from the global point of view of *life*, is worth the extent of the *transformations of energy* needed to realize it; or, if you like, whether the gain is worth the expense of energy. For we live in a world of scarcity in which every expenditure shows up somewhere else as a waste.

Within modern societies, the division of labour ensures that different groups are allocated different tasks which, taken together, constitute praxis. For our purposes, this division of labour engenders specialists of practical knowledge. In other words, in and through this particular group, *disclosure* is isolated as a moment of action and posed for itself. The ends are defined by the ruling class and are realized by the working classes, but the study of the means to them is reserved to a group of technicians who belong to what Colin Clark calls the tertiary sector, made up of scientists, engineers, doctors, lawyers, jurists, academics and so on. These men as individuals do not differ from other men, since each of them, whatever he does, discloses and preserves the being that he surpasses by his project of organizing it. On the other hand, the social function which is assigned to them consists of the critical examination of the field of the possibles; neither the evaluation of ends, nor in most cases (there are exceptions: surgeons for example) their realization, falls within the province of these specialists. Such technicians of practical knowledge do not yet, as a group, qualify as intellectuals, but it will be from their midst – and nowhere else – that intellectuals will be recruited.

To understand better what intellectuals are, let us see how, in France, they came into being. Up to about the 14th century, the cleric, a servant of the Church, was in his own way the holder of a body of knowledge.

Typically, neither the barons nor the peasants knew how to read. Reading was the *province of the cleric*. But the Church wielded economic power (it possessed immense wealth) and political power (as evidenced by the truce of God* which it imposed on the nobility and was generally able to enforce). It was, as such, the guardian of an *ideology* – Christianity – which expressed it and which it inculcated in other classes. The cleric was the mediator between lord and peasant; he enabled them to recognize each other in so far as they possessed (or believed they possessed) a common ideology. He preserved dogmas, and transmitted and adapted traditions. In his capacity as a servant of the Church he was not a specialist in any one branch of knowledge. He offered a mythical image of the world, a totalitarian myth which, while expressive of the class consciousness of the Church, defined the place and destiny of man in a wholly sacred universe; it reinforced, of course, the existing social hierarchy.

The specialist in the field of practical knowledge appeared with the development of the bourgeoisie. The merchant class, as it crystallized, entered into conflict with the Church, whose principles (the just price, condemnation of usury) fettered the development of commercial capitalism. However, it adopted and preserved the ideology of the clerics without troubling unduly to define its own ideology. But from amongst its own sons it chose its technical auxiliaries and advocates. Merchant navies presupposed the existence of scientists and engineers; double-entry book-keeping needed calculators who would develop into mathematicians; unconditional property and contracts multiplied the demand for lawyers; medicine evolved and anatomy provided an inspiration for bourgeois realism in the arts. A new stratum of 'experts in means' thus arose from within the ranks of the bourgeoisie: they constituted neither a class nor an elite, but were wholly integrated in the vast enterprise that was mercantile capitalism, and provided it with the means to self-reproduction and expansion. These scientists and experts were not the guardians of any *ideology*, and their function was certainly not to provide the bourgeoisie with one. They were to take little part in the

* Translator's note: A ruling by the Church dating from the 11th century forbidding any act of violence or hostilities between armies from Friday evening to Monday morning.

conflict that ranged the bourgeoisie against the ideology of the Church. The formulation of ideological problems was left to the clerics, who split into opposing camps in the name of synthetic universality, at the time when the development of commerce had turned the bourgeoisie into a force to be reckoned with. There sprang from their efforts to adapt a sacred ideology to the demands of a rising class, simultaneously, the Reformation (Protestantism was the ideology of mercantile capitalism) and the Counter-Reformation (the Jesuits contended with the reformed Church for the bourgeoisie: thanks to them, the notion of usury gave way to that of credit). The men of knowledge lived through these conflicts, interiorized them, were deeply affected by the contradictions of the epoch, but were not their principal agents.

As it happened, no adaptation of sacred ideology could ultimately satisfy the bourgoisie, whose interests now demanded a *desacralization of every sphere of practical activity*. It was this secularization – beyond all inter-clerical conflicts – that the technicians of practical knowledge had unwittingly prepared by rendering bourgois praxis aware of its own nature, and defining the time and space of the circulation of commodities. As one sacred field after another was laicized, God was obliged to retire back to Heaven: from the end of the 17th century, he became a *Hidden God*. At this time, the bourgeoisie felt a compelling need to affirm itself as a class with a global conception of the world, that is to say an ideology: such was the content of what has been called 'the intellectual crisis of Western Europe'. This ideology was not created by clerics but by specialists of practical knowledge: men of the law (Montesquieu), men of letters (Voltaire, Diderot, Rousseau), mathematicians (d'Alembert), a tax-farmer (Helvetius), doctors, etc. They took the place of clerics and called themselves *philosophers*, that is to say 'the lovers of Wisdom'. Wisdom was equated with Reason. Over and above their specialist labours, they were called upon to create a rational conception of the Universe which would embrace and justify the *actions* and *demands* of the bourgeoisie.

They were to use the analytic method of reasoning which was the method of research that had proved its efficacy in the sciences and technologies of the time. They were now to apply it to the problems of history and society: it was their best weapon against the traditions, privileges and myths of the aristocracy, long founded on an irrational syncretism. Prudence, however, led them in turn to give a syncretic guise to the vitriols they prepared for the corrosion of aristocratic and theocratic myths. As a single example, I will cite the idea of *Nature*, a compromise between the rigorous object of the exact sciences and the Christian world created by God. *Nature* was the one and the other at the same time. It was in the first instance the idea of a totalizing and syncretic unity of everything that exists – and thus referred back to a divine Reason; but at the same time it was the idea that everything is subject to laws and that the world consists of an infinite number of causal series, in which each object of knowledge is the fortuitous effect of the juncture of several of these series, which eliminate any need for a Demiurge. The ample shelter of this well-chosen concept allowed thinkers to be Christians, deists, pantheists, atheists or materialists; the men of the time either dissimulated their deepest convictions behind this façade without ever believing in it, or they deceived themselves and became believers and non-believers *at the same time*. Most of the *philosophes* fell into the second category – for although they had developed specialist skills of practical knowledge, they were still influenced by the beliefs inculcated into them in their earliest childhood.

Henceforward, their task was to forge weapons for the bourgeoisie in its struggle against feudalism and to bolster its proud consciousness of itself. By extending the idea of *natural law* to the economic sphere – an inevitable but fundamental error – they both secularized the economy and converted it into a domain external to man: a system of inflexible laws whose constraints permitted no modification. The economy was part of Nature – here too one could only command Nature by obeying it. When the *philosophes* demanded liberty, the right of free inquiry, all they were doing was demanding an independence for thought that was necessary to conduct practical research (which they were performing at the same time). But for the bourgeois class, the target of this demand was above all the abolition of feudal shackles on commerce, and the victory of liberalism or free economic competition. In the same way, *individualism* appeared to bourgeois proprietors as the validation of *real* property – a relationship without intermediaries between the possessor and the goods possessed – as against feudal property, which expressed above all a relationship between men themselves. The notion of *social atomism* was the outcome of the application of the scientific thought of the period to society: the bourgeois made use of it in order to reject social 'organisms'. Equality between all social atoms was a necessary consequence of the scientific ideology which derived from analytical Reason: the bourgeoisie made use of it to discredit the nobility by pitting the *rest* of society against it. In fact at the time, as Marx said, the bourgeoisie saw itself as the universal class.

In short, the *philosophes* did what intellectuals are criticized for doing today – they used their skills for another end than that towards which they were supposed to be working; they developed a bourgeois ideology based on a mechanistic and analytical scientism. Should we view them as the first intellectuals? Yes and no. It is true that aristocrats attacked them, at the time, for meddling in affairs that had nothing to do with them. The nobles and the prelates reproached them for doing this: but *not* the bourgeoisie. For the fact was that their ideology did not arise out of thin air: the bourgeois class produced it in a raw and diffuse state in and through *its* commercial practice. This class was becoming aware that it needed such an ideology to achieve full consciousness of itself through a system of signs and symbols – and to dissolve and destroy the ideologies of the other classes in society. The *philosophes* can thus be seen as *organic* intellectuals, in the sense that Gramsci gave to the word. They were born into the bourgeois class, and they took upon themselves the task of expressing the *objective spirit* of this class. Where did this organic accord come from? Firstly, from the fact that they were engendered by this class, borne along by its successes and saturated by its customs and attitudes. Secondly and above all, from the fact that the advance of scientific and practical research, and the progression of the rising class, moved forward together. The ensemble of ideas and values composed of a spirit of contestation, a rejection of the principles of authority and the fetters on free commerce, a conviction of the universality of scientific laws and a belief in the universality of man by contrast with feudal particularism, culminated in the twin formulas: every man is a bourgeois; every bourgeois is a man. This ideological complex has a name: bourgeois *humanism*.

This was its golden age. The *philosophes*, born, educated and moulded within the bourgeoisie, fought in consonance with it to bring its ideology to light. That age is now distant. Today the bourgeois class is in power, but no one any longer believes it to be a universal class. This alone would suffice to make its 'humanism' obsolete; all the more so since this ideology was adapted to a capitalism of family enterprises, and bears no relation to the era of monopolies. Yet it lingers on; the bourgeoisie persists in calling itself humanist, the West has baptized itself the Free World, and so on. However, in the last third of the 19th century and, particularly from the Dreyfus affair onwards, the grandsons of the *philosophes* became *intellectuals*. What does this mean?

Intellectuals are still recruited from the ranks of the technicians of practical knowledge. But in order to define them we must enumerate the *modern* characteristics of this social category.

(1) The technician of practical knowledge is recruited *from above*. In general he is no longer a member of the ruling class, but it is this class that defines his *being* by its allocation of *jobs*: an allocation that is a function of the exact nature of *its* priorities (for example, according to the level of industrialization), and of the social needs determined by *its* particular options and interests (a society in part *chooses* the number of its deaths according to the fraction of surplus-value it assigns to medical research). The job, as a position to be filled and a role to be played, defines *a priori* the future of an abstract but *awaited* man. Such and such a number of places for doctors, teachers, etc., in 1975 means for a whole category of adolescents at once a specific structuration of the field of their possibilities, of studies to be undertaken, and at the same time a *destiny*. In fact, it sometimes happens that the job awaits them even *before* their birth, as their *social being*. This being is nothing other, in effect, than the unity of the functions they will have to fulfil day in, day out. In this way the ruling class determines the number of technicians of practical knowledge in accordance with the dictates of *profit*, which is its supreme end. It decides at the same time what fraction of surplus-value it will devote to their salaries, in keeping with the level of industrial development, the state of the business cycle, and the appearance of new needs. (Mass production, for example, involves a considerable expansion of the advertising industry, and thus calls into being a growing army of applied psychologists, statisticians, copy-writers and designers; while

the adoption of 'human engineering' involves the direct participation of applied psychologists and of sociologists.) Today the situation is clear enough: industry is trying to extend its control over the university to force it to abandon the old obsolete humanism and replace it with specialized disciplines, destined to supply firms with testers, supervisors, public relations officers, and so forth.

(2) The ideological and technical formation of the specialist in practical knowledge is also defined by a system that is instituted from above (primary, secondary and higher education) and hence is necessarily *selective*. The ruling class regulates education in such a way as to give its technicians (a) the ideology it judges suitable for them (primary and secondary education) and (b) the knowledge and skills to enable them to perform their functions (higher education).

It thus educates them *a priori* to fulfil two roles: it turns them simultaneously into specialists in research and servitors of hegemony, that is to say custodians of tradition. In their second role they become 'functionaries of the superstructures', to use another of Gramsci's expressions. As such, they are granted a certain degree of power – that of 'exercising the subaltern functions of social hegemony and political government' (testers perform policing functions, teachers implement the selection procedures, etc.). They are implicitly entrusted with the task of transmitting received values (adapting them as the need arises, to changing circumstances) and if necessary combating the ideas and values of all other classes, by deploying their specialized knowledge. At this level they are the agents of an ideological *particularism*, which is sometimes openly admitted (the aggressive nationalism of the Nazi theoreticians) and sometimes concealed (liberal humanism, with its false universality). It is worth noting in passing that they are in this respect expected to concern themselves with things that have nothing to do with them. Yet no one would dream of calling them *intellectuals*, since they merely camouflage the dominant ideology as scientific laws. In the colonial epoch, psychiatrists conducted so-called rigorous studies to establish the inferiority of Africans, for example, on the basis of the anatomy and physiology of their brains. In this way, they contributed to the maintenance of bourgeois humanism – all men are equal *except* colonials who are merely shadows of men. Other studies established in the same way the inferiority of women: humanity was bourgeois, white and masculine.

(3) Class relations automatically regulate the selection of the technicians of practical knowledge: in France there are hardly any workers in this social category, because of the enormous difficulty for a working-class child to *acquire* higher education; a somewhat greater number of peasants can be found in this category, because the most recent waves of rural emigration have been to some extent absorbed in civil administration in the towns. But above all this category consists of sons of the petty bourgeoisie. A system of scholarships (education is free, but one needs money to live) allows the state to adopt this or that recruitment policy according to the circumstances. We should add that even for middle-class children, the field of possibilities open to them is rigorously limited by family resources: six years of medical training puts too much of a strain on the budget of a lower-middle class family. Thus his whole situation is rigorously defined for the technician of practical knowledge. He is born, in general, into the middle ranks of the middle classes, where from earliest childhood a particularist ideology of the ruling class is inculcated in him, while his work invariably ranges him in any case with the middle classes. This means that in general he has no contact whatever with workers: in fact he is an accomplice to their exploitation since, after all, he lives off surplus value. In this sense his social being and his destiny come to him from without: he is a middle man, a middling man, a middle-class man. The general ends towards which his activities lead are not *his* ends.

It is at this point that the intellectual makes his entrance. His emergence is rooted in the fact that the socialized worker whom the ruling class has made a technician of practical knowledge suffers at various levels from a fundamental contradiction.

(1) He has been a 'humanist' from his earliest childhood – which means that he was taught to believe that all men are equal. Yet, if he considers himself, he becomes aware that he is living proof that all men are *not* equal. He possesses a measure of social *power* by virtue of his knowledge become skill. This knowledge came to him, the son of a civil servant or manager or member of the liberal professions, as a *heritage*: culture resided in his family even before he was born into it. Thus to be born into his family and to be born into culture were one and the same thing

for him. And if he happens to be one of the few who have risen from the ranks of the working class, he will have succeeded only by traversing a complex and *invariably unjust* system of selection which has eliminated most of his comrades. He is thus always the possessor of an unjustified privilege even, and in a certain sense above all, if he has brilliantly passed all the tests. This privilege, or monopoly of knowledge, is in radical contradiction with the tenets of humanist egalitarianism. In other words, he ought to renounce it. But since he *is* this privilege, he can only renounce it by abolishing himself, a course which would contradict the instinct for life that is so deeply rooted in most men.

(2) The *philosophe* of the 18th century had, as we have seen, the luck to be born as an organic intellectual of *his own* class. This meant that the ideology of the bourgeoisie – which contested the obsolete forms of feudal power – seemed to arise spontaneously out of the general principles of scientific research, an illusion which derived from the universalism of the bourgeoisie: in opposition to the aristocracy, which deemed itself particularized by virtue of descent and race, the bourgeoisie took itself to be the universal class.

Today, the bourgeois ideology with which the technicians of practical knowledge are initially impregnated by their education in the 'humanities', contradicts the other component part of themselves, their function as researchers, equipped with specific knowledges and methods. They are universalist because they seek universal forms of knowledge and practice. But if they apply their methods to an examination of the ruling class and its ideology – which is also *their own* – they cannot hide from themselves the fact that both are surreptitiously particularist. At that moment, in their very research, they discover alienation: they become aware that they are the instruments of ends which remain foreign to them and which they are forbidden to question. This contradiction stems not from themselves but from the ruling class itself. We can see this clearly in an example taken from Japanese history.

In 1886 Arinari Mori reformed the Japanese educational system: primary education was to be based on the ideology of militarism and nationalism, it was to nourish in the child loyalty to the State and submission to traditional values. But at the same time Mori was convinced (we are talking about the Meiji era) that if education were to be limited to these basic conceptions, Japan would be unable to produce the scientists and technicians necessary for its industrialization. Thus, for the same reason, 'higher' education had to be given a certain amount of freedom in order to stimulate research.

Since then the Japanese educational system has been drastically changed, but I have cited this example in order to show that the contradiction experienced by the technicians of practical knowledge is created by the contradictory needs of the ruling class. In effect, it is the dominant class which fashions the contradictory mould which awaits the technicians from their earliest childhood, and which turns them into men-in-contradiction, since the particularist ideology of obedience to a state, to a political policy, to a ruling class, must enter into conflict in their case, with the free and universalist spirit of research which is also conferred on them from without, but *at a later date*, when they are already submissive. In France, this contradiction is the same: from childhood they are screened from social reality – the exploitation of the majority by a minority – by a false universality. Under the name of humanism the true condition of the workers and peasants and the class struggle is concealed from them. A lying egalitarianism masks the imperialism, colonialism and racism which are the ideology of these practices. When they start their higher education, most of them have already been imbued since infancy with a belief in the inferiority of women. Liberty, exercised by the bourgeoisie alone, is presented to them as a formal universality – everyone has the right to vote. Peace, progress and fraternity ill conceal the mechanisms of selection which make each of them a 'competitor' against each other, or the wars of imperialism such as the US aggression in Vietnam. Recently, they have been made to learn or recite pretentious prattle about 'affluence', whose only function is to dissimulate the fact that two-thirds of humanity live in a state of chronic under-nourishment. To give any appearance of unity to all these contradictory thoughts, to check the freedom of research in the name of ideas which are manifestly false, it is consequently necessary to fetter free scientific and technical thought with norms which do not belong to science, and to erect external barriers to the spirit of inquiry, while trying to believe and make others believe that they are inherent to any inquiry. In short, scientific and technical thought can develop its universality only *under control*. Thus in spite of its kernel of freedom, universality and rigour, science – subordinated to particularism – becomes ideology.

(3) Whatever may be the goals of the ruling class, the technician's activity is first and foremost *practical*: in other words, his goal is what is useful. Not what is useful to this or that social group, but what is useful without specification or limits. When a doctor is engaged in research to find a cure for cancer, his quest does not specify, for example, that only the *rich* are to be cured, for the simple reason that degrees of wealth have nothing to do with cells of cancer. The indetermination of the patient to be cured is necessarily conceived as a universalization: if it is known how to cure one man (obviously characterized by socio-professional traits which fall outside the scope of research) then *all* men may be cured. But in reality the doctor finds that he is caught within a system of relations defined by the ruling class in terms of *scarcity* and *profit* (the supreme end of the industrial bourgeoisie). The result will be that his research, limited by the funds made available for it and – if he finds a cure – by the high price of initial treatments, will only benefit a minority. (We should add that his discoveries can be shelved for commercial reasons by this or that organization: a first-class remedy devised in Rumania for maladies of old age can be secured in certain countries but not in France, because of the resistance of the local pharmaceutical companies; other medicaments may exist in laboratories for several years but cannot be bought anywhere, while the public is kept ignorant of them, etc.). In many cases, with the complicity of the technicians of practical knowledge in question, privileged social groups rob discoveries of their *social utility*, and transform it into a utility for the minority at the expense of the majority. For this reason new inventions frequently remain for a long time instruments of frustration for the majority: such is one of the meanings of *relative impoverishment*. Thus the technician who creates inventions for *all* men may become – at least for a time whose length can rarely be predicted – simply an agent of the pauperization of the working class. This process is particularly obvious in the case of major improvements in industrial products, which are promptly utilized by the bourgeoisie to increase its profits.

Thus the technicians of knowledge engendered by the ruling class are always torn by an inner contradiction. On the one hand, in their capacity as salaried employees and minor functionaries of the super-structure, they are directly dependent on the managers of private or state enterprises and are defined in this particularity as a specific stratum within the tertiary sector. On the other hand, in as much as their speciality is always the universal, these specialists embody a contestation of the very particularisms with which they have been injected and which they cannot contest without contesting themselves. They insist there is no such thing as 'bourgeois science' and yet their science is bourgeois by virtue of the *limits* imposed on it, and they know it. All the same, it is true that in the phase of research proper they work in an atmosphere of freedom, which makes the return to their real condition all the more bitter.

The powers that be are not unaware of the fact that the reality of the technician's activity is a ceaseless reciprocal contestation between the universal and the particular, and that the technician therefore represents, at least potentially, what Hegel called an 'unhappy consciousness'. For this reason authorities regard him as extremely *suspect*. They accuse him of being someone 'who is forever saying no'; although they know perfectly well that contestation is not a mere character trait but a necessary procedure of scientific thought. For scientific thought, while it is tra-ditionalist to the extent that it accepts a corpus of accumulated knowledge, is negative to the extent that the object of study *contests itself* within it and thereby renders possible further scientific advance. The upshot of the Michelson–Morley experiment* was to put in question the whole of Newtonian physics. But this contestation was in no way sought as such. Progress in the measurement of speed (*technical* progress in *instrumentation*, linked to industrial development) led Michelson and Morley to attempt to measure the velocity of the earth. Their measurement re-vealed a wholly unexpected contradiction; they took cognizance of it only in order the better to overcome it with a new contestation – which was in effect forced on them by the object. Fitzgerald and Einstein may thus be seen not so much as scientists contesting a previous system, but

---

*Translator's note: the Michelson–Morley experiment of 1887 was set up to attempt to measure the velocity of the earth through a 'fixed' frame of reference (the aether) by the effect which it was anticipated this velocity would have on the velocity of light. The failure of the experimenters to detect any such effect was the starting point of Einstein's theory of relativity in 1905.

rather as exploring what had to be abandoned in the system in order to integrate into it the results of experience at least cost. No matter: in the eyes of authority, if technicians of knowledge are such that current means are disputed in their work, they will eventually start to dispute current ends – the abstract postulates of the ruling class and the aggregate unity of current means. Thus the researcher is simultaneously indispensable and yet suspect in the eyes of the dominant class. He cannot fail to experience and interiorize this suspicion, and to become suspect *from the outset* in his own eyes.

Thereafter there are two possible lines of development:

(i) The technician of knowledge accepts the dominant ideology or adapts himself to it: in the end, in a state of wholly bad faith, he puts the universal to the service of the particular; he practices self-censorship and becomes *apolitical, agnostic,* etc. It can also happen that he is politically coerced into abandoning a valid dissent and renounces his ability to question the world, at the price of considerable damage to his skills. In this case, his rulers typically say with satisfaction of a man, 'he is no intellectual'.

(ii) If the technician of practical knowledge becomes aware of the particularism of his ideology and cannot reconcile himself to it: if he sees that he has interiorized authoritarian principles in the form of self-censorship; if he has to call in question the ideology that formed him to escape malaise and mutilation; if he refuses to be a subaltern agent of bourgeois hegemony and to act as the means towards ends which he is forbidden to know or to dispute – then the agent of practical knowledge becomes a monster, that is to say an intellectual; *someone who attends to what concerns him* (in exteriority – the principles which guide the conduct of his life; and in interiority – his lived experience in society) and whom others refer to a man *who interferes in what does not concern him.*

In a word, every technician of knowledge is a *potential intellectual* since he is defined by a contradiction which is none other than the permanent tension within him between his universalist technique and the dominant ideology. But in reality a technician cannot simply decide to become an intellectual. Such a conversion will depend in part on his personal history, which may determine whether the tension which characterizes him is released; while in the last analysis only social factors can complete the transformation.

Among the latter figure first and foremost the policy adopted by the ruling classes and the living standard they promise their intellectuals – in particular their students. Low salaries are certainly a way of intensifying their dependence. But they may also incite technicians of knowledge to revolt by revealing the real position reserved for them in society. Then again the ruling class may be unable to provide all its students with the jobs which have been promised them: those who fail to find employment will fall below the standard of living – no matter how low – typical of technicians, and will tend to develop solidarity with the less favoured social classes. Unemployment of this kind, or demotion to less well-paid and less honorific employment, is often the outcome of a process of selection within the educational system; but the negative product of such selection (the eliminated student) cannot contest the filtering mechanisms of which he is a victim without contesting the whole of society. There are also certain historical conjunctures in which the traditional values and dominant ideology of a society are violently opposed by the working class, inducing profound transformations within the ruling class itself.

At such times, numerous specialists in knowledge are transformed into intellectuals because the contradictions which have erupted in society bring home to them their own contradiction. If, on the other hand, the dominant classes seek to augment the impact of ideology at the expense of that of science, it is they who intensify the inner tension within technicians and are responsible for their transformation into intellectuals – by reducing the quota of technique, science and free research to a level below what such technicians can accept. In Japan, in recent years, the capitalist State has forced teachers of history to deform historical truth; even where the latter had till then been solely concerned with teaching or establishing facts, they were thereby impelled to oppose, in the name of their own professional conscience and scientific standards, a ruling ideology which they had otherwise hitherto passively accepted. Usually all these diverse determinants operate *at the same time*: for their totality, however contradictory it may be, reflects the general attitude of a society towards its specialists. But these pressures can ultimately do no more than bring the specialist to consciousness of his own *constitutional contradiction*. The intellectual is thus someone who becomes aware of the opposition, both within himself and within society, between a search for practical truth (with all the norms it implies) and a ruling ideology (with its system of traditional values). Although this new awareness must, *in order to be real*, operate in the case of the intellectual *first and foremost* at the level of his professional activities and functions, it is nothing other than an unmasking of the fundamental contradictions of the society: that is to say, the struggle between classes and within the dominant class itself, the organic conflict between the truth the latter needs for its own purposes and the myths, values and traditions with which it seeks to infect other classes in order to ensure its hegemony.

The intellectual, the product of a class-divided society, testifies to these conflicts because he has interiorized them. He is thus a product of history. In this sense no society can complain of its intellectuals without accusing itself, for it has the intellectuals it makes.

2. THE FUNCTION OF THE INTELLECTUAL

A. *Contradictions*

We have defined the intellectual in his *existence*. We must now discuss his *function*. But does he have one? It is clear, in effect, that no one has given him a mandate to exercise a function. The dominant class attaches no importance to him: all it is willing to acknowledge is the technician of knowledge and the minor functionary of the superstructure. The under-privileged classes cannot engender him since he derives from the specialist in practical truth who in turn is created by the options of the dominant class, which allocates a fraction of surplus value to produce him. As for the middle classes – to whom he belongs – although they originally suffer from the same inner divisions, reproducing within themselves the discord between the bourgeoisie and the proletariat, their contradictions are not experienced at the level of myth versus scientific knowledge, or particularism versus universalism: thus the intellectual cannot knowingly be mandated to express them.

Let us say that the intellectual is characterized as having a mandate from no one, and as receiving his statute from no authority. He is, as such, not the product of a particular decision – as are doctors, teachers, etc., in as much as they are agents of authority – but the monstrous product of a monstrous society. He is claimed by no one and recognized by no one (neither the State, nor the power-elite, nor the lobbies, nor the organizations of the exploited classes, nor the masses). We can be sensible of what he *says* but not of his existence. For example, discussing a diet and the reasons for it, we may say more or less inanely: 'It was *my* doctor who told me that', whereas if an intellectual's arguments take effect and are widely accepted, they will be presented in *themselves*, without any reference to he who first developed them. They will become an *anonymous* outlook, the common property of all. The intellectual is suppressed by the very manner in which his products are used.

Thus no one concedes him any rights or status. In fact, his existence cannot be admitted, since it cannot even admit itself. It is simply the lived impossibility of being a pure technician of practical knowledge in our societies. This definition reveals the intellectual as the most disarmed of men: he certainly cannot belong to an elite because, at the outset, he disposes of no *knowledge* and, consequently, no *power*. He cannot hope to teach, even though he is often recruited from amongst the ranks of teachers, because he is initially one who is ignorant. If he is a professor or a scientist, he does *know* certain things even if he cannot derive them from true principles. But as an intellectual, he is *searching* for other things: the restrictions, violent or subtle, of universality by particularism, and the envelopment of truth by myth have made him essentially an *investigator*. He investigates *himself* first of all in order to transform the contradictory being assigned to him into a harmonious totality. But this cannot be his only object, since to find his inner secret and resolve his organic contradiction, he must proceed to apply the rigorous methods he uses as a specialist technician of practical knowledge to the society of which he is a product – to its ideology, its structures, its options and its praxis.

The principles which govern these methods are: freedom of research (and contestation); rigour of inquiry and proof; quest for truth (disclosure of being and its conflicts); universality of results obtained. Nevertheless, these abstract principles do not suffice in themselves to constitute an adequate method for the intellectual's pursuit of his object, for the specific object of his inquiry is two-fold, in effect, and each aspect is both the complement and converse of the other. The intellectual will both seek to understand *himself* within society, in so far as he is a product of society, and at the same time to study the total society which produces, at a certain point in time, intellectuals like himself. The result is a perpetual reversal of perspectives: the self is referred to the world and the world is referred to the self. The object of the research of an intellectual can thus never be the object studied by anthropology. For the intellectual cannot consider the social whole *objectively*, because he discovers it within himself as his fundamental contradiction. Nor, on the other hand, can he be satisfied with a merely *subjective* questioning of himself, since he is precisely inserted into a determinate society that has fashioned him. From these remarks we may conclude that:

(1) The object of the intellectual's inquiry demands a specialized knowledge of the abstract method of which we have spoken. Within this constant reversal of perspectives that is necessary to overcome his inner contradiction, the two moments – the interiorization of exteriority and re-exteriorization of interiority – must be rigorously linked. Such a linkage of contradictory terms is nothing other than the *dialectic*. The dialectic is a method that the intellectual is not qualified to teach. When he awakens to his new condition and seeks to overcome his 'difficulty in being', he is not familiar with any dialectical procedure. It is his object that will impose it on him little by little, since it is a two-fold object and each of its faces refers to the other. Yet even at the end of his quest the intellectual will not have a rigorous knowledge of the method that has imposed itself on him.

(2) In any case the ambiguity of his object separates the intellectual from the realm of *abstract universality*. The mistake of the *philosophes* was to believe that they could directly apply a universal (and analytic) method to the society in which they existed, when precisely *they lived within it*: for in fact it conditioned them historically in such a way that its ideological presuppositions infiltrated their positive research and even their negative will to combat them. The reason for their error is obvious: they were *organic intellectuals* working for the very class that had produced them, and their universality was simply the false universality of the bourgeoisie,

which took itself to be a universal class. Thus when they sought man, they got no further than the bourgeois. True intellectual investigation, if it is to free truth from the myths which obscure it, implies a traversal of research through the singularity of the researcher. The latter needs to situate *himself* in the social universe in order to be able to grasp and destroy within and without himself the limits that ideology imposes on knowledge. It is at the level of the *situation* that the dialectic of interiorization and exteriorization is operative; the intellectual's thought must ceaselessly turn back on itself in order always to apprehend itself as a *singular universality* – a thought secretly singularized by the class prejudices inculcated in him since childhood, even while it believed itself to be free of them and to have attained the universal. To take just one example, if we wish to combat racism (as an ideology of imperialism) it is not enough simply to oppose it with universal arguments that are drawn from anthropological science. Such arguments may be convincing on the level of universality – but racism is a concrete everyday attitude, and consequently a man can sincerely hold anti-racist opinions of a universal type, while in his deepest recesses, under the influence of his childhood, he remains a racist – so that one day he will involuntarily behave like one in ordinary life. Thus the intellectual's labour will come to nothing, even if he demonstrates the aberrant character of racism, unless he constantly returns to himself to liquidate the traces of racism within him left over by his childhood, by a rigorous investigation of the 'incomparable monster' that is his self.

At this level the intellectual, who by virtue of his work as a technician of knowledge (endowed with a certain salary and standard of living) can be classified as a petty-bourgeois promoted by a selective educational process, must ceaselessly combat his own class – which, itself moulded by the culture of the ruling class, necessarily reproduces within him a petty-bourgeois ideology and petty-bourgeois thoughts and sentiments. The intellectual is thus a technician of the universal who realizes that in his own field, universality does not exist ready-made; but perpetually remains to be achieved. One of the principal traps an intellectual must avoid in this enterprise is to universalize too fast. I have seen some who were in such a hurry to pass over to the universal that during the Algerian war they condemned Algerian terrorism in exactly the same breath as

French repression. Such a judgement was the very pattern of a false bourgeois universality. What these intellectuals failed to understand was that the Algerian rebellion – an insurrection of the poor, disarmed and hunted by a police regime – could not but choose *guerrilla war and the use of bombs*. Thus, the true intellectual, in his struggle against himself, will come to see society as the arena of a struggle between particular groups (particularized by virtue of their structure, their position and their destiny) for the statute of universality. In contradiction to the tenets of bourgeois thought, he will perceive that *man does not exist*. But by the same token, once he knows he is not yet a man, he will grasp – .within himself and then outside himself, and vice versa – man as a *task*. As Ponge has said: man is the future of man. In opposition to bourgeois humanism, an intellectual who achieves self-awareness necessarily comes to see both his own singularity and its adumbration of man, as the distant goal of a practical and daily enterprise.

(3) For this reason, a criticism often made of intellectuals is senseless – the general prejudice that an intellectual is an abstract being who lives in a world of pure universality, who is familiar only with 'intellectual' and purely negative values, whose 'cerebral' reasoning is impervious to the appeals of sensibility. The origin of these criticisms is obvious: the intellectual is an agent of practical knowledge, *first and foremost*, and it is only rarely that he ceases to be so when he becomes an intellectual. It is true that he claims to apply methods of the exact sciences outside their familiar domain, in particular to dissolve the dominant ideology both outside and within himself – an ideology that is presented to him in the form of confused and elusive thoughts and 'affective' or 'vital' values, so called to magnify their fundamentally irrational character. But his goal is to realize the practical subject and to discover the principles of a society capable of engendering and sustaining such a subject. In the interim he pursues his investigation at all levels and attempts to modify *himself* in his *sensibility* as well as his *thoughts*. This means that as far as possible he seeks to produce, both in himself and in others, a true unity of the personality, a recuperation by each agent of the ends imposed on his activity (which would, by the same stroke, become different ends), a suppression of alienations, a real freedom for thought – by defeating *external* social prohibitions dictated by the class structure, and

internal inhibitions and self-censorship. If there is *a* sensibility which he rejects, it is a *class* sensibility – for example the 'rich' and variegated sensibility of racism; but he rejects it in favour of a richer sensibility, that implies human relations of reciprocity. There is no certainty that he will achieve this completely, but at least he will indicate the path towards it, both to himself and to others. What he contests, by contrast, is simply ideology (and its *practical* consequences) – in so far as ideology, whatever its origin, is a mendacious and imperspicuous substitute for a class consciousness. Thus his contestation is merely a *negative moment* of a praxis which he is incapable of undertaking alone, a praxis which can only be brought to fruition by the totality of oppressed and exploited classes, and whose positive meaning – even if he can only glimpse it – is the advent in a distant future of a society of free men.

(4) This dialectical action of one singular universal on other singular universals should never, therefore, be conducted in the abstract. The ideology to be combated by the intellectual is constantly actualized in *events*. We should be clear on this point: ideology comes to us not so much in the form of a set of clearly defined propositions, but rather as a way of expressing and masking particular events. Racism, for example, is sometimes – but rather rarely – manifested in books (as in the case of Drumont's *La France Juive*), but it will be found much more frequently as the hidden motor of events, such as the Dreyfus affair; or in the justifications casually and indirectly furnished by the mass media for racist violence – whether as legal persecution (Dreyfus), lynching, or intermediate forms – which themselves constitute one of the principal aspects of racism. To discharge himself of the clinging racism against which he must always struggle, the intellectual can express his ideas in a book. But the most important thing he can do is tirelessly to denounce *in acts* the sophisms which attempt to justify the condemnation of a Jew *on the grounds that he is a Jew*, or to excuse a particular pogrom or some massacre. In short, the intellectual must work *at the level of events* to produce other concrete events that will combat pogroms or racist verdicts in the courts, by revealing the violence of the privileged in all its nakedness. By *event* I mean a fact that is the bearer of an idea, in other words, a singular universal – for the universality of the idea is limited by the singularity of the fact, a *dated* and *localized* event that *takes place* at a

certain point in the history of a nation, and which resumes and totalizes it to the extent that it is a totalized product of it. This means, in effect, that the intellectual is constantly confronted with the concrete, and can only make a concrete response to it.

(5) The intellectual's most immediate enemy is what I will term the *false intellectual* and what Nizan called a watch-dog – a type created by the dominant class to defend its particularist ideology by arguments which claim to be rigorous products of exact reasoning. In actual fact, representatives of this category share the same origins as true intellectuals: they too begin as technicians of practical knowledge. It would be simplistic to imagine that the false intellectual is merely an individual who has 'sold out' – unless we understand the bargain that makes a technician of knowledge into a false intellectual as a little less crude than is normally implied. Let us say that certain subaltern functionaries of the superstructure feel that their interests are tied to those of the dominant class – which is true – and refuse to feel anything else – which is to suppress the opposite sentiment, that is also true. In other words, they ignore their alienation as men (actual or potential men) and think only of their power as functionaries. They wear the appearance of intellectuals and also start by contesting the ideology of the dominant class – but their's is a pseudo-contestation, whose rapid exhaustion merely serves to demonstrate that the dominant ideology is resistant to all contestation. In other words, the false intellectual, unlike the true, does not say *no*, but rather cultivates the 'no, but . . .' or the 'I know, but still . . .' attitude. These arguments are capable of seducing the true intellectual, who typically is only too inclined – in his capacity as a functionary – to entertain such attitudes himself, and to use them to revert again from monster to pure technician. But he is also necessarily impelled to refute such arguments, precisely because he is *already* the monster that they cannot convince. He will thus reject 'reformist' propositions, and in doing so will tend to become more and more *radical*. In actual fact radicalism and intellectual commitment are one and the same; it is the 'moderate' arguments of reformists which logically radicalize the intellectual, by showing him that he must either reject the basic principles of the ruling class or serve it by merely appearing to reject them. For example, many false intellectuals in France declared during the French war in Indo-China

or the Algerian war: 'Our colonial policy is not all it should be: there is too much inequality in our overseas territories. But I am against all violence, whatever its origin: I wish to be neither executioner nor victim, and for this reason I am opposed to the revolt of the natives against the settlers.' To any radicalized thinker, it is clear that such a pseudo-universalist position amounts to the following: 'I am in favour of the chronic violence that the settlers inflict on the colonial peoples (super-exploitation, unemployment, under-nourishment, police terror) – which is in any case a minor evil that will be righted in the long run; but I am against the violence that the colonial peoples seek to exercise in order to liberate themselves from their oppressors.' It is then obvious enough that once the use of counter-violence against the oppressors is vetoed, mild reproaches to them count for very little (such as: 'grant equal pay, or, at least make a gesture towards it'; 'a little more justice, for goodness sake!'). Such reproaches are patently a façade since the false intellectual seeks to prevent the real strength of the oppressed from transforming them into demands backed by arms. If the colonial population does not rise *en masse*, the settlers are well aware that it will find no organized force in the metropolitan country to support it. Colonial authorities thus have no reason to object to the false intellectual, whose discourse helps to divert the colonial population from revolt by luring it towards the mirage of reformism. Intellectual radicalism is thus normally fortified and developed by the arguments and attitudes of the false intellectuals. In the permanent dialogue between true and false intellectuals, reformist arguments and their practical consequences (preservation of the *status quo*) necessarily tend to revolutionize true intellectuals, since they demonstrate that reformism merely performs the double function of serving the dominant class while allowing the technicians of practical knowledge to maintain an illusory distance from their employers, in this dominant class.

All those who adopt a universalist perspective *here and now* are *re-assuring* to the established order: the universal today is made up of false intellectuals. True intellectuals – uneasily aware of their essentially monstrous character – are by contrast *disquieting*: for they suggest that the human universal is *yet to come*. Many false intellectuals enthusiastically joined Gary Davis's movement for 'world government' after the Second World War. They hoped to become citizens of the world *overnight* and to establish the reign of Peace on Earth. 'Very good', a Vietnamese of the time might say to a false French intellectual of this type: 'Now make a start by demanding peace in Vietnam, since that is where the fighting is.' 'Not on your life,' the intellectual would reply: 'that would only help the Communists.' Such an attitude wants peace in general, but no particular peace, whether to the advantage of imperialism or of its colonial victims. But he who calls for universal peace, but no particular peace, merely confines himself to a *moral* condemnation of war – something everyone repeats, even President Johnson. It is because of the role of false intellectuals that the popular image of an intellectual (as I explained in the first lecture) is of a moralist and idealist, who pronounces *moral* condemnations of war and dreams in this violent world of a day when ideal peace will finally reign – a peace that will not be a new human order founded on the abolition of all wars by the victory of the oppressed, but a spiritual idea of a peace descended from heaven. It is for this reason that the true intellectual, as a *radical* thinker, is neither a moralist nor an idealist: he knows that the only peace worth having in Vietnam will cost blood and tears; he knows that peace will only come after the withdrawal of American troops and the end of American bombing – *therefore* after the defeat of the United States. In other words, the nature of his contradiction obliges him to *commit himself* in every one of the conflicts of our time, because all of them – class, national, and racial conflicts – are particular effects of the oppression of the under-privileged and because, in each of these conflicts, he finds himself, as a man conscious of his own oppression, on the side of the oppressed.

Nonetheless, it must be repeated, his position is not a *scientific* one. He gropingly applies a rigorous method to unknown objects which he demystifies by demystifying himself; he pursues a work of practical exposure by combating ideologies and revealing the violence they mask or justify; he labours in order that a social universality may one day be possible where all men will be *truly* free, equal and fraternal, certain in his knowledge that on that day, and not before, the intellectual as a species will disappear, and men will at last acquire practical knowledge in liberty and harmony. For the moment, all he can do is seek and stumble, with no other guide than his dialectical rigour and radicalism.

B. *The intellectual and the masses*

The intellectual stands alone because no one has mandated him. Now one of his contradictions is that he cannot liberate himself unless others liberate themselves at the same time. For every man possesses personal goals which are perpetually *stolen* from him by the system. Alienation even extends into the ranks of the ruling class itself, whose members work for inhuman ends which do not belong to them, that is to say fundamentally for *profit*. Thus the intellectual, once he grasps his own contradiction as an individual expression of objective contradictions, is in solidarity with every man who struggles for himself and for others against these contradictions.

However it would be wrong to imagine that the intellectual could accomplish this task by simply *studying* the ideology inculcated into him (for example by subjecting it to ordinary critical methods). In actual fact it is his *own* ideology – it manifests itself both in his mode of life (in so far as he is a *real* member of the middle classes) and in his *Weltanschauung*. In other words it is the tinted glasses through which he normally looks at the world. The contradiction from which he suffers is at first experienced only as suffering. In order to examine it, he must *take his distance* from it – and this he cannot do without assistance. In effect, this historical agent is entirely conditioned by his circumstances and his consciousness is precisely the opposite of an *overview*. If he sought to project himself into the future in order to know himself (as we can know past societies), he would miss his goal completely; he has no knowledge of the future, and even if he were to guess an aspect of it, it would be as still imbued with his own current prejudices – and thus would reproduce the very contradictions he sought to look back upon. If he were to try to place himself theoretically outside society in order to judge the ideology of the dominant class, *at best* he would take his contradictions with him; at worst he would identify with the big bourgeoisie which is economically situated *above* the middle classes and overlooks them, and he would then accept its ideology without demur. It follows that if he wishes to understand the society in which he lives, he has only one course open to him and that is to adopt the point of view of its most underprivileged members.

The under-privileged do not represent universality, which is non-existent today, but they do represent the *immense majority*, particularized by the oppression and exploitation which make of them the products of their products, and rob them of their ends (as the technicians of practical knowledge are likewise robbed) by reducing them to particular means of production, defined by the instruments they fashion and the tasks these utensils assign to them. Their struggle against this absurd particularization leads them in their turn to seek universality – not, of course, the universality of the bourgeoisie (when it views itself as a universal class) – but a concrete universality of negative origin, born of the liquidation of particularisms and the advent of a classless society. The only way the intellectual can really distance himself from the official ideology decreed from above is by placing himself alongside those whose very existence contradicts it. The urban and rural proletariat, by nature, prove that our societies are particularist and class-divided. The fact that two billion people out of a world population of three billion are under-nourished today reveals another fundamental truth of our present societies – belying the myth of affluence invented by false intellectuals. The degree of consciousness achieved by the exploited classes is *variable* – they may at times be deeply imbued with bourgeois ideology; but they nevertheless remain characterized by an *objective intelligence*. This intelligence is not a gift, but is a product of their *point of view* of society, the one and only radical perspective on it – whatever their *political attitudes* may be (in some cases resigned dignity or reformism, to the extent that their objective intelligence has been obscured by values inculcated by the dominant class). This objective perspective gives rise to a *popular mode of thought*, which spontaneously views society from its foundations upwards, starting with the lowest level of the social hierarchy that is most susceptible to radicalization. This popular vision captures the dominant classes and their allies as in a *tilt shot* angled from below, in which they appear not as cultural elites but as enormous statues whose pedestals press down with all their weight on the classes which reproduce the life of the society. Here there is no mutual recognition, courtesy or non-violence (as between bourgeois who look into each other's eyes at the same height), but a panorama of violence endured, labour alienated and elementary needs denied. If the intellectual can adopt this simple and radical perspective, he would see himself *as he really is*, from below – rejecting his class and yet doubly conditioned by it (born into it as a psycho-social 'background' and reinserted into it as a technician of knowledge), weighing on the popular classes as a charge on the surplus-value they produce. He would then clearly perceive the ambiguity of his position and, if he applied the rigorous methods of the dialectic to these fundamental truths, he would learn in and through the popular classes the true nature of bourgeois society. He would abandon what few reformist illusions he has left, and would become a revolutionary. He would understand that the masses must imperatively break the idols that crush them. His new task would then be to combat the perpetual re-emergence *within the people* of ideologies which paralyse them. But at this level, new contradictions arise.

(1) In the first place, the under-privileged classes do not as such produce intellectuals, since it is precisely the accumulation of capital which allows the dominant classes to create and to augment *technical capital*. Of course, the 'system' recruits a few technicians of practical knowledge from the exploited classes (in France, about 10 per cent); but even if these technicians come from the people, they are immediately integrated into the *middle classes* through their work, their salary and their standard of living. In other words, the under-privileged classes do not produce organic representatives of the objective intelligence which is theirs. Until the day of the revolution, an organic intellectual of the proletariat will remain a contradiction in terms. Besides, since such an intellectual would be born into classes who demand the universal because of their very situation, he would never be the monster we have described as an unhappy consciousness (if he could exist at all).

(2) The second contradiction is a corollary of the first. If the intellectual, who cannot be organically produced as such by the under-privileged classes, nevertheless seeks to rally to them in order to assimilate their objective intelligence and to inform his trained methods with their popular principles, he will promptly and *justifiably* encounter the distrust of those with whom he wishes to ally. In effect workers are bound to see him as a member of the middle classes – in other words, of strata which are by definition accomplices of capital. The intellectual is thus necessarily separated by a gulf from those men whose point of view he wants to

adopt – that of *universalization*. He is, in fact, constantly attacked for this by the false intellectuals who are in the pockets of the established order of the ruling class and its allies: 'You are a petty-bourgeois who has imbibed bourgeois culture from birth and lived amongst the middle classes; how dare you claim to represent the *objective spirit* of the working classes; you have no contact with them and they want nothing to do with you.' In point of fact it seems as if there is a vicious circle here: in order to struggle against the particularism of the dominant ideology, it is necessary to adopt the point of view of those whose very existence condemns it. But to adopt this point of view, an intellectual must never have been a petty-bourgeois, since his education has irretrievably infected him from the start. Moreover, since it is the contradiction between particularizing ideology and universalizing knowledge that makes a petty-bourgeois into an intellectual, to adopt this point of view it would be necessary *not to be an intellectual*.

Intellectuals are perfectly well aware of this new contradiction: many of them come to grief over it and go no further. They either assume a position of *too great humility* towards the exploited classes (hence their long-standing temptation *to refer* to themselves as proletarians, or to try to *become* proletarians), or they fall into systematic suspicion of each other (each suspects that the ideas of the other are secretly conditioned by bourgeois ideology, because every intellectual is *tempted* by his petty-bourgeois background and sees in others a reflection of himself); or finally, in desperation at the distrust of which they are the object, they retreat and – unable to revert to simple technicians of knowledge at peace with themselves – they become *false intellectuals*.

Joining a mass party – another temptation – does not resolve the problem. The distrust remains. Discussion of the precise role of intellectuals and theoreticians in the Party recurs again and again. This has happened many times in France. The same pattern occurred in Japan, around 1930, in the time of Fukumoto, when the communist Mizuno left the Japanese CP and accused it of being 'a theoretical discussion group dominated by the petty-bourgeois ideology of corrupted intellectuals'. Who in that epoch could claim that he represented or theorized the objective intelligence of the working class? Those who insisted, for instance, that the Meiji restoration was a bourgeois revolution? Or those who denied this? If it is the Party leadership which decides the matter on practical political grounds, who can be sure that when these change, its personnel and opinion will not be changed too? If this should happen, it is safe to predict that those who retained the condemned theory a moment too long will be denounced as 'corrupt intellectuals' – in other words as intellectuals *tout court*, since corruption is precisely the fundamental characteristic which every intellectual rebels against once he has discovered it inside himself. Thus if petty-bourgeois intellectuals are led by their own contradictions to align themselves with the working class, they will serve it at their risk and peril; they may act as theorists but never as organic intellectuals of the proletariat, and this contradiction, no matter how well it may be understood, will never be resolved. Thus our axiom is confirmed that intellectuals cannot receive a mandate from *anyone*.

C. *The role of the intellectual*

These two complementary contradictions are awkward but not as serious as they might appear to be at first sight. The exploited classes, in actual fact, do not need an *ideology* so much as the practical truth of society. That is to say, they have no need of a mythical representation of themselves; they need knowledge of the world in order to change it. This means that they demand to be *situated* (since knowledge of one class implies knowledge of all the others and of the balance of forces between them), and that they aspire to discover their *organic goals* and the praxis which will enable them to reach them. In short, they need to posess their own practical truth, which means they seek to grasp themselves both in their *historical particularity* (such as two industrial revolutions have made them, with their class memory, or material residues of past structures; workers in St Nazaire, for example, are contemporary witnesses to an older form of the proletariat) and in their *struggle for universalization* (that is to say, against exploitation, oppression, alienation, inequality, the sacrifice of labour to capital). The dialectical relationship between these two exigencies is what is called *class consciousness*. Now it is at this level that the intellectual can serve the people. Not as a technician of universal knowledge, since he is *situated*, as are the 'under-privileged' classes themselves. But precisely in so far as he is a *singular universal*, since an intellectual achieves self-consciousness by simultaneously discovering his class particularism and his task of universality – which is to contradict and surpass his particularity towards a universalization of the particular, starting from his original particularism. But since the working class seeks to change the world by taking itself as it is as the point of departure, instead of posing itself at the outset as universal, there is a parallelism between the effort of the intellectual to achieve universalization and the spontaneous movement of the working class. In this sense, although the intellectual can never be originally *situated* within this class, it is a gain that he has become conscious of his *situated condition*, even as a member of the middle class. His task is not to deny his situation, but to use his experience of it to *situate* the working class, and his universalist techniques to illuminate the efforts of this class to achieve universalization. At this level, the contradiction which produces an intellectual offers him the means to grasp the historical singularity of the proletariat with universal methods (historical research, structural analysis, dialectics) and its strivings towards universalization in their particularity (as they issue from a singular history and preserve it to the very extent that they call for the *incarnation* of a revolution). It is by applying the dialectical method, by grasping the particular in the demands of the universal and reducing the universal to the movement of a singularity towards universalization, that the intellectual – defined as a man who has *achieved consciousness of his own constituent contradiction* – can help the proletariat to achieve its own self-consciousness.

However, his class particularity may vitiate over and over again his efforts as a theoretician. Thus the intellectual must forever struggle against the *ideology* which forever rises anew within him, perpetually recreated in novel forms by his original situation and formation. He has two resources he should use simultaneously in this struggle:

(1) *Perpetual self-criticism:* he must not confound the universal – which he practices as a specialist in the field of practical knowledge: $y=f(x)$ – with the singular efforts of a particularized social group to achieve universalization. If he poses as the guardian of the universal, he lapses at once into the particular and again becomes a victim of the old illusion of the bourgeoisie that takes itself for a universal class. He must strive to remain aware of the fact that he is a petty-bourgeois breaking out of his

mould, constantly tempted to renourish the thoughts of his class. He must remind himself that he is never secure from the danger of lapsing into universalism (which thinks of itself as already *completed* and as such, excludes the effort of various particularities towards universalization), into racism, nationalism, or imperialism. (In France the so-called 'respectful left' is one which respects the values of the right even though it believes it does not share them – such was 'our left' during the Algerian war.) At the very moment when the intellectual is denouncing these attitudes, he is always liable to be infected by them: American Blacks have good reason to denounce with horror the paternalism of many intellectual and anti-racist whites. Thus an intellectual cannot join workers by saying: 'I am no longer a petty-bourgeois; I move freely in the universal.' Quite the contrary; he can only do so by thinking 'I am a petty-bourgeois; if, in order to resolve *my own* contradiction, I have placed myself alongside the proletariat and peasantry, I have not thereby ceased *to be* a petty-bourgeois; all I can do, by constantly criticizing and radicalizing myself, is step by step to refuse – though this interests no one but myself – my petty-bourgeois conditioning.'

(2) *A concrete and unconditioned alignment with the actions of the underprivileged classes.* Theory, in effect, is nothing but a moment of praxis: the moment of assessment of the field of possibilities before it. Therefore, if it is true that theory illuminates praxis, it is equally true that it is conditioned and *particularized* by the total enterprise undertaken, since before posing itself for itself, it arises organically within an action which is *always particular*. The role of the intellectual is thus not to judge an action before it has begun, nor to urge that it be undertaken, nor to supervise its development. On the contrary, it is to *join it in mid-course* in its elemental forms (a wild-cat strike, or a stoppage that has already been canalized by a trade union), to integrate himself in it, participate in it physically, allow himself to be captured and borne along by it and only then, to the extent that he judges it necessary, to decipher its nature and illuminate its meaning and possibilities. In so far as a common praxis integrates him into the general movement of the proletariat, he can grasp, within its internal contradictions (the action is particular in its origins, universalizing in its ends) both the particularity and the universalizing ambitions of this movement, as a force at once familiar

(the intellectual shares the same goals and runs the same risks) and foreign, that has borne him a long distance from where he once stood, yet remains *given and out of reach*: excellent conditions for grasping and defining the particularities and universal exigencies of *a* proletariat. How can a specialist in universality best serve the movement of popular universalization? Both in his capacity as one who can never be assimilated, and remains excluded even during violent action, and as a divided consciousness, that can never be healed. The intellectual will never be either completely inside the movement (thus lost within a too great proximity of class structures) nor completely outside it (since as soon as he begins to act, he is in any case a traitor in the eyes of the ruling class and of his own class, one who uses the technical knowledge they allowed him to acquire against them). Outlawed by the privileged classes, suspect to the under-privileged classes (because of the very culture he puts at their disposal), he can begin his work. And what exactly is his work? One could, I believe, describe it in the following terms:

(1) He must struggle against the perpetual rebirth of ideology amongst the popular classes. In other words, he should attack externally and internally every ideological representation that they entertain of themselves or their power (the 'positive hero' the 'personality cult', the 'glorification of the proletariat', for example, all of which may appear to be products of the working class but are in fact borrowed from bourgeois ideology: as such, they must be destroyed).

(2) He must make use of the capital of knowledge he has acquired from the dominant class in order to help raise popular culture – that is to say, to lay the foundations of a universal culture.

(3) Whenever necessary and particularly *in the present conjuncture*, he should help to form technicians of practical knowledge within the under-privileged classes, since these classes cannot themselves produce them, in the hope that they will become the organic intellectuals of the working class, or at least, technicians who are as near as possible to such intellectuals (who cannot yet in fact be created).

(4) He must recover his own ends (universality of knowledge, freedom of thought, truth) by rediscovering them as the real ends sought by *all those in struggle* – that is, as the future of man.

(5) He should try to radicalize actions under way, by demonstrating

the ultimate objectives beyond immediate aims – in other words, universalization as a historical goal of the working class.

(6) He must act as a guardian of the historical ends pursued by the masses, against *all political power* – including the power of mass parties and apparatuses of the working class itself. Since an end is always, in effect, the unity of its means, he must examine the latter in the light of the principle that all means are good if efficacious, *provided* they do not deform the end pursued.

The last task raises a new difficulty. In as much as an intellectual puts himself at the service of a popular movement, he must observe its discipline, and refrain from weakening the organization of the masses. But in as much as he must clarify the practical relationship between means and ends, he can never renounce his critical faculties if he is to preserve the fundamental meaning of the ends pursued by the movement. But this contradiction need not detain us: *it is the natural element of the combatant intellectual,* which he will live *in tension,* with more or less success. All we can say on this subject is that there should be intellectuals associated with the political leadership of popular parties or organizations – in a situation of maximum discipline and minimum criticism. It is equally necessary that there should be intellectuals outside parties, united with the movement as individuals from the outside, in a situation of minimum discipline and maximum criticism. Between these two extremes (we could say, the opposite poles of opportunism and ultra-leftism) there is a marsh of intellectuals shifting from one position to the other, non-party members who nevertheless respect discipline and critical party members who are always on the brink of leaving; through them a sort of osmosis takes the place of antagonisms – one man enters the party as another man leaves. No matter: antagonisms may diminish, but perpetual contradictions and dissensions are the lot of the social group we call intellectuals – all the more so in that a fair number of *false* intellectuals have normally slipped into their ranks, police agents capable of understanding the problems of the intelligentsia. The swarm of disputes that make discord the normal internal statute of the intelligentsia will astonish only those who believe we live in the era of the universal rather than that of universalizing endeavour. What is certain is that thought progresses by contradictions. It should be stressed that contemporary divergences can become so accentuated that they divide intellectuals very deeply (after a defeat, or during a decline, after the Twentieth Congress or in consequence of the Sino-Soviet split) and that in such cases they usually threaten to weaken both the movement of thought and the popular movement itself. For this reason intellectuals must try to establish, maintain or re-establish an antagonistic unity amongst themselves – in other words, a dialectical consensus that contradictions are necessary and a unitary supersession of opposites is always possible, and that therefore, rather than trying obstinately to convert others to one's own point of view at all costs, intellectuals should seek to create by mutual understanding of conflicting theses the condition for surpassing them.

At this point, we reach the term of our inquiry. We know that an intellectual is an agent of practical knowledge and that his principal contradiction (professional universalism versus class particularism) impels him to join the movement of the under-privileged classes towards universalization, for fundamentally they are moving towards the same goals as himself, whereas the dominant class reduces him to the rank of a means towards a particular end which is *not his own* and which, consequently, he is powerless to criticize.

It remains true that, even so defined, the intellectual has a mandate from no one; suspect to the working class, a traitor to the dominant class, a fugitive from his own class who can yet never wholly escape it, he rediscovers his own contradiction once again, modified and deepened, even within the ranks of popular parties. If he joins one of these parties, he will still be at once solidary and excluded, since he always remains in latent conflict with political authority. Everywhere the intellectual is *unassimilable*. His own class wants no more of him than he of it, but no other class opens to welcome him. How then can we speak of the *function* of an intellectual? Is he not rather *one man too many*, a *defective* product of the middle classes, compelled by his imperfections to live on the fringe of the under-privileged classes without ever becoming part of them? Today, many people from all classes think that the intellectual arrogates functions to himself that do not exist.

In one sense, this is true. The intellectual, indeed, is well aware of it. He cannot ask anyone to legitimize his 'function'. He is a by-product of our societies, and the contradiction within him between truth and belief, knowledge and history, free thought and authoritarianism, is not the outcome of an intentional praxis but of an internal reaction - that is to say the system of relations between mutually incompatible structures within the synthetic unity of a person.

But on closer inspection we find that the intellectual's contradictions are the contradictions inherent in *each* one of us and in the whole society. Our ends are robbed from all of us – we are all means towards ends which escape us, ends which are fundamentally inhuman; we are all torn between objective thought and ideology. The only difference is that, in general, these contradictions remain at the level of lived experience and find expression either in a straightforward denial of basic needs or in a diffuse dissatisfaction (among the white collar workers of the middle classes, for instance) whose causes are not perceived. This does not mean that people do not suffer from these contradictions – on the contrary, they can die or go mad from them. But in general they lack, for want of technical knowledge, a reflective consciousness of their situation. Yet each of us, though we may not be aware of it, spontaneously strives to achieve this consciousness, which would permit man to reassert his mastery over this savage society that turns him into a monster and a slave. The intellectual, because of his own contradiction, is driven to make this effort for himself, and consequently *for everyone* – and it is this that becomes his *function*. In one sense he is suspect to all, since he is a disputant *from the outset* and thus a potential traitor, but in another sense, he makes an effort to achieve consciousness *for all*. Of course, everyone can repeat the performance afterwards. However, to the extent that he is a situated and historical being, the disclosure he attempts to accomplish is always liable to be limited by re-emergent prejudices, or by confusion of a completed universality with an ongoing universalization, as well as by simple ignorance of history (inadequacy of instruments of research). But (a) he expresses society, not as it will be for a future historian, but as it is now *for itself* – and his degree of ignorance therefore represents the *minimal ignorance* that structures his society; (b) he is not, consequently, infallible – on the contrary he is often mistaken; but his errors, to the extent that they are inevitable, indicate the *minimum* coefficient of mistakes to which under-privileged classes are liable in any historical situation.

Through the intellectual's struggle against his own contradictions inside him and outside him, a historical society gains a perspective – a hesitant, doubtful perspective, conditioned by external circumstances – *on itself*. It attempts to think itself *practically*, that is to say to determine its structures and its ends; in short, to universalize itself on the basis of methods which the intellectual derives from his techniques of knowledge. In a certain sense the intellectual becomes *a guardian of fundamental ends* (the emancipation, universalization and hence humanization of man). But let us be clear on one point: within society, the technician of practical knowledge possesses in his capacity as a subaltern functionary of the superstructures, a certain amount of power. The intellectual, on the other hand, though he springs from this technician, is *powerless*, even if he is linked to the leadership of a party. For at another level this link returns him to the role of a subaltern functionary of the superstructures and, while accepting this role for reasons of discipline, he must also always contest it, by constantly watching over the relationship between means chosen and organic ends. As such, his function can vary from testimony to martydom: established power, whatever its complexion, typically seeks to make use of intellectuals as instruments of its propaganda, but it distrusts them and always makes them the first victims of a purge. No matter: as long as he can write and speak, the intellectual must defend the popular classes against the hegemony of the dominant class and against the opportunism of popular apparatuses.

When a society loses its ideology and its system of values as a result of a great upheaval (such as military defeat, or enemy occupation) it often happens that it will – almost without being aware of it – expect its intellectuals to liquidate the old system and recreate a new one. Yet, of course, its intellectuals will not be content simply to replace an outworn ideology with another, just as particularist, that merely facilitates the reconstruction of the same type of society as before. They will attempt to abolish all ideology and to define the *historical ends* of the exploited classes. Thus it comes about that when the dominant class regains the upper hand, as it did in Japan towards 1950, it attacks intellectuals for having failed in their duty – that is to say, for not having *dressed up* the old ideology in order to *adapt* it to the new circumstances (in other words, for not having behaved in conformity with the general idea of a technician of practical knowledge). At the same time, it may happen that the exploited classes (either because living standards are rising, or because the dominant ideology remains powerful, or because workers temporarily blame intellectuals for their setbacks, or because they need a *pause* in their struggle) condemn the past actions of the intellectual, and relegate him to solitude. But this solitude is his *lot*, since it arises from his own contradictions: he can no more escape from it when he exists in symbiosis with the exploited classes whose *organic* intellectual he can never be, than he can abandon it at the moment of defeat by making false and futile retractions (unless he is to become a pseudo-intellectual). In actual fact, when he is working with the exploited classes, his *apparent* communion does not mean that he is necessarily right, any more than his near-total solitude in moments of retreat mean that he is necessarily wrong. In other words, numbers have nothing to do with the problem. The intellectuals' duty is to live his contradiction *for all* and to surpass it *for all* by his radicalization (in other words, by the application of techniques of truth to lies and illusions). Precisely because of his contradiction, he tends to become a guardian of democracy: he challenges the abstract character of the rights conferred by bourgeois 'democracy', not because he wishes to suppress them, but because he seeks to complete them with the concrete rights of socialist democracy – while preserving, in either form of democracy, the *functional* truth of freedom.

3. IS THE WRITER AN INTELLECTUAL?

I

We have defined the situation of the intellectual in terms of the contradiction within him between practical knowledge (truth, universality) and ideology (particularism). This definition applies to teachers, scientists, doctors, and others. But by this criterion, is the writer an intellectual? On the one hand, he exhibits most of the fundamental characteristics of intellectuality. On the other hand, his social activity as a 'creator' does not *a priori* appear to have universalization or practical knowledge as its end. If beauty can be seen as a particular mode of unveiling the world, the role of *contestation* in a beautiful work of art would seem to be minimal – indeed, in a certain sense, inversely proportional to its beauty. Moreover, it would appear that excellent writers (e.g. Mistral) can draw their strength from established traditions and ideological particularism. Writers may also oppose the development of theory (in as much as theory interprets the social world and the place they occupy in it) in the name of lived experience (their particular experiences) or of absolute subjectivity (the cult of the Ego; Barrès and the enemy – the barbarians, the engineers – in the *Jardin de Bérénice*). For that matter, is it correct to describe whatever it is that a reader learns from a writer as *knowledge*? And if so, should we not define the writer in terms of his choice of a particularism? But this would prevent the writer from living within the scope of the contradiction that makes someone an intellectual. For while the intellectual vainly seeks integration into society, only to encounter solitude, does not the writer *choose* solitude from the outset? If this were indeed the case, then the writer's sole task would be *his art*. Yet we all know that some writers *are committed* and struggle for universalization alongside or among intellectuals. Is this to be explained by factors external to their art (the historical conjuncture) or is commitment an imperative which, in spite of all we have said above, is somehow inherent in their art? These are the questions we must now examine together.

2

The role, object, means and end of writing have all changed in the course of history. We have no intention of considering the problem here in its generality. We shall confine our observations to the contemporary writer, the *poet* who has declared himself to be a *prose-writer* and lives in the post-World War II world. This is an epoch in which naturalism is no longer readable, realism is questionable, and symbolism has lost its vigour and its modernity. The only firm ground we have as a starting point is that the contemporary writer (1950–70) is a man who has taken *ordinary* language as his material: by ordinary language I mean whatever serves as a vehicle for all the propositions of the members of a single society. Language, we are told, is a means of *self-expression*. We also commonly hear that *expression* is the stock-in-trade of the writer – in other words, he is someone who has *something to say*.

But everyone has *something to say*, from the scientist reporting the results of his experiments to the traffic policeman reporting an accident. And none of them needs a writer to express it for them. More precisely, such subjects as laws, social structures, mores (anthropology), psychological or metapsychological processes (psychoanalysis), events which have *occurred* and ways of living (history) – none of these constitute what a writer *has to say*. We have all had the experience of meeting someone who says: 'Ah! If only I could tell the story of my life – it would make a novel! You're a writer – I'll tell it to you, and you can write it down.' Here the shoe is on the other foot – the writer becomes aware that the very people who regard him as someone who has something to say, regard him at the same time as someone who has *nothing to say*. In effect, people find it quite natural to tell us the story of their life because they think the *important* thing (both for them and for us) is that we possess (in varying degrees) the technique of narrative, and that we can take the content of our story from anywhere. This is an opinion often shared by critics. For example, those who said 'Victor Hugo is a form in search of a content' forgot that a form demands certain types of content and excludes others.

3

What seems to justify this point of view is that for the purposes of his art the writer can only rely on ordinary language. Usually, as it happens, a man who has *something to say* chooses the means of communication that will transmit a maximum of information and a minimum of *misinformation*. An example of such a means of communication is a technical language: it is conventional and specialized; new words are introduced corresponding to precise definitions; its code is, as far as possible, protected from the distorting influences of history. The language of ethnologists is a good case in point. Now ordinary language (which acts, incidentally, as the basis for a large number of technical languages, leaving a certain imprint of imprecision on all of them) contains a maximum of *misinformation*. That is to say, since such elements as words or rules of syntax mutually condition each other and have no reality other than through their interrelations, to speak is in fact to recreate the entire language as a conventional, structured and *particular* ensemble. At this level, its particularities do not represent a body of information about the object the writer is discussing; although they can become a body of information about the language – for the purposes of a linguist. But at the level of signification they are either simply superfluous or positively harmful – because of their ambiguity, because of the very limits of the language viewed as a structured totality, because of the variety of meanings that history has imposed on them. In short, the *word* the writer uses possesses a much denser *materiality* than, for instance, the mathematician's symbols, which effaces itself before its signified. One might say that the *word* tends both to point vaguely in the direction of the signified and to impose itself as a *presence*, drawing the reader's attention to its own density. This is why it has been possible for people to say that to name something means both to *present* the signified and to kill or bury it in the mass of the word.

The words in ordinary language are at one and the same time *too rich* (they largely overflow their concept, because of their long existence, the combination of shocks and rites which make up their 'memory' or 'living past') and *too poor* (they are defined in relation to the whole of the language as a fixed determination of it, rather than as a supple possibility of expressing something new). In the exact sciences, when a new phenomenon is discovered, a word to name it is simultaneously invented by a few and rapidly adopted by all in the scientific community – entropy, complex numbers, transfinity, tensors, cybernetics, or operational calculus. But even though it sometimes happens that a writer feels called upon to invent a word, in general he rarely makes use of this procedure in order to transmit a knowledge or register an emotion. He prefers to utilize a 'current' word and charge it with a new meaning that becomes superadded to its old ones – one might say that he has vowed to utilize the *whole* of ordinary language and nothing but ordinary language, with all the misinformative features that hamper it. If then the writer adopts ordinary language, he does so not simply as a means for transmitting knowledge, but also as a means for *not* transmitting it. Writing means both possessing language ('The Japanese naturalists', a critic said, '*conquered* prose from poetry') and not possessing it, in so far as language is something *other* than the writer and *other* than men. A specialist language is the conscious creation of the specialists who use it; its conventional character is the outcome of synchronic and diachronic *agreements* established between themselves. For example, a phenomenon is often named, at the beginning, by two or more words, but with the passing of time, one of them becomes dominant and the others drop away. In this sense, the young student of the discipline in question is led tacitly to accede to these agreements as well. He simultaneously learns the thing, and the word that designates it, and he thereby becomes, as a collective subject, *master of his technical language.* The writer, on the contrary, knows that ordinary language is developed by men who speak *without agreement* with each other. Conventions are established through the activities of these men, but in so far as the groups they constitute are *other* for each other and thus other than themselves, and in so far as the whole of language develops in an apparently autonomous fashion as a materiality which mediates between men to the extent that men are mediators between its different aspects (a materiality I have elsewhere called *practico-inert*). Now the writer is interested in this materiality in so far as it seems to possess a life of its own and eludes him, in common with all the other speakers of the language. In French there are two genders – masculine and feminine – which can only be understood in terms of each other. Now as it happens, these two genders designate not only men and women, but in addition – in each case, via a long history – objects which in themselves are neither masculine nor feminine but neuter. In these cases a sexual dichotomy is devoid of conceptual significance. It becomes positively *misinformative* when it goes so far as to reverse genders, so that a feminine gender applies to men and a masculine gender to women. One of the greatest of modern writers, Jean Genet, delighted in such phrases as this: 'Les brûlantes amours de la sentinelle et du mannequin.'* The word *amour* is masculine in the singular and feminine in the plural; *la sentinelle* is a man, and *le mannequin* is a women. Of course this sentence transmits an item of information: a certain soldier and a women from the world of fashion-parades love each other passionately. But it transmits this information in such a bizarre way that it can be said to be deformed as well: the man is feminized and the woman masculinized. Let us say

---

*Translator's note: Literally: 'the ardent passion the sentry and model feel for each other'. The point of the sentence is that the word *sentinelle* (a masculine concept) is grammatically feminine and the word *mannequin* (a feminine concept) is grammatically masculine.

that the sentence is eroded by a falsely informative materiality. To sum up, it is *a writer's sentence*, in which the information is invented in such a way that the pseudo-information is richer than it.

It was on the strength of this that Roland Barthes made his distinction between *écrivants* and *écrivains* – 'literal writers' and 'literary writers'. The literal writer uses language to transmit information. The literary writer is a custodian of ordinary language, but he goes beyond it, for his material is language as non-significance or misinformation. He is an artisan who produces a certain verbal object by working on the materiality of words; for him, meaning is the means and non-meaning the end.

Coming back to our first description, we can say that the prose-writer has *something to say*, but that this something is nothing *sayable*, nothing conceptual or conceptualizable, nothing that signifies. We do not yet know what this something is nor whether, in the writer's quest for it, he must make an effort towards universalization. All we know is that this object is formed by his work on the particularities of a historical and national language. The object thus formed will be: (1) a concatenation of significations which control each other (for example, a *story* that is being told); (2) and yet, viewed as a totality, other and more than this: the wealth of non-signifying elements and of misinformation closes back, as it were, on the order of significations.

If to write is to *communicate*, the literary object appears as a form of communication *beyond language* – a form of communication that rests on the non-signifying silence enclosed by the words (though also produced by them). Thus the phrase: 'this is just literature' typically means: 'you speak in order to say nothing'. It remains to ask ourselves what this *nothing is*, this silent non-knowledge that the literary object has to communicate to the reader. The only way to reach an answer is to go back from the *signifying content* of literary works to the fundamental silence which surrounds them.

4

The signifying content of a literary work may refer to the *objective* world (by this I mean both society, the social ensemble of the Rougon-Macquart, and the objectified universe of inter-subjectivity, as in Racine or Proust or Nathalie Sarraute) or to the *subjective* world (here it is no longer a question of analysis nor of distanciation, but of complicit adhesion, as in *The Naked Lunch* by Burroughs). In each of the two cases the content, taken on its own, is abstract in the original sense of the word, that is to say it is cut off from the conditions which would be necessary to make it an object capable of existing on its own.

Let us consider the first case. Whether the work attempts to disclose the social world *as it really is* or to demonstrate the inter-psychology of various groups, it must be assumed – if we merely consider the set of significations it proposes – that the author enjoys a complete *overview* of his object. The writer thus appears to possess a consciousness similar in type to a 'bird's-eye view': desituated, he glides above the world. To know the social world is to claim to be exempt from its conditioning; to know the domain of inter-subjective psychology is to claim to be exempt as a writer from psychological conditioning. Now it goes without saying that the novelist can never make such a claim: Zola saw the *world-that-Zola-saw*. Not that what he saw was pure subjective illusion – naturalism in France drew from the sciences of the time and Zola was, moreover, a remarkable observer. But what reveals Zola in his writings is a point of view, an atmosphere, a particular selection of details, a narrative technique, a certain rhythm of episodes. Thibaudet called Zola an *epic* writer, and there is a considerable element of truth in this. But he should also be called a *mythic* writer, because his characters are frequently myths as well. Nana, for example, is in part the daughter of Gervaise, the girl who went on to become one of the great prostitutes of the Second Empire, but she is above all a myth – the *femme fatale* who starts life as a luckless child in the down-trodden proletariat and avenges her class on the males of the dominant class. It would be interesting to go through Zola's works and catalogue his obsessions – sexual and other – as well as to trace his diffuse feeling of guilt.

Besides, it would be difficult for anyone who had studied Zola not to *recognize* him if he were given a chapter to read from one of his works without being told the name of the author. But recognition is not the same as cognition. We read the epic-mythical description of the exhibition of linen-wares in *Au Bonheur des Dames* and we say: 'This is Zola!' for in it Zola is patent – recognized but unknowable, because he had no knowledge of himself. Zola was a product of the society he described and observed it with the eyes it had given him. Was this author totally unaware of the fact that he put *himself* in his books? Of course not: had the naturalist writer not wanted readers to recognize and admire him, he would have abandoned literature for scientific pursuits. The most objective of writers will always strive to be an invisible but *felt* presence in his books: he seeks to be present in them and moreover he cannot help but be so.

Conversely, those who write their fantasies in perfect complicity with themselves necessarily deliver the presence of the world to us – precisely in so far as this world conditions them, and their place in society partially explains their style of writing. It is just when they are most in harmony with themselves, that they can readily be seen as a particularization of bourgeois idealism and individualism. Why is this so? Well, it so happens that the exact sciences, and anthropology in particular, cannot offer us an exact account of what we are. Everything they state is true – the facts cannot be otherwise – but the scientific attitude presupposes a certain *distance* between knowledge and its object. This is a valid assumption in the natural sciences (macrophysics) and in anthropology, to the extent that the scientist can situate himself in a relationship of exteriority to the object under study (ethnographic material, primitive societies, quantifiable social structures, statistical patterns of behaviour, etc.). But the assumption is no longer valid in microphysics, where the experimenter is objectively part of the experiment. And this particular condition refers us back to a capital feature of human existence, which Merleau-Ponty termed our *insertion in the world* and I have called our *particularity*. Merleau-Ponty went on to say: we have the capacity to see because we are visible. What this comes down to is the proposition that we can only see the world *in front of us* because it has *constituted* us from behind as *visual* beings, who are therefore necessarily also *visible* beings. In fact there is a fundamental link between our own being (the multiple determinations that we have to exist) and the being in front of us, that is there to be seen. The apparition that is constituted in a world that produces me by assigning me through the banal singularity of my birth to a *unique adventure*, while at the same time conferring on me by my situation (the son of a man, of a petty-bourgeois intellectual, of such and such a family) a *general destiny* (a class destiny, a family destiny, an historical destiny), is none other than what I call *being-in-the-world* or the *singular universal*. This apparition is fated to expire in a universe which I interiorize by my very project to wrest myself free of it, an interiorization of the exterior accomplished by the very moment in which I exteriorize my interiority. This can be put in yet another way: I, as a part of an ongoing totalization, am the product of this totalization and thereby express it entirely; but I can only express it by turning myself into a totalizer, that is to say by grasping the world in front of me in a practical disclosure. This is the explanation for the fact that Racine reproduces his society (his epoch, its institutions, his family, his class, etc.) by disclosing and producing *inter-subjectivity* in his works; and for the fact that Gide reveals the world that both produces and conditions him in his advice to Nathanael, or in the most intimate pages of his journal. The writer is not a special case: he too cannot escape his insertion in the world, and his writings are the very type of a singular universal. Whatever their category, literary works always have two complementary facets: the historical singularity of their being, and the universality of their aims – or vice versa, the universality of their being and the singularity of their aims. A book is necessarily a part of the world, through which the totality of the world is *made manifest*, although without ever being fully disclosed.

This perpetually dual character of a literary work is what constitutes its richness, its ambiguity and its limitations. This duality was not explicitly apparent to classical or naturalist writers, although they were not entirely unaware of it. Today it is clear that it is not simply a passive determination of the literary work; for the latter can have no other end than to exist on both planes at once, because its very structure as a singular universal prevents any possibility of positing a unilateral end. The writer utilizes language in order to produce a two fold object which testifies, in its being and in its end, both to its singular universality and to its universalizing singularity.

However we must be quite clear here. I know or can find out that I am determined universally; I know or can find out that I am part of an ongoing totalization that is totalized, and that my slightest gesture will retotalize it. Certain human sciences – marxism, sociology, psycho-analysis – provide me with the tools I need in order to know my *place* and the general lines of my development. These are the facts in my own case. I am a petty-bourgeois, the son of a naval officer. I was fatherless. One of my grandfathers was a doctor and the other a teacher. I was fed bourgeois culture such as it was spooned out between the years 1915 and 1929, when my studies officially came to a close. These facts, linked to certain objective data of my childhood, endowed me with a predisposition towards a certain neurotic reaction. If I examine this ensemble in the light of anthropology, I shall acquire a certain type of knowledge about myself which, far from being useless to the writer, is *indispensable* today to deepen and develop literature. But it is indispensable in order to illuminate the literary option proper, to situate it externally, and to clarify the writer's relationship with the world in front of him. But no matter how precious it may be, knowledge of myself and of others in our pure objectivity does not constitute the fundamental object of literature, since such knowledge represents universality *without* the singular. Nor, conversely, is the literary object created by a total complicity with fantasies. What constitutes the object of literature is being-in-the-world – not in so far as it is treated externally, but in so far as it is *lived* by the writer. For this reason literature, though it must today rest more and more on universal scientific knowledge, is not concerned with transmitting items of information from any given sector of that knowledge. Its subject is the unity of the world, a unity that is ceaselessly called into question by the twofold movement of interiorization and exteriorization or, if you like, by the impossibility of the part being anything other than determined by the whole or of merging with the whole that it negates by the very determination (*omnis determinatio est negatio*) that is conferred on it by the whole. The distinction we make between the world in front and the world behind should not blind us to the fact that the two are continuous – they make but one. Flaubert's hatred of the bourgeoisie was his way of exteriorizing the interiorization of his *bourgeois-being*. The 'fold in the world' of which Merleau-Ponty used to speak is today the only possible object for literature. The writer will restore, for example, a landscape, a street scene, an event:

(1) In so far as these singularities are embodiments of the whole, which is the world;

(2) Simultaneously, in so far as the way in which he expresses them

testifies to the fact that he is himself a separate embodiment of the same whole (the world interiorized);

(3) In so far as this insurmountable duality reveals a rigorous unity that haunts the object produced without ever being *visible* in it. In effect, the individual was originally this unity, but his existence destroys it as a unity to the very extent that it manifests it. Since even the destruction of this existence would not restore it, the writer is better advised to try to make it felt in the ambiguity of his work, as the impossible unity of a suggested duality.

If such is in fact the aim of the modern writer – whether or not he is conscious of it – then a number of consequences for his works will follow:

(1) First of all, it is true that fundamentally the writer has *nothing* to say. We should understand by this that his basic aim is not to communicate *knowledge*.

(2) But he *communicates*, all the same. For he presents the human condition in the form of an object (the work) such that it can be grasped in its most radical depth (being-in-the-world).

(3) But this being-in-the-world is not presented in the same way as I am referring to it here, by verbal approximations that still strive towards universality (for I describe it in so far as it is the mode of being of all men – which could be expressed by saying: man is the son of man). The writer can testify only to his own being-in-the-world, by producing an ambiguous object which suggests it allusively. Thus the real relationship between reader and writer remains non-knowledge: when reading a writer's work, the reader is referred back indirectly to his own reality as a singular universal. He realizes himself – both because he enters into the book and does not completely enter into it – as another part of the same whole, as another view-point of the world on itself.

(4) If the writer has *nothing* to say, it is because he must present *everything* – in other words, the singular and practical relationship of the part to the whole which is being-in-the-world; the literary object must testify to the paradox of man in the world, not by providing information about men in general (which would make the author no more than an amateur psychologist or sociologist) but by simultaneously objectifying and subjectifying being-in-the-world – being-in-*this*-world – as a

constitutive and unsayable relationship between everyone and every-thing, and between each man and all others.

(5) If the work of art has all the characteristics of a singular universal, everything happens as if the author had taken the paradox of his human condition as a *means*, and the objectification of this condition *in the midst of the world* as an *end*. Thus beauty today is nothing other than the human condition presented not as facticity but as the product of a creative free-dom (that of the author). And, to the extent that this creative freedom aims at communication, it addresses itself to the creative freedom of the reader and solicits him to recompose the work by reading it (for reading, too, is creation); in other words, it invites him freely to grasp his own being-in-the-world as if it were the product of his freedom – as if he were the responsible author of his being-in-the-world even while suffering it, or if you like, as if he was the world incarnated in liberty.

Thus the literary work of art cannot be life addressing itself directly to life and seeking to realize – by emotion, sexual desire and so on – a symbiosis between writer and reader. On the contrary, by addressing itself to freedom, it invites the reader to assume responsibility for his own life (but not for the circumstances which modify it and can make it intolerable). It does so not by edifying but, on the contrary, by demanding an aesthetic effort to recompose it as the paradoxical unity of singularity and universality.

(6) We can now understand that the total unity of the *recomposed* work of art is silence – that is to say, the free incarnation, through words and beyond words, of being-in-the-world as non-knowledge folding back over a partial but universalizing knowledge. It remains to ask ourselves how the author can engender an underlying non-knowledge – the object of his book – by means of significations; in other words, how he can fashion silence with words.

It is here that we can see why the writer is a specialist in ordinary language, that is to say the language that contains the greatest quantity of *misinformation*. In the first place, words have two aspects as *being-in-the-world*. On the one hand they are objects that have been sacrificed: for they are always surpassed towards their significations, which – once understood – become in their turn polyvalent verbal schemas which can be expressed in a hundred different ways, hence with other words. On the other hand, they are material realities: in this sense they possess an objective structure which imposes itself and can always affirm itself at the expense of meaning. The words 'frog' and 'ox' have sonorous and visual values: they are presences. As such, they contain an important quotient of non-knowledge. Much more so than mathematical symbols. The expression 'The frog that wants to become as big as an ox'* contains, in an inextricable blend between materiality and meaning, much more corporeal density than the expression '$x \rightarrow y$'. The writer chooses to use ordinary language not *in spite of* this material weight but *because of it.* His art lies in his ability to attract the reader's attention to the materiality of any given word, even while conveying as exactly as possible a meaning through it, so that the object signified is at once beyond the word and yet incarnated in its materiality. Not that the word 'frog' bears any resemblance whatever to the animal itself. But *precisely for this reason*, the word should produce for the reader the pure and inexplicable material presence of a frog.

No element of language can be invoked without the whole of language foregathering behind it, in all its riches and restrictions. In this sense ordinary language differs from technical languages, of which each relevant specialist may feel himself co-author, since they are the object of intentional conventions. Ordinary language, on the contrary, imposes itself on me in its entirety in as much as I am *other* than myself and in as much as it is the conventional but involuntary product of each man as *other than himself* through and for others. To explain: in a market situation, I hope for my own good that the price of a certain commodity will be as low as possible; but the very fact of my subjective demand for it has the effect of raising its price: since for the sellers who supply it, I am *an other*, like all the others and, as such, I act in opposition to my own interests. It is the same in the case of the common language: I speak it and, in the same breath, I am, as an other, spoken by it. Needless to say, these two facts are simultaneous and dialectically linked. No sooner have I said: 'Good morning, how are you?' than already I no longer know whether I am making use of language or whether language is making use of me. I use it – I wanted to greet a particular man that I am pleased to see again; it uses me – all I have done is re-actualize (with a particular intonation, it is

*Translator's note: A phrase taken from one of La Fontaine's fables.

true) a commonplace of discourse that is affirmed through me. From this moment, the whole of the language comes into play; in the conversation that follows, I will see my intentions deflected, limited, betrayed and enriched by an articulated ensemble of morphemes. In this way language, a strange bonding device, unites me *as other* to an other *in his capacity as an other* to the very extent that it unites the two of us in so far as we are *the same* – that is to say, subjects communicating intentionally with each other.

Far from attempting to suppress this paradoxical situation, the writer seeks to exploit it to the maximum and to make his *being-in-language* the expression of his *being-in-the-world*. He employs phrases for their value as agents of ambiguity, as a way of 'presenting' the structured whole of language; he plays on the plurality of meanings; he uses the history of words and of syntax to overcharge them with unusual secondary meanings. So far from trying to struggle against the limitations of his language, he uses it in such a way as to make his work virtually incommunicable to all but his compatriots, accentuating its national particularism at the very moment that he suggests universal meanings. But to the extent that he makes the non-significant the proper matter of his art, he does not produce mere absurd word-games (though a passion for puns, as can be seen from the case of Flaubert, is not a bad preparation for a literary career), but aims instead to present obscured significations as they are filtered through his being-in-the-world. His *style*, in effect, communicates no knowledge: it produces the singular universal by showing simultaneously language as a generality that produces and wholly conditions the writer in his facticity, and the writer as an adventurer, turning back on his language, and assuming its follies and ambiguities in order to give witness to his practical singularity and imprison his relationship with the world, as lived experience, in the material presence of words. Take the sentence: 'the self is hateful: you, Miton, can cover it, but you can never remove it'.* The meaning in this sentence is universal, but the reader masters it through its abrupt non-signifying singularity, its style, which henceforth will attach itself so closely to it that he will not be able to think the idea other than through this singularization – in other words, other than through Pascal thinking it. Style is the whole of language

*Translator's note: A passage from Pascal's *Pensées*.

surveying itself, by virtue of the mediation of the writer, from the perspective of singularity. It is no more, of course, than a means – though a fundamental means – of presenting being-in-the-world. There are a hundred others, all of which should be used simultaneously, and which deliver the writer's *style of living* (supple or hard, a devastating vivacity of attack or, on the contrary, a slow start, careful preparations, leading up to brusque compressions). Everyone knows what I am talking about here – all those characteristics which conjure up so much of a man that we can virtually feel his breath, *without giving us any knowledge of him.*

(7) This fundamental way of using language cannot even be attempted if the writer does not simultaneously seek to convey meanings. Without meaning, there can be no ambiguity, and the object does not come to dwell in the word. How else could we speak of ellipses? Ellipses of what? The essential task of the modern writer is to work on the non-signifying element of ordinary language to enable the reader to discover the being-in-the-world of a singular universal. I propose to call this task a search for *significance* (*sens*). Such a significance is the presence of the totality in the part. The style of a writer lies in this respect in his interiorization of exteriority; within any singular effort to surpass conditions towards meanings, it is what might be called the *flavour* of the epoch or the *taste* of the historical moment, as they appear to an individual singularly formed by the same history.

But although style is fundamental, it remains in the background since all it figures is the writer's insertion in the world. Much more prominent is the signifying ensemble that corresponds to the world in front of him, such as it appears in its universality from a viewpoint conditioned by the world behind him. Yet the meanings of words are nothing more than quasi-meanings, and taken together they constitute no more than a quasi-knowledge. For firstly, they are chosen as means of significance and are rooted in it (in other words, they arise from style, are expressed by style, and, as such, are dimmed by their origin); while secondly, they seem to have been cut out of the universal by a singularity (thus they comprise, in themselves, the unity and explosive contradiction of the singular and the universal). Everything presented in a novel can be given an appearance of universality, but the appearance is a counterfeit which belies itself and is belied by the rest of the book. Akinari, in *Le Rendez-vous aux Chrysanthèmes*, begins in these terms: 'The inconstant person establishes relationships easily, but they are only of short duration; the inconstant person, once he has broken with you, will never inquire after you again.' Here we would seem to have a series of universal propositions. But within *the story* this universality is counterfeit. To start with, two tautological judgements provide us with a definition – one that we already *knew* – of inconstancy. But what is their role here, since the story is not about inconstancy but, on the contrary about a marvellous constancy? The sentences thus refer us back to Akinari's singularity. Why did he choose this phrase? It occurred in the Chinese story which he used as his inspiration, though he altered the tale totally. Did he leave the phrase in by accident? Or to give a clear indication of his source? Or to surprise the reader by suggesting that it was inconstancy that prevented a friend from appearing at a rendezvous, and then later revealing his incomparable fidelity? Anyway, the phrase is indirectly problematical and its universal object is contradicted by the singularity of the reasons why the writer included it. Style constitutes the expression of our invisible conditioning by the world behind us, and meanings constitute the practical efforts of an author thus conditioned to attain *through this conditioning* the elements of the world in front of him.

(8) These few observations, in effect confirm that a literary work today is faced with the task of simultaneously demonstrating the twin facets of being-in-the-world. It must constitute itself a self-disclosure of the world through the mediation of a singular part produced by it, such that the universal is everywhere presented as the generator of singularity, and singularity as the enveloping curve and invisible limit of universality. In a literary work, objectivity should be discerned on every page as the fundamental structure of the subjective and, conversely, subjectivity should everywhere be visible as the impenetrability of the objective.

If the work has this dual intention, it matters little what formal structure it assumes. It may, as in the case of Kafka, appear as an objective and mysterious narrative, a sort of symbolism without symbols and or anything precisely being symbolized, in which metaphors never indirectly convey information, but the writing constantly indicates those modes of being-in-the-world that are lived as indecipherable. It may, as in Aragon's later novels, take shape as a work in which the author openly intervenes in his narrative in order to limit its universality at the very moment when he appears to want to extend it. Or again, it may quite simply assume the guise, as in Proust, of a work in which a fictitious character – sibling of the narrator – intervenes in the story as judge and protagonist, instigator and witness of the whole adventure. The relation between the singular and the universal can equally be captured in a hundred other ways (Robbe-Grillet, Butor, Pinget, etc.). None of these forms has any precedence over the others – their choice depends on the enterprise in question. To claim the contrary is to lapse *both* into formalism (the universalization of a form that can only exist as *one* expression of a *singular* universal: for example, the *vous* in *La Modification** is valid only in its context – but there it is perfectly valid) and into reism (the conversion of a form into a *thing*, an etiquette, a ritual, whereas it is simply the inner unity of a content).

On the other hand, no work is valid unless it accounts, in the mode of non-knowledge, or lived experience, for *everything:* that is to say, the social past and the historical conjuncture, in so far as they are *lived* without being *known*. It follows that the singular is visible only as the non-signifying particularization of membership in a community and its objective structures. Conversely the quasi-meanings suggested by a work have significance (*sens*) as objective structures of the social, only if they appear to be concrete because lived from a particular anchorage. An objective universal will never be attained by a work of literature: but it remains the horizon of an effort of universalization which is born from singularity and preserves it while negating it.

The literary work must therefore appertain to the whole epoch, in other words to the situation of the author in the social world, and on the basis of this singular insertion, to the entire social whole – in so far as this insertion renders the author, like any other man, a being *concretely* in question in his being, who *lives* his insertion into the world in the form of alienation, reification, frustration, want, solitude, against a *suspected* background of possible plenitude. The totalization accomplished by the literary work is itself, at the same time, historically particularized as a simple moment of a wider on-going totalization. A writer today can only

*Translator's note: Michel Butor: *La Modification*.

live his being-in-the-world in the specific form of a being-in-*one*-world. In other words, he cannot avoid being affected in his life by the contradictions of the whole planet (such as the contradiction between atomic war and people's war, with its permanent reminder of man's capacity today either to destroy the human species, or to advance towards socialism). Any writer who did not attempt to render the world of the atomic bomb and space flights, in so far as he has experienced it in obscurity, impotence, and disquiet, would be recounting an abstract world, not that in which we live; he would be a mere entertainer or charlatan. The precise form in which such an insertion into the present world conjuncture is conveyed is of little importance: a vague anguish drifting from page to page is enough to demonstrate the existence of the bomb. There is no need whatever to speak openly of nuclear weapons. The totalization of a writer, on the contrary, occurs in the domain of non-knowledge; conversely, in so far as life is the ultimate foundation of everything and the radical negation of anything that threatens it, such a totalization is not passively interiorized but appropriated from the viewpoint of the unique importance of life. The ambivalence which underlies any literary work was well captured by Malraux in his dictum, 'A life is worth nothing – and nothing is worth a life.' The phrase succinctly combines the viewpoint of the world behind us (producing and crushing each life with indifference) and the viewpoint of each singularity which flings itself against death and affirms itself in its autonomy.

The commitment of the writer is to communicate the incommunicable (being-in-the-world as lived experience) by exploiting the misinformation contained in ordinary language, and maintaining the tension between the whole and the part, totality and totalization, the world and being-in-the-world, as the *significance* of his work. *In his professional capacity itself*, the writer is necessarily always at grips with the contradiction between the particular and the universal. Whereas other intellectuals see their function arise from a contradiction between the universalist demands of their profession and the particularist demands of the dominant class, the inner task of the writer is to remain on the plane of lived experience while suggesting *universalization* as the affirmation of life on its *horizon*. In this sense, the writer is not an intellectual *accidently*, like others, but *essentially*. Precisely for this reason, the literary work itself demands that he situate himself *outside it*, on the theoretical-practical plane where other intellectuals are already to be found. For this work is both a restitution, on the plane of non-knowledge, of the experience of being in a world which crushes us, and a lived affirmation that life is an absolute value and an appeal for freedom addressed to all other men.

A Friend of the People

Since May 1968 there has been a break between the traditional conception of the left-wing intellectual and a new conception of the revolutionary intellectual forged in struggle. Many well-meaning intellectuals of the post-war era now find themselves confronted with a political situation they no longer understand. What do you think of this development?

To answer that we must first define what an intellectual is. Some people think of him as a person who works exclusively with his intelligence, but this is a poor definition. No type of work is a pure exercise of the intelligence; for that matter no type of work can dispense with intelligence either. A surgeon, for example, can be an intellectual and yet his work is manual. I do not think intellectuals can be defined exlcusively in terms of their profession – but all the same, we need to know in which professions we are likely to find them. I should say they can be found in the occupations which I would call the techniques of practical knowledge. In fact all knowledge is practical, but this has been realized only recently. This is why I use the two words together: the technicians of practical knowledge develop or utilize by means of exact disciplines a body of knowledge whose end is, in principle, the good of all. This knowledge aims, of course, at universality: a doctor studies the human body *in general* in order to cure, in any particular person, a disease whose symptoms he discovers and against which he develops a remedy. But the technician of practical knowledge can just as well be an engineer, a scientist, a writer or a teacher. In each case, the same contradiction is to be found; the totality of their knowledge is conceptual, that is to say universal, but it is never used by *all* men; it is used, in the capitalist countries, *above all* by a certain category of persons belonging to the ruling classes and their allies. Thus the application of the universal is never universal, it is particular; it concerns *particular people*. A second contradiction follows from this, that concerns the technician himself.

The technician's procedure is universal in his professional work, in his method of obtaining knowledge, but he finds that *in fact* he typically works for the privileged classes and is therefore objectively aligned with them: at this level, he himself is at stake. We still have not defined the intellectual yet: all we have are technicians of practical knowledge who either accommodate themselves to their contradiction or manage to avoid suffering from it. But when one of them becomes aware of the fact that despite the *universality of his work* it serves only *particular interests*, then his awareness of this contradiction – what Hegel called an 'unhappy consciousness' – is precisely what characterizes him as an intellectual.

You feel that in spite of May 1968 the traditional mission of the intellectual is the same?

No. But first we must know what this 'mission' was, and who gave it to him. In fact, because he was both universal and particular, the intellectual denounced each particularized use of the universal, and in each specific case he tried to indicate the principles of a universal policy, designed to achieve the good of the greatest number.

Thus the classical intellectual was the type who would say: watch out, they are holding this up to you today as the application of a universal – for example, a law that is supposed to be applied universally, under which people are arrested impartially. Now this is not true, says the intellectual. Laws are not universal, for such-and-such a reason, and on the other side, there is such-and-such a particular interest that is served by these laws; there is a particular class and a particular policy that led to such-and-such an individual being arrested or such-and-such a war being continued. The classic example of an intellectual's activity can be seen in the opposition to the Vietnam war: a certain number of intellectuals joined parties or organizations denouncing the war in Vietnam, and they made use of their specialized knowledge to show, let us say, that a particular type of defoliant had been sprayed over the fields of Vietnam, or that the justifications for the war offered by the Americans could not bear serious examination. In the former case they might be chemists, in the latter historians and jurists who could base their arguments on international law (while denouncing certain particularist

features of it at the same time). But they must be called 'classical intellectuals' – to use your phrase – because even though they suffer from their
contradiction, they still consider that it renders them useful to everyone and, consequently, they refuse to call themselves into question as
individuals. Yet, in their very practice, there is as it were a hint – which
they conceal from themselves – of this contestation. Since they aim to
suppress *outside* themselves the antagonism between the universal and
the particular which constitutes them, they should also try to suppress it
within themselves; in other words, the universalist society they aspire to
objectively *has no place* for the intellectual.

*Was there really a break in May? Does the classical conception of the role of
the intellectual still remain present, or is there scope for a new conception?*

To tell the truth, in most cases there has been little change and the
classical intellectual is still as ubiquitous as ever. The reason is that he
likes his role: he is a well-paid technician of practical knowledge, who –
for example – on the one hand teaches physics, and on the other protests
against repression at meetings. He is ill at ease *in principle*, and thinks
that by virtue of this feeling – which represents an awareness of his
contradiction – he can be useful, since his contradiction is the contradiction of the whole society.

*One might say that you acted as guide for a whole generation of French
intellectuals, and yet you were one of the first suddenly to become aware of the
failure of a large part of this generation and the need today for a new political
outlook on the part of intellectuals?*

I certainly would not say I was one of the first. The correct analysis was
largely the work of students. The students who had become technicians
of practical knowledge, even in their first year at university, immediately
felt the real problem: whatever happened, they were going to be turned
into wage-workers for capital or minions of its repression. Those who
saw this said to themselves: we don't want this. Or more precisely they
said: we no longer want to be intellectuals, we want the knowledge that
we acquire (the acquisition is the first problem – subsequently there is
the problem of knowledge itself), which is a universalist knowledge, to
be used for the benefit of everyone. When the rank and file committees
against the war in Vietnam started to appear, for example, the students

came to realize that their apprenticeship under bourgeois orders was in no way cancelled merely by their belonging to a committee against the war in Vietnam. Organization of demonstrations by committees cannot in itself alter the very kernel of the nature of the intellectual in our society, as someone who is condemned to be in perpetual contradiction, in so far as he does the opposite of what he wants to do and helps to oppress the people he should want to liberate. I see for example teachers I knew, who go on behaving today like classical intellectuals. Some of them did very courageous things during the Algerian war, saw their apartments bombed, etc. Yet these same people, as teachers, remained educationally elitist. In the educational system they never moved from the plane of the particular, while elsewhere they were in complete support of the FLN, and thus in support of the total liberation of Algeria, displacing the universal onto it. They made use of their knowledge and their mode of reasoning, formed by their studies and their practical experience, to serve ideas which were genuinely universal – for example, the right of a people to determine its own future; yet at the same time they remained selectionists as teachers and taught their courses according to the plans laid down by the university. Such people never dreamt of contesting themselves as intellectuals. They found a good conscience in their bad conscience, because of what they were doing – or thought they were doing – for Algeria or Vietnam. The classical intellectual is the sort of person who retrieves a good conscience from his guilty conscience by actions (in general, the writing of articles, pamphlets, etc.) that his conscience impels him to do in other fields. In May 68 these people did not go the same way as the others at all. Doubtless they supported the students and strikers, but they failed at the outset to understand that this was a movement contesting themselves. Some of them were visibly confounded, and cherished a nagging hostility to the events of May when suddenly they felt the movement was contesting *them* in their capacity as *intellectuals*, whereas until then the intellectual had always been there to help others, to be available – the natural person to provide the theories, the ideas.

But these intellectuals were attacked for the very form of their knowledge, which you described a moment ago as 'universal', and which the Chinese with justice say may be universal, but remains nonetheless bourgeois – since in its very form it is already particularized?

Agreed, but this was only discovered later. What I mean is the classical intellectual of the 1950s was the sort who thought that mathematics represented a totally universal body of knowledge. He did not distinguish between a way of learning and applying mathematics which would itself be universal, and a particularist way of learning it

To sum up, the real break occurred in May, when the intellectuals came to understand that it was they themselves and the very form of their knowledge that were being called into question?

The form of their knowledge, and the nature of their *real existence*. One should not say that the classical intellectual was simply the victim of a contradiction: full stop. Such intellectuals have got to feel that this contradiction needs to be suppressed within themselves. Basically it is quite true that their contradiction is the same as that of the society as a whole, and it is certain that an intellectual is a wage-earner, and that his real problems are the problems of wage-earners in general: he has a knowledge and a power that are at the disposal of a certain kind of society. Yet these fine people who on the one hand supported the Algerian FLN, the Vietnamese NLF, and adopted vanguard positions in all fields, on the other hand remained in spirit wholly in the service of a situation that made them actually harmful. They were not simply un fortunate people who had their contradictions like anyone else, but were harmful precisely in the sense that they were immediately recuperable. But in May it was not the 'established' intellectuals, who had passed their exams and were handling real money, but the apprentice intellec- tuals, who understood the situation and said to themselves: one thing we *do not* want is to be like that.

By the end of May, science students were leftist politically, but there was absolutely no political analysis of their own scientific knowledge.

True – I noticed it at meetings; there was a mixture of paternalism – in so far as people assumed that knowledge was after all an essential element in political power – and of *ouvrierism*, that is say a complete abandonment of culture. The real problem was seldom brought out.

So from May onwards it was the apprentice intellectuals – young people – who refused to become personages of the traditional type defined by a function and a salary, for after all this is what defines a man – what he earns and what he does. You remarked that it is not strictly universal knowledge that is taught in our educational system, but bourgeois knowledge universalized, and I would agree. But if the intellectuals had thought this in 1968, they would never have gone ahead with the May revolt. Because at a given moment they had to have the idea of a universal in order to understand that this universal presupposes a universal society.

The matching of society to knowledge?

Exactly. But had they realized something more difficult, namely that what they possessed was not universal knowledge but only a particularized culture, the shock would have been less violent. Whereas they thought: we have or can have a universal knowledge, but what can we do with it in this society?

We came out into the streets as a result of the first line of analysis, and came to the second . . .

Only later, I agree. But the two have also been necessarily linked and discovered together, above all in certain fields, for example psychiatry (I am thinking of Gorizia).*

In your opinion, what stage has been reached in the process of re-education of the intellectuals – to use a Chinese expression? In other words, to what extent has the barrier between culture and politics been broken down? How far has the process of re-education gone?

It has only just begun. Had the movement and the violent contestation of May 68 continued, had there not been the betrayal and the relative defeat of June, I think that many people would have adopted much more radical positions than they have now. Because a lot of them were already shifting rapidly.

So on the one hand you have the classical intellectuals and on the other, amongst the students, people who have completely broken with the traditional

---

* Translator's note: An Italian counter-psychiatric community.

identity of the intellectual, who have gone off to work in factories, and after two or three years no longer speak the same language at all. Their language has become simplified, their relationship with the proletariat has become real. They have become new men, for example the ex-students working at Renault: their language has been completely transformed. This change-over is much more difficult for thirty, forty or fifty year old intellectuals, but it is occurring. What kind of role could they play?

Well, those who have really changed realize that there is no longer any other way of conceiving universal ends than by forging a direct relationship with those who demand a universal society, i.e. with the masses. But this does not mean that they should follow the example of the classical intellectuals, and 'speak' to the proletariat – in short, to produce a theory that is sustained by the masses in action. This is an attitude that has been completely abandoned.

While we are on this subject, what do you think of the collapse of the writers' organizations that sprang up in May '68 (Hotel de Massa, Writers-Students Committee)?

What happened was this: they all thought that May was an opportunity to put into effect ideas they had conceived before. I think they were people who were on the sidelines (former Communists, in many cases). They tried in vain to fit May into their preconceived schemata.

So you think there is little to be expected from groups of intellectuals who were more or less established (even if they were young) before May 68?

That is what I think, yes.

There is little hope of re-educating them?

Little hope. Because you must not forget – an intellectual is generally an individualist. Not all of them, but writers for example are always saddled with their individualism, despite everything . . .

So we cannot expect much of people who have already a certain cultural output behind them, but a kind of re-education is possible for a new type of intellectual, one who has still not produced anything culturally?

Right. Deutscher laid a lot of stress on what he called 'ideological interest'. He meant, for example, that if you have written a lot of books, these can thereafter become your ideological interest. In other words, it is not simply your ideas that are there, but real, material objects, and these are your interest. This is not necessarily to say that what counts is the money these books bring in – what is important is that they are your objectification. This objectification of yourself is there, it exists – and at any particular moment you have to repudiate it or change it or accept it completely, but any way you look at it you are confronted with something that makes you different from the man who, let us say, punches tickets on the underground all day. He has no ideological interest. Take myself, for instance. I have a certain number of books behind me. I may not always agree with what I wrote earlier, but these books constitute my ideological interest – for the idea of seeing them entirely suppressed is repugnant to me, certainly not because I am particularly proud of them, but because of the kind of person I am. That's how people are – you have a past that you can't repudiate. Even if you try to, you can never repudiate it completely because it's as much part of you as your skeleton. This gives rise to a problem – what can you ask of a forty-five year old who already has an extensive production behind him?

In short, there are two types of intellectual – those who refuse out of hand to involve themselves, and those whom Musil describes in The Man Without Qualities *as 'back-view writers' who sign all the petitions, are at all the political rallies, play a useful role and yet never cross a certain threshold, no matter how honest or rigorous they may be?*

Except that this is a new problem, for there was no such thing as our latter-day ultra-left before. There used to be nothing to the left of the Communist Party. There was only one course open in 1936, or in 1940–41, and that was to go along with the Party. If you didn't want to join it because you were not entirely in agreement with it, you were a fellow traveller, but you couldn't do any more. There would not have been any point in going to work in a factory then. It would have made no sense.

Then how do you see the new mission of the intellectual? 'Mission' is hardly the right word, anyway.

He must first of all suppress himself as an intellectual. What I mean by intellectual, here, is a man with a guilty conscience. What he should learn to do is to put what he has been able to salvage from the disciplines that taught him universal techniques, directly at the service of the masses. Intellectuals must to learn to understand the universal that the masses want, in reality, in the immediate, this very moment.

The concrete universal?

The concrete universal. And conversely, while learning the language of the masses, they can give a certain expression to the techniques they possess. For example, I think that a newspaper today that is created for the masses should comprise a certain proportion of intellectuals and a certain proportion of workers, and that the articles should be written neither by the intellectuals nor by the workers, but by both together. The workers explain what they are and and what they are doing, and the intellectuals are there to understand, to learn and at the same time to give things every so often a certain type of generalization.

Do you think that apprenticeship in the language of the masses completely changes the form of universal knowledge?

No, I do not. At least not at the moment. This is a very important problem that touches on culture, and culture is a very difficult problem.

A problem that is always being side-stepped . . .

Yes, because we still lack the means to deal with it.

A personal, or rather a personalized question. To what extent did May change you culturally?

May in itself had no immediate effect on me, but its consequences did. During May I was like everyone else – I grasped nothing of what was going on at the time. I understood what was being said, but not the deeper meaning of the events. In fact, my evolution developed from the aftermath of May to my 'entry' into *La Cause du Peuple*. I questioned myself more and more as an intellectual. Basically, I was a classical intellectual.

Since 1968 I hope I have changed a bit, although I haven't had the opportunity of doing very much. To direct a paper nominally as I do, or even to distribute it in the streets, is still not real work, that is to say it is not writing in the conditions we talked of. The problem I face in my own case is that of an intellectual sixty-five years old, who for the last twenty-five to twenty-seven years has wanted to write a *Flaubert*, using well-known methods, scientific methods if you like, or at any rate analytical methods, to study a man. Then May 68 happens. I have been deep in this project for fifteen years. What do I do? Abandon it? That wouldn't make sense, and yet, as someone has rightly remarked 'the forty volumes of Lenin constitute an oppression for the masses'. It is a fact that the masses have neither the time nor the means at the present moment to tackle this type of knowledge, which is an intellectual's knowledge. So what should I do? This is a precise and practical problem – what should you do when you've been working on a book for fifteen years, when in the long run you have not changed much, since you can never discard the whole of your childhood? What should you do? I decided to finish the book, but as long as I go on working on it, I remain at the level of the traditional intellectual.

Will you finish it in the way you originally envisaged?

Of course. It wouldn't make sense otherwise. But you see, this case is a good example of a contradiction – you go as far as possible in one direction, but in another you finish what you have to do . . . I could only abandon this work with difficulty, for after all it would mean renouncing the work of many years.

But you have abandoned things in the past – for example The Roads to Freedom *and other works you had begun?*

Yes, but that was because of internal difficulties.

Yet The Roads to Freedom *could speak directly to the masses; it was a far more popular literary work than your* Flaubert *will ever be?*

Very true. But this is a problem I cannot resolve. Should there not be a type of research and culture that is not directly accessible to the masses and which nevertheless is mediated to them by one means or another? Isn't specialization still insurmountable in our day? Or, even more problematically, does writing this *Flaubert* make any sense at all (I'm not talking about its merits)? Is it a work which necessarily will be buried, or on the contrary is it a work which may in the long run prove to be of some use? You can't tell. For example, I don't like what so-and-so writes, but I can't say whether his or someone else's work might not be useful to the masses one day, for reasons that are obscure to us now. I can't tell – how could I?

Indeed. Mallarmé himself, in 'L'Humanité Dimanche', has become Comrade Mallarmé. So, between May 68 and the time when you took over the direction of 'La Cause du Peuple', something happened which wasn't enough to stop you writing your Flaubert but which . . .

But which radicalized me in another direction. Now I consider myself available for any correct political tasks requested of me. It wasn't as a liberal defending the freedom of the press that I took over the direction of *La Cause du Peuple*: I didn't do it for any reason like that. I did it as an act which committed me to the side of people with whom I got on well, but whose ideas I certainly don't entirely share. Yet it's not a purely formal commitment.

We should also like you to say something to us about the strengths and weaknesses of the revolutionary press.

Firstly, no paper has found the correct tone – not even *La Cause du Peuple*. It has a certain tone, but there is no link between theory and practice.

It's also a problem to know what sort of information to give. Systematic exaggeration of minor events is often of dubious help.

Obviously it's undesirable. Moreover, as I see it, the revolutionary press should give a true account not only of successful actions, but of unsuccessful ones too. As long as you keep up a triumphalist tone, you stay on the same terrain as *L'Humanité*. This is something to be avoided. There are certain well-tried techniques of lying that I do not like. What needs to be said, on the contrary, is the truth – which means saying such-and-such was a failure, and this is why; or again, such-and-such was successful, and this is why. It's always more valuable to report the truth; the truth is revolutionary and the masses have a right to it. This is what has never been done. Just imagine what it must have been like for a worker of my age who had been a Stalinist and then, one fine day, was told brutally and without any explanation that Stalin was nothing. Such workers were left high and dry with no further word of explanation. What kind of behaviour is that? Is that the way to treat a man? This was a terrible experience – it threw people into a kind of despair. What is even more serious is the fact that the bourgeois press tells more of the truth than the revolutionary press, even when it is lying. The bourgeois papers lie less. They lie more skilfully. They manage to discredit, but they stick to the facts. It's terrible to think that the revolutionary papers, far from being more truthful than bourgeois papers, are less so. But what is also necessary is that we – who are also the masses – learn to live with the truth. Revolutionaries don't want to know the truth; they have been brainwashed. They live in a sort of dream-world. We have to create a desire for the truth, in ourselves and in others.

A desire that May didn't generate, perhaps?

True, May didn't generate this desire. Partly because of a lyrical quality that we shouldn't reject.

The problem now is to try to define a new role for intellectuals. Because in fact, since May, they have continued to play no other role than that of support, or surety for a mass movement (of students or workers) that was already there: for example, in the CNPF* occupation.

I'll limit myself to a single observation: you still see them as intellectuals. I don't approve of that.

You're right; it's a mistake on our part.

Yes, it's a mistake. Listen, what is needed in this connection is collective work. That's what is lacking. If you want to recapture that 'organic union' that existed in the nineteenth century – an organic union of workers are intellectuals – you have to work in mixed cells. Let's have done with these separate cells cut off from each other. This is the only way you'll ever change intellectuals. And, on the other hand, this gives

---

*Translator's note: CNPF is the Confédération National du Patronat Français (the French Employers Federation).

them the opportunity within the group to test their opinions from time to time against their own practice. I think that's the way in which they should work.

Do you think the intellectuals who occupied the CNPF could find a different type of intervention in mass movements?

That seems highly unlikely to me. You know how difficult it is with intellectuals . . . I have much more hopes of the young. When I talk of organizations bringing workers and intellectuals together, I'm thinking of twenty to thirty year olds, the young people thrown up by May.

Index